METHODS AND ANALYSIS ON TOURISM AND ENVIRONMENT

TOURISM AND HOSPITALITY DEVELOPMENT AND MANAGEMENT

Additional books in this series can be found on Nova's website
under the Series tab.

Additional e-books in this series can be found on Nova's website
under the e-book tab.

ENVIRONMENTAL RESEARCH ADVANCES

Additional books in this series can be found on Nova's website
under the Series tab.

Additional e-books in this series can be found on Nova's website
under the e-book tab.

METHODS AND ANALYSIS ON TOURISM AND ENVIRONMENT

JOSÉ MONDÉJAR JIMÉNEZ
MANUEL VARGAS VARGAS
F. JAVIER ORTEGA ROSELL
AND
ESTEBAN PEREZ CALDERON
EDITORS

nova publishers

New York

Library of Congress Cataloging-in-Publication Data

Methods and analysis on tourism and environment / Josi Mondijar Jiminez, Manuel Vargas Vargas, F. Javier Ortega Rosell, Esteban Perez Calderon.
    pages cm.
 Includes index.
 ISBN: 978-1-62417-824-5 (hardcover)
 1. Tourism--Environmental aspects. 2. Tourism--Research. 3. Environmental management. 4. Sustainable development. I. Mondejar-Jimenez, Jose
 G156.5.E58M47 2013
 338.4'791--dc23
                              2013007520

Published by Nova Science Publishers, Inc. † New York

CONTENTS

In: Methods and Analysis on Tourism and Environment   ISBN: 978-1-62417-824-5
Editors: J.M.Jiménez, M.V.Vargas, F.J.O.Rosell et al. © 2013 Nova Science Publishers, Inc.

Chapter 1

STATUS AND TRENDS OF CHINA'S TOURISM DEVELOPMENT

Yanyun Zhao, Xu Qin, Fan Wu and Yang Zhao
Renmin University of China, China

ABSTRACT

This chapter utilizes the data found in the China Statistical Yearbook to outline the level and structure of China's tourism development, and summarizes its characteristics from the aspects of scale, structure, quality, function and innovation. Based on "The 12th five-year plan" for China's tourism industry issued by the National Tourism Administration of the People's Republic of China, this chapter also predicts the trends of China's tourism development, not only at the overall level of its industrialization, commercialization, modernization and internationalization, but also at the regional level, and puts forward corresponding suggestions. Based on the analysis of national tourism as a whole, this chapter also illustrates the local development of China's tourism with Beijing, the capital of China.

1. INTRODUCTION

In recent years, China's tourism has made great progress, not only in the domestic market, but also in the outbound and overseas market, which greatly promotes the spiritual civilization and corporeal civilization construction of China, as well as the influence and status of China in international tourism development.

The environment for tourism development is getting improved, not only by increasing tourism consumption, promotion of science and technology, but also by the support of national policies. Recently, the National Tourism Administration of the People's Republic of China has issued "The 12th five-year plan" for China's tourism industry, and local tourism administrations have also issued "The 12th five-year plan" for their own tourism industry. The plans provide significant directions for the future development of national and local tourism industry, and will surely achieve remarkable effects.

From a local perspective, China also makes great achievements. As the capital of China, Beijing is a typically famous oriental city, classical as well as modern. Its world-renowned historical and modern attractions, sound policy support, as well as good consumption environment help fascinate large amounts of both overseas and domestic tourists to Beijing and greatly promote its tourism development.

2. LEVEL AND STAGE OF CHINA'S TOURISM DEVELOPMENT

2.1. Domestic Tourism

Average annual growth rate of domestic tourism earnings between 1990 and 2009 is 24.04%, as can be seen in figure 1. During the same period, domestic visitor number grows at an average rate of 10.61%. Domestic Tourism development climbs up to a higher stage at a faster pace after the decline in 2003 when SARS (Severe Acute Respiratory Syndrome) was widespread in China.

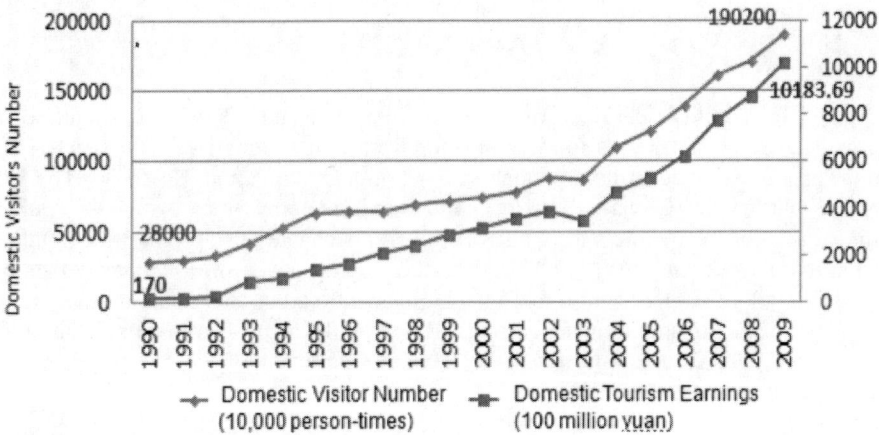

Figure 1. Domestic Visitor Number and Tourism Earnings.

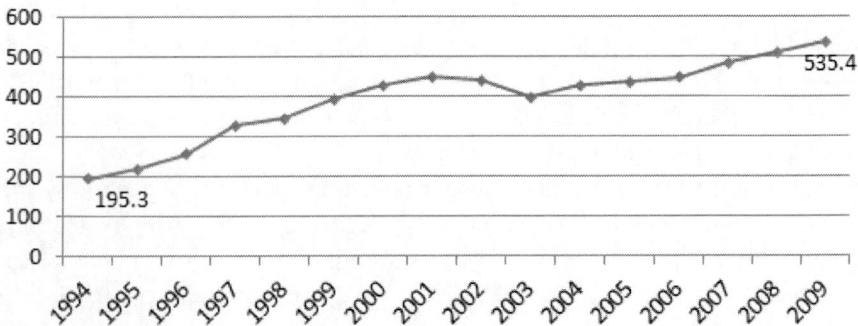

Figure 2. Domestic Tourism Expenditure per Capita (Yuan).

As figure 2 shows, domestic tourism expenditure per capita in 2009 reaches 535.4 yuan, which is 1.74 times more than that in 1994. 2001-2003 is the depression of China's tourism due to the influence of SARS. Although China experienced Wenchuan Earthquake, international financial crisis and H1N1 afterward, domestic tourism expenditure per capita keeps growing steadily. Tourism has become an important way of entertainment for Chinese people, and promotes the spiritual civilization and corporeal civilization construction.

2.2. Outbound Tourism

As figure 3 shows, outbound tourism was not influenced by SARS in 2003 and keeps growing fast. The number of Chinese outbound visitors grows at an average rate of 17.24% annually between 1993 and 2009, and rises at a faster pace right after 2003. China's position as Asia's largest outbound tourist country is consolidated. China's outbound tourism plays a very important role in promoting the global tourism market to step out of the recession during the financial crisis. The reception quality of outbound tourism destinations and the security mechanisms for outbound tourists have been further improved, laying a solid market foundation for China's internationalization strategy of tourism industry in the international market.

2.3. Overseas Tourism

Overseas tourism keeps showing steady growth at an increasing pace during 1978-2007 period, as figure 4 shows, except when both the overseas visitor number and the foreign exchange earnings from international tourism declined in 1989 and 2003. The growth rate of China's overseas tourism keeps among the highest in the world in the past five years, although the development of overseas tourism declined in 2008 and 2009. In 2009, the number of global international tourists dropped by 4%, while Chinese overseas tourist number only dropped by 2.7%.

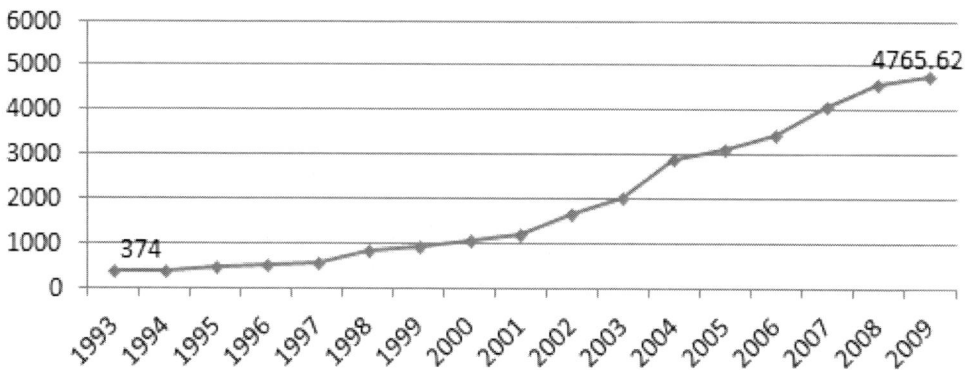

Figure 3. Number of Chinese Outbound Visitors (10,000 person-times).

Figure 4. Overseas Visitor Number and Foreign Exchange Earnings from International Tourism.

Among overseas tourists, as figure 5 shows, the proportion of the tourists from Japan, Korea, Russia, US, Malaysia and Singapore exceeds 5%. China's tourism has made great progress in the multilateral and bilateral cooperation with US, Russia, EU, ASEAN, Japan and Korea, and formed an effective operating mechanism. China's overseas tourism has also played an important role in civil diplomacy and trade in services. The influence and status of China in international tourism development have been further promoted.

2.4. Tourism Market Structure

China's domestic visitor proportion has kept growing since 2005, as figure 6 shows, while the overseas proportion kept declining, and the outbound proportion fluctuated around 2%. Domestic market keeps most important in China's tourism no matter how the structure fluctuates. Domestic visitor proportion is as high as 91.61% in 2009.

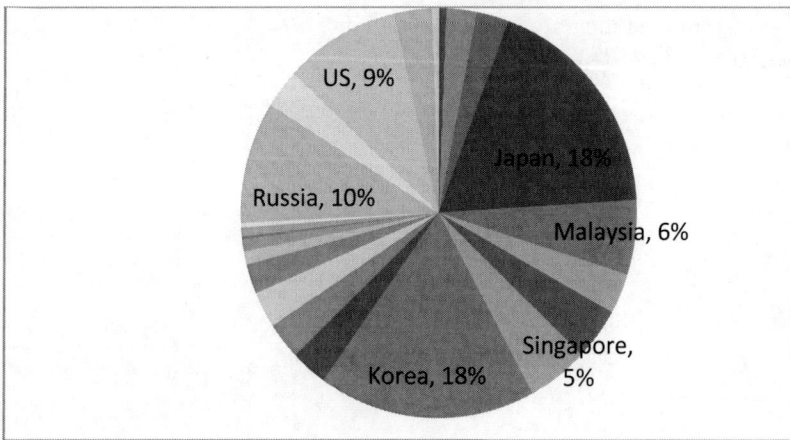

Figure 5. Structure of overseas tourists.

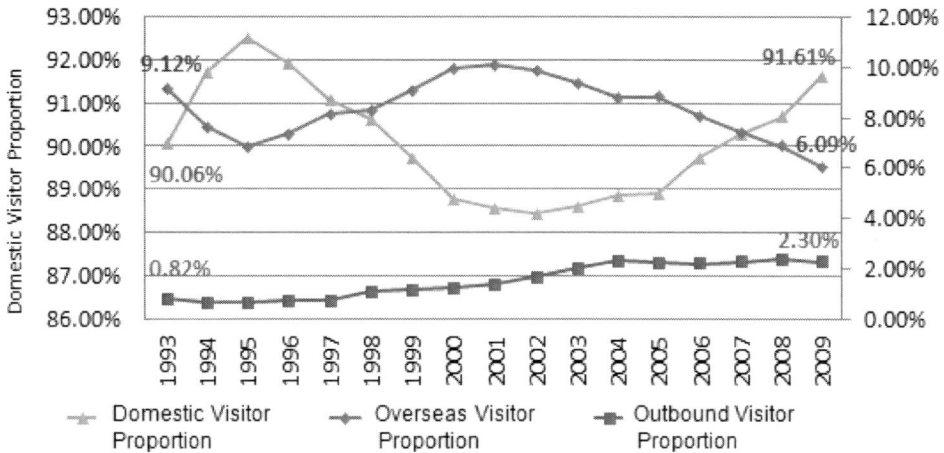

Figure 6. Structure of China's Tourism Market.

3. CHARACTERISTICS OF CHINA'S TOURISM DEVELOPMENT

3.1. Continuously Expanded Scale

China's tourism has been promoted by 2008 Beijing Olympic Games, 2010 World Expo and Asian Games, while it also experienced the attack of Wenchuan Earthquake, International Financial Crisis and H1N1. Nevertheless, China resisted the adverse effects, and showed strong adaptability. Total tourism earnings exceed 1 trillion yuan for the first time. Overseas visitor number and foreign exchange earnings step into the top 5 in the world for the first time.

3.2. Gradually Optimized Structure

Tourism system construction has achieved significant breakthroughs. Tourism products are diverse. Travel services are relatively complete. Modern tourism industry system is competitive. Three markets are developing coordinately with domestic market as the core part.

3.3. Obviously Improved Quality

The competitiveness of tourism has been promoted significantly. The development of tourism elements has become more mature, and the investment and financing system has been improved a lot. Holiday products and special tourism products are now the investment hot spots. Overseas listing is an important financing channel for emerging tourism enterprises. The incorporation of other industries into tourism accelerates the marketing process of tourism.

3.4. Effectively Released Function

Tourism becomes an important drive force to expand domestic demand, adjust structure, promote growth, and benefit people's life. State council requires tourism to grow into a mainstay industry and modern service industry, and implement a series of strategic measures, including 2004-2010 National Red Tourism Development Plan, Guidance on Accelerating Tourism Development to Promote Employment, and Guidance on Accelerating Rural Tourism Development

3.5. Significantly Effective Innovation

Local government plays a leading role in tourism development. Horizontal and vertical cooperation among tourism sectors get further enhanced. Regional tourism cooperation is in the ascendant. Industry management innovation gains more and more attention. Travelling management system gets further improved.

4. ENVIRONMENT FOR CHINA'S TOURISM DEVELOPMENT

There are three basic judgments on the environment of China's tourism development during the next five years. First, tourism will be still lat the new stage of fast growth. Second, domestic tourism will become the basis of industry development. Third, tourism is going to step into the best period in the history. The reasons are mainly as follows:

4.1. Tourism Consumption Stepping into the Era of Mass

In the recent ten years, GDP grows at the average annual growth rate of 10%. GDP per capita has reached $3000. With the development of the well-off society, average consumption level will keep sustainable growth, and inhabitant consumption pattern is turning from material consumption to both material and service consumption. China has just realized the goal that each inhabitant should travel once per year, while the annual travelling times per capita has already gone beyond seven in developed countries as US, Japan, Korea. China's tourism consumption has reached explosive growth baseline according to the economic development law. With the duration of public holidays, rest days and paid vacation approaching the level of developed countries, tourism is going to be the basic part in urban inhabitants' life.

4.2. Domestic Demand Expansion Policy as a Strong Driving Force

Facing the challenge and complex domestic and international situation brought about by international financial crisis, Chinese government put forward a series of plans and strategies, and achieved remarkable improvement. However, with the increasing influence of European debt crisis, RMB appreciation pressure, and the risk of "double dip" in the world economy, domestic demand is in urgent need of expansion. Tourism, as an important industry to expand demands and promote consumption, is sure to play a greater role. Besides, motivated by increasing transportation infrastructure, financial subsidies and tax cuts, surge in household car ownership will definitely promote the growth of tourism market.

4.3. Strong Support of National Great Strategies

"Opinions of the State Council on Accelerating the Development of Tourism" issued in 2009 provides tourism with strong support: 1) Deepen the reform and opening up of tourism. 2) Optimize the environment for tourism consumption. Gradually establish a tourist destination evaluation mechanism based on tourist evaluation. Price adjustment should be announced to the society six months in advance, etc. 3) Encourage civilized and healthy way of travelling. 4) Accelerate the tourism infrastructure construction. 5) Promote the diverse development of tourism products. 6) Promote the integration of tourism and culture, sports, agriculture, industry, forestry, business, irrigation, environmental protection, meteorology, etc. 7) Improve tourism service level. 8) Promote energy saving and environment protection. 9) Increase government investment and financial support.

Tourism also becomes the main content in the 25 great regional strategies promulgated by the Chinese government in the recent years. For example, Hainan is required to construct an international tourist island. Guangxi is required to construct a national tourism comprehensive reform pilot area.

4.4. Strong Promotion of Science and Technology Development

With the development of technology, the incorporation of tourism and information industry becomes the inevitable trend. The development of tourism can't leave new technology. Wide application of tourism e-business technology, such as 3G and mobile business, will surely promote the deeper integration of tourism and information.

5. TRENDS OF CHINA'S TOURISM DEVELOPMENT

The development of China's tourism will focus on the principle of industrialization, commercialization, internationalization and modernization.

5.1. Industrialization of Tourism Elements

Accelerate the integration of tourism and relative industries, such as culture and sports. Promote the innovation of industrial development pattern, and strengthen the input of new elements and the application of modern industrial operation mode.

5.2. Commercialization of Tourism Resources

Accelerate the change of government functions, and strengthen public service system. Relax the entry conditions of tourism market to break the industry and regional barriers. Encourage various kinds of ownership enterprises to invest in tourism industry. Accelerate the reform of industry association, and improve its development capacity. Promote the grouping, networking and branding development of tourism. Chinese tourism enterprises will strive for entering world top 500 in the next five years.

5.3. Modernization of Tourism Development Pattern

Strengthen the application of information technique and modern corporate management structure and business pattern into tourism. Promote the integration of tourism and modern service industries, such as finance, insurance, information, and cultural and creative industries. Promote the upgrading of tourism products and service to satisfy the diverse modern demands.

5.4. Internationalization of Tourism Spatial Layout

Take tourism as an important channel to improve the national image, and exert its public diplomacy functions. Apply the international standard to China market, and improve the quality and management of tourism service. Develop a group of international tourism cooperation regions, and improve China's rule-making power in the international tourism market. Combine the strategy of "going out", and accelerate the construction of the overseas reception system.

6. SPATIAL DISTRIBUTION OF CHINA'S TOURISM

According to the regional overseas visitor number in 2009, the regional layout of China's tourism can be shown on the map of China. Figure 7 clearly shows that, there exist significant gaps among eastern, middle and western regions. The overseas visitor numbers in most of the western regions are below one million, which shows that western tourism is still at its initial stage and is in urgent need of industrialization. The overseas visitor numbers in most of the middle regions are between one million and two million. The numbers in the eastern region are generally above two million, and go beyond five million in the Yangtze River Delta formed by Zhejiang, Jiangsu and Shang. The overseas visitor number in Guangdong, located in the Pearl River Delta, is even as high as 27.48 million.

It is clearly pointed out in "The Twelfth Five-Year Guideline of China's tourism industry" that, tourism development has to observe the overall national policy for regional development, take high-speed transport system as the core, take urban group as the basis, and take fostering tourism gathering area as the important task. Only by following the principle of internationalizing the eastern region, urbanizing the middle region, industrializing the eastern region, will all the regions develop coordinately.

6.1. Coordinate Development of Four Main Regions

6.1.1. Internationalization of East Region

Develop the Bohai Sea Ring Area, the Yangtze River Delta, and the Pan-Pearl River Delta Tourism Demonstration Region. Develop International tourism products, such as business exhibition, coastal vacation, and urban tourism, etc.

6.1.2. Civilization of Middle Region

Rely on tourism resources of mountains, rivers, villages and metropolitan. Explore the tourism of eco-adventure, folk culture, religious pilgrimage, world heritage, as well as red tourism and rural tourism.

6.1.3. Industrialization of Western Region

Utilize the folk custom, history, ecology, and rural resources. Reform Silk Road tourist area, tourist areas along the Qinghai-Tibet Railway, the North Bay tourist area, and Shangri-La tourist area。

6.1.4. Industrial Upgrading of the Northeast

Improve brand awareness of snow tourism, border tourism, and forest eco-tourism. Promote the integration of tourism and industry.

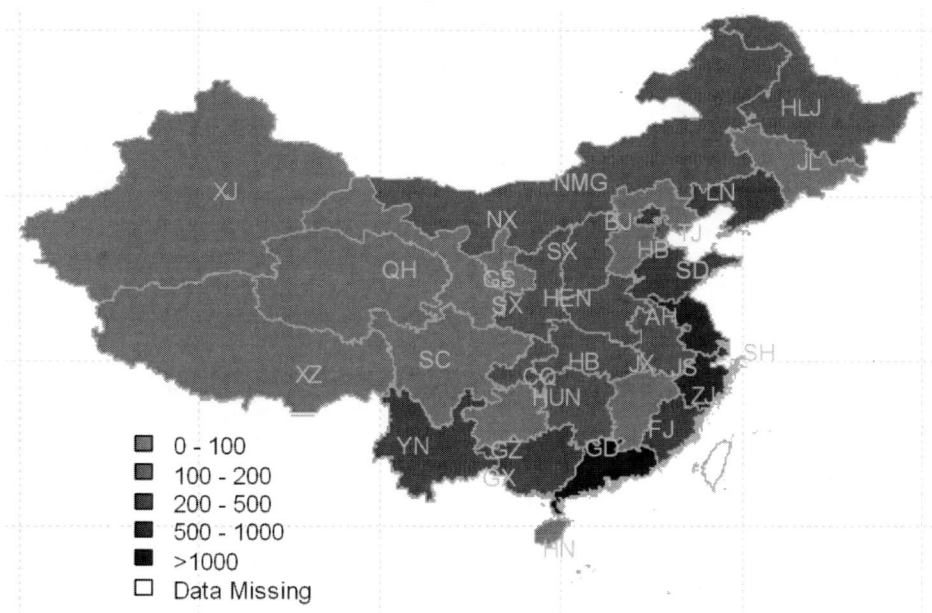

Figure 7. 2009 Regional Overseas Visitor Number (10,000 person-times).

6.2. Increasing Regional Tourism Cooperation

Observe the principles of overall planning, win-win benefits, complementation of advantages, exchange of information, share of resources and markets. Develop the regional tourism cooperation depending on resources, capital, information, transportation, personnel, product and market, and find the optimal combination to realize a win-win development. Construct regional cooperation demonstration regions, such as the Bohai Sea Ring Area, the Yangtze River Delta, the Pan-Pearl River Delta, the Silk Road, the areas along the Qinghai-Tibet Railway, the northeast old industrial base, the areas along the Beijing-Hangzhou Grand Canal and the Wuling Mountains.

7. LOCAL TOURISM DEVELOPMENT — WITH BEIJING AS AN EXAMPLE

7.1. Rich Resources of Beijing's Tourism

On one hand, having a profound history of more than 3000 years, being a capital for different dynasties for over 850 years and its splendid culture all indicate how classical it is. One the other hand, its modern side is proved by the existence of SOHO Modern City, SanLiTun Bar Street, the National Grand Theater, the Bird Nest along with the Water Cube.

As a world-renowned resort for travelling, Beijing embraced advantaged tourism resource. It has 201 tourist attractions of level A in total, such as the forbidden city --- the largest imperial palace in the world, the BaDaLing Great Wall ---one of the eight miracles on earth, the imperial garden the Summer Palace and so forth. There are over 7300 cultural and historic relics interspersing among Beijing and six of them belong to the World Heritage Sites. At the same time, it has 98 national key cultural preservation centers and 327 regional ones.

7.2. Level and Stage of Beijing's Tourism Development

7.2.1. Domestic Tourism

In the year 2010, Beijing hosted 179,000,000 domestic tourists up by 1.67 times compared to the year 1994 ---the number of which is 67,100,000 --- with the tourism incomes at 242.51 billion yuan, up by 7.14 times than the year 1994 --- the number of which is 29.8 billion. After a thorough view of the development from 1994 to 2010, it can be easily seen that domestic tourists enjoys a steady increase except for the year 2003, when the amount of tourists declined drastically under the influence of SARS. Then in 2008, although the number of tourists decreased to some extent because of the Olympic Games, tourism income increased. One possible explanation for this is tourists might spent longer in Beijing or the expense of each tourist increased which shows that the market of being is constantly being optimized. The Bird Nest, Water Cube and the Olympic Sports Park together attracted large numbers of domestic visitors after the Beijing Olympic Games, which results in a noticeable increase in the number of tourists.

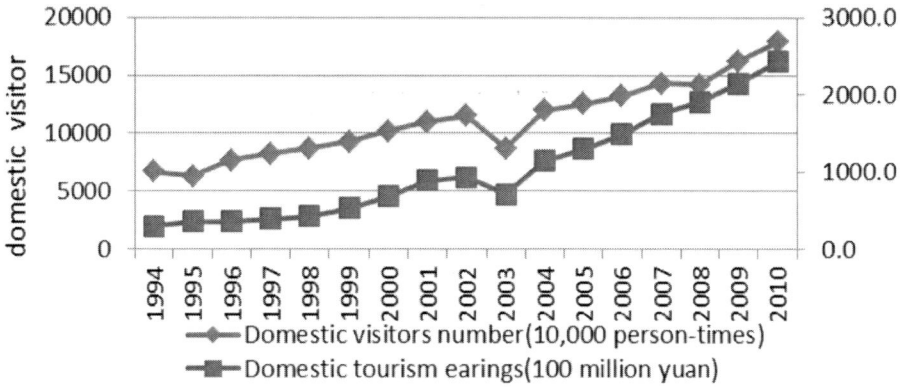

Figure 8. Domestic Visitor Number and Tourism Earnings.

7.2.2. Overseas Tourism

In the year 2010, Beijing hosted 4,901,000 overseas tourists up by 1.41 times compared to the year 1994 --- the number of which is 2,030,000 --- with the tourism incomes at 5,044,000,000 dollars, up by 2.51 times than the year 1994 --- the number of which is 2,009,040,000 dollars.

The data shows that from 1994 to 2007, the overseas tourism experienced three declines in the number of tourists, each in year 1998, year 2003 and year 2008, and the number began to increase instantly in the next year. After a thorough understanding of the whole situation, it can be concluded that the flood in the summer of 1998 and the Finance Crisis in Asia is responsible for the decline in 1998, the explosion of SARS led to the decline in 2003, while the reason for the decline in 2008 is two-fold. On one hand, the adjustment of visa policy and other policy makes it more difficult to go to Beijing because of the Olympic Games; one the other hand, global financial crisis broke out in this year.

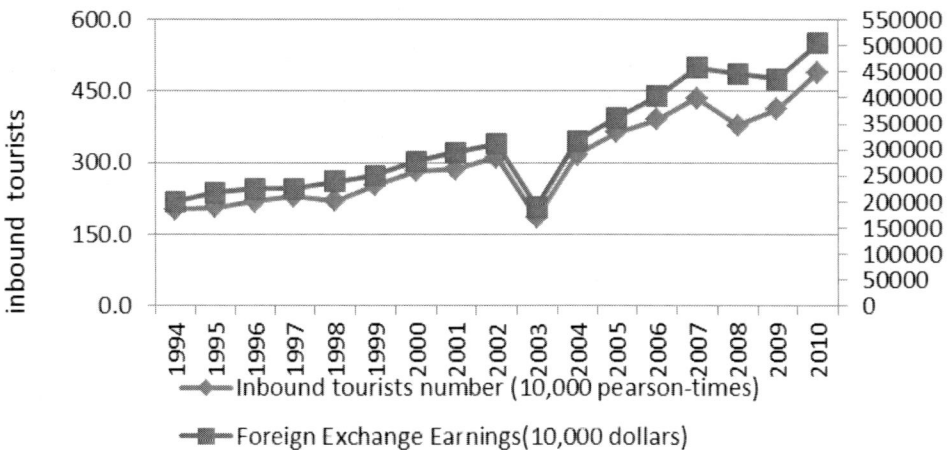

Figure 9. Overseas tourists Number and Foreign Exchange Earnings from International Tourism.

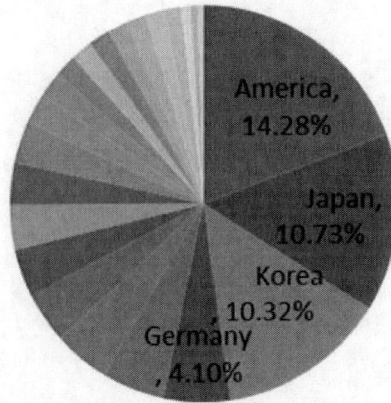

Figure 10. Structure of overseas tourists.

In 2010, 14 percent of the international tourists are our countrymen from Hong Kong, Macao and Taiwan and foreigners posses the other 86 percent. Among all the continents, tourists from Asia are the most which means the number of visitors who chose short-journey in international travelling is proportionately larger than the long ones. Among the foreigners, Americans, Japanese, Koreans, and Germans have a proportion of more than 4 percent while Russians, Britishers and Canadians are more than 3% of the total amount of tourists.

It shows that the number of tourists from Hong Kong, Macao and Taiwan declined by 1.72 percent, among which tourists from Macao declined by 13.2 percent, Taiwan increased to some extent --- an increase about 13 percent. When it comes to foreign countries, except for New Zealand, the number of which declined compared with the year 2009, tourists from all the other countries increased at different rates and the highest five countries are Mongolia, Korea, Indonesia, Malaysia and Thailand.

7.2.3. Tourism Market Structure

The whole process of development indicates that though fluctuation exists in the proportion of domestic tourists and international tourists, undoubtedly, the domestic tourism market is the most important market in the tourism of Beijing.

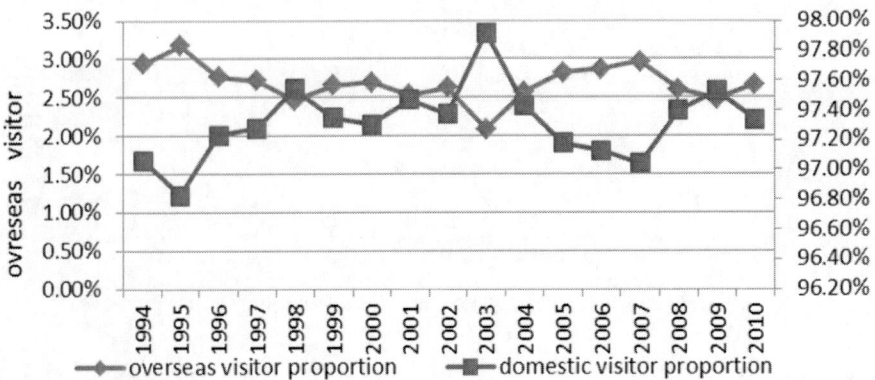

Figure 11. Structure of Beijing's Tourism Market.

7.3. Tourism Consumption in Beijing

In order to compare the traveling income from foreigners with the one from domestic market, all the earnings are needed to exchange into RMB, based on the average exchange rate in each year. As the Figure 12 shows, the average traveling consumption of foreigners is much higher, which means this will be a potential market. According to the trend of the amount of the consumption during 1994 to 2009, the average income of tourism from foreigners has descended slightly, while the income coming from internal people (except people from Beijing itself, the same below) has enhanced.

Figure 5, which is the change of domestic and foreign tourism earnings in Beijing during 1994 to 2009 indicates that the total amount of domestic tourism earnings in Beijing (except the income from Beijing itself, the same below) has been rising rapidly and obviously, while the amount of foreign tourism earnings, which is less than the amount of local earnings all along, keeps even.

Based on these two figures, although the average consumption of foreigners is much higher, it has a trend of decline; however the consumption of domestic people moves contrarily. Moreover, the people coming from other areas in China, whose group is still growing these years, are far more than the people from foreign. Thus, domestic tourism earnings are much more than foreign tourism earnings.

Currently, the tourism earnings in Beijing mainly come from domestic travelers, whose potential of consumption has been exposed gradually.

7.4. Tourism Consumption Structure in Beijing

Since lots of factors, like economics, politics and cultures, may influence the consumption, people from different areas will have different spending habits. So the analysis will be processed in three parts: general analysis, lateral comparison and vertical comparison.

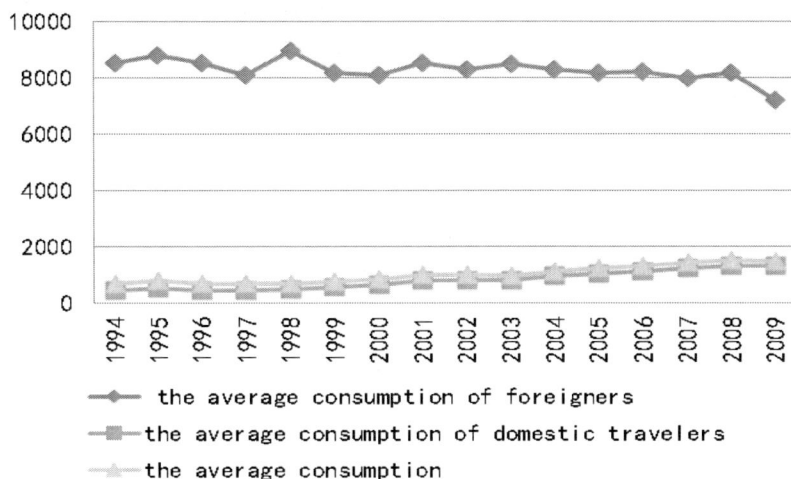

Figure 12. The Average Consumption of Tourism in Beijing.

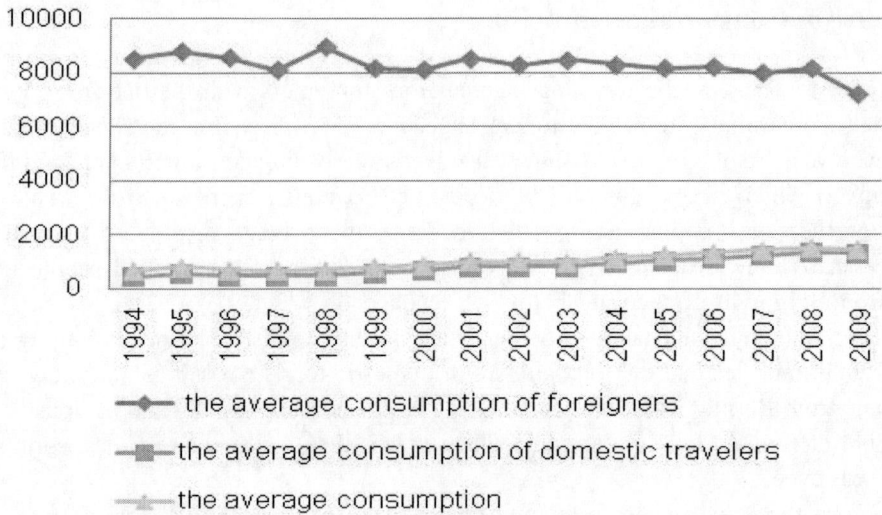

Figure 13. The Total Consumption of Tourism in Beijing.

7.4.1. General Analysis

The proportion of the cost of food and beverages, accommodation, shopping and traffic will be analyzed in this part.

Figure 7 shows the consumption of travelers in Beijing in 2009. In order to get the general proportion of the cost, the foreign exchange earnings, adjusted by the average exchanged rate in 2009, have been weighted averaged with the consumption of domestic tourism of the corresponding items.

As it shows in the figure, the cost of shopping and long-distance traffic are the two biggest expenses, about 60% of the total expenses. Among them, the air transport cost stands the largest proportion, far more than the rail and road. This is mainly due to the higher price of civil aviation as well as the preference of convenience and comfort when traveling. After these two costs, the cost of food and beverages, about 20%, and accommodation, about 17%, are two major consumer items as well. In addition, the cost of scenic tours, city transportation, entertainment, postal and telecommunications are also in a certain proportion of total spending.

7.4.2. Lateral Comparison

This part mainly discusses whether the source of tourists will influence the consumption structure through analyzing the differences of spending habits between domestic tourists (except visitors lived in Beijing, the same below) and foreign tourists.

According to Figure 8, the difference of consumption structure between these two kinds of people is significant.

Firstly, the foreign tourists spend much more money on transportation of both civil aviation and city transportation because of the spatial difference.

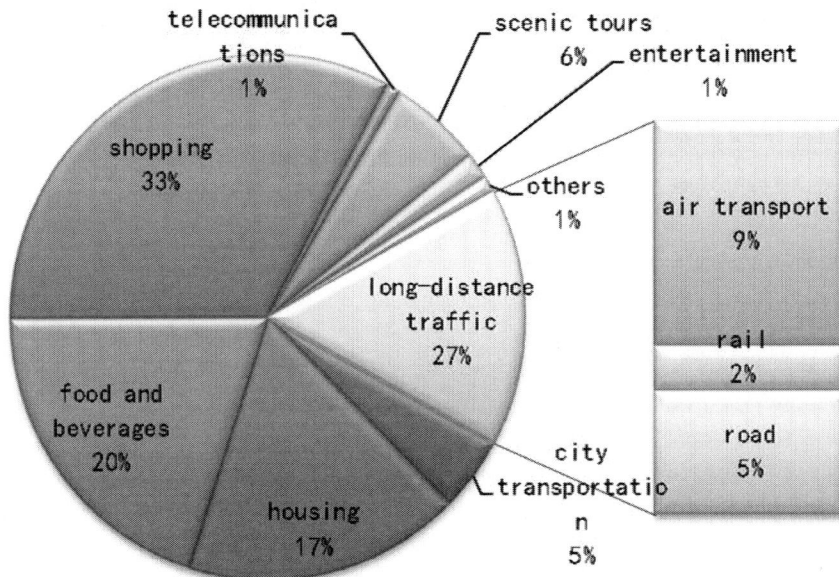

Figure 14. The Consumption Structure of Tourism in Beijing (2009).

Secondly, the proportion of spending of domestic tourists on food and beverages and accommodation is higher; especially in the food and beverages, the proportion of domestic ones' is 14% higher. This phenomenon is due to the discrepancy in the catering culture: Chinese people places great emphasis on the quality of catering, particularly when they are traveling, and eating tasty food has become an important part of traveling in China; foreigners, however, will pay more attention and money on other items.

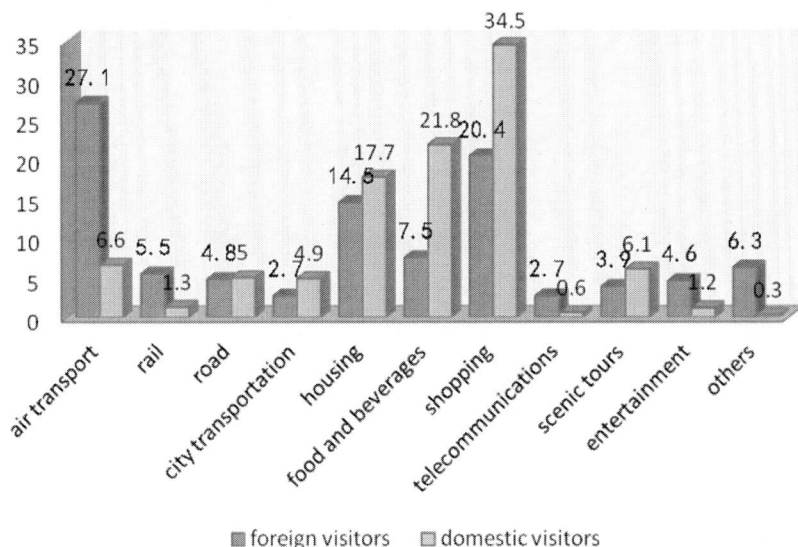

Figure 15. The Comparison of the Structure of Consumption Between the Domestic Tourists and Foreign Visitors in 2009.

Other aspects of consumption of domestic tourists are much higher than that of foreign visitors, including the expense of tourist attractions. Foreigners are more willing to spend their money on cultural and entertaining items, almost equal to the money spent on scenic spot visiting; nevertheless Chines prefer to pay more money for scenic spots visiting rather than spend money on cultural and entertaining items, which is only 1.2% of their total expenses.

7.4.3. Vertical Comparison

This part primarily analysis the time series data of the consumption of each item, which shows the change of consuming structure.

Figure 9 indicates the variation tendency of the consuming structure in Beijing between 2005 and 2009. According to the graph, the construction of consumption hasn't changed much since 2005, except the proportion of the money spent on shopping, which is increasing year by year. This phenomenon not only means the spending habits of visitors has changed, but indicates that along with the rapid growing of tourism, the synergy of the tourism and retail trade has emerged. In response to this trend, analysis of tourist spending habits to meet the demand will have a positive effect on the further development of the tourism economy.

When considering the consuming structure of different tourists separately, we could find that the tendencies differ. Not like the overall structure, the consuming structure of both domestic tourists and foreign tourists has changed.

Figure 10 shows the proportion of hotel expense of foreign visitors enhanced sharply in 2006, and then fell back to the former level. And the proportion of shopping expenses of foreign visitors keeps smooth.

On the other hand, the proportion of shopping and food expenses has risen, which demonstrates that the overall change of the structure is mainly caused by the change of domestic visitors' spending habits; besides, the proportion of money spent on visiting scenic spot of domestic travelers has dropped.

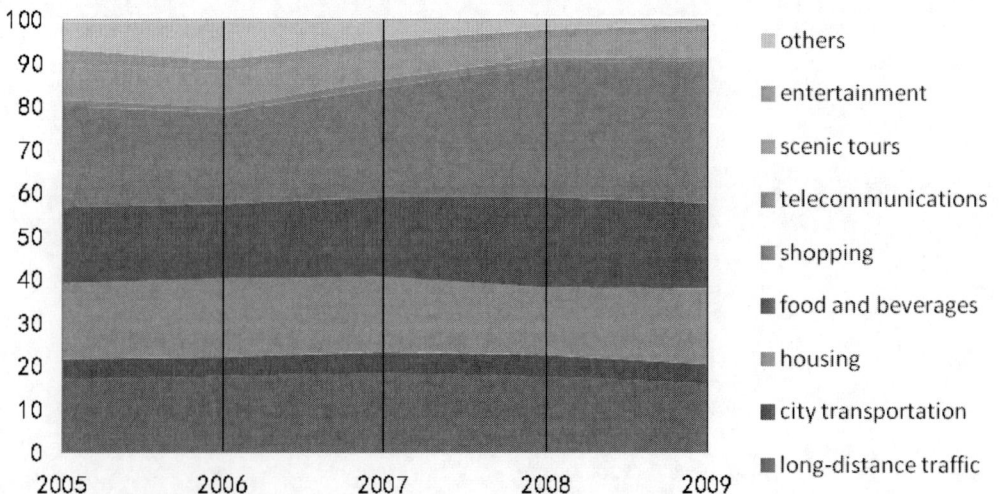

Figure 16. The Structure of Consumption of Tourists in Beijing (2005 to 2009).

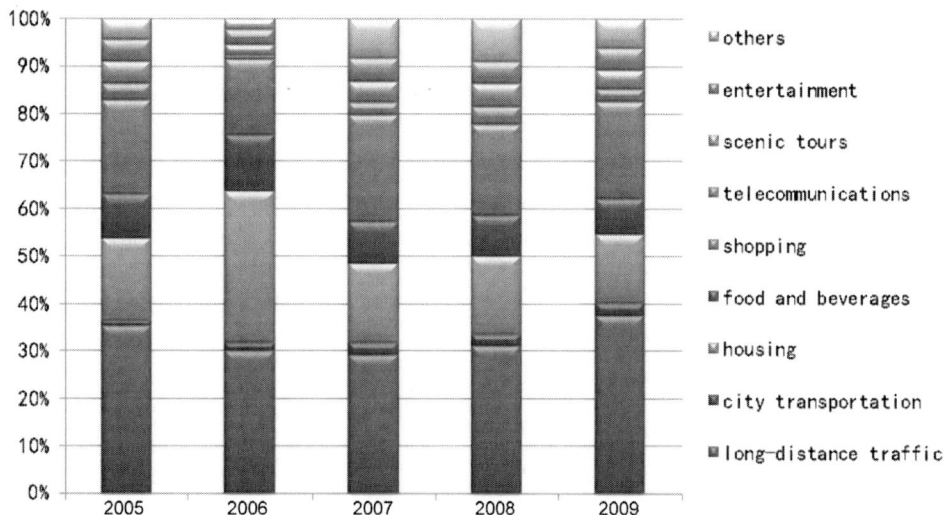

Figure 17. The Structure of Consumption of Foreign Visitors (2005 to 2009).

CONCLUSION

Both domestic and foreign tourism in China are developing coordinately, which consolidates the leading status of China's tourism in the world. China's tourism has made progress in domestic and international market exploitation, industrial system, industry function release, as well as institutional innovation. National strategy for tourism development becomes more clearly. The environment for China's tourism also greatly promotes its improvement. Significantly increasing tourism consumption, domestic demand expansion policy and other national great strategies all play as a strong driving force.

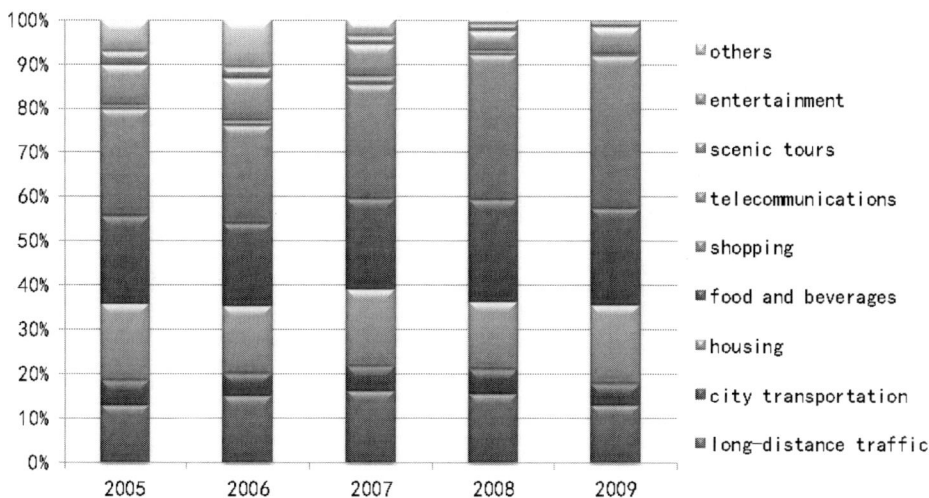

Figure 18. The Structure of Consumption of Domestic Visitors (2005 to 2009).

With the development of China's tourism, its elements will be more industrialized, its resources will be more commercialized, its development patterns will be more modernized, and its spatial layout is getting more internationalized. Moreover, the internationalization of east region, the civilization of middle region, industrialization of western region, and the industrial upgrading of northeast region are all in progress.

According to the analysis of Beijing's tourism, it can be observed that visitors spend most of their money on shopping and transportation, and the next two items are the expenses of food and beverages and accommodation. In order to promote the development of tourism economy and stimulate relative consumption, these four aspects should be mainly focused on.

The distinction of consumption structure indicates that the consumption habits of visitors from different areas differ. Therefore, it is better to provide varied service to cater the need of different people. For example, the travel agency could provide more cultural or recreational events to foreign visitors while offer more opportunities, like taking tasty food and shopping, to domestic travelers.

Since consumption habits have changed recently, the travel agency should adjust to such tendency. Also, the agency should find out the detail of "others", for the cost of "others" has increased among foreign visitors. Since domestic visitor pay more and more money on shopping and food, the tourism make a great contribution on catering industry and retail trade, which leads to the economic prosperity.

REFERENCES

Beijing Municipal Bureau of Statistics (2011). *Beijing Statistical Yearbook -2011*. Beijing: China Statistics Press.

Beijing Tourism Administration (2011). *The 12th five-year plan for Beijing's tourism industry*, Beijing: China Statistics Press.

National Bureau of Statistics (2001). *China Statistical Yearbook -2011*. Beijing: China Statistics Press.

National Tourism Administration of the People's Republic of China (2011a). *The 12th five-year plan for China's tourism industry*. Beijing: China Statistics Press.

National Tourism Administration of the People's Republic of China (2011b). *Opinions of the State Council on accelerating the development of tourism*. Beijing: China Statistics Press.

In: Methods and Analysis on Tourism and Environment   ISBN: 978-1-62417-824-5
Editors: J.M.Jiménez, M.V.Vargas, F.J.O.Rosell et al. © 2013 Nova Science Publishers, Inc.

Chapter 2

TOURISM POTENTIAL OF THE SHEIKH ABD EL-QURNA TOMBS (WEST BANK OF LUXOR, EGYPT)

María José Viñals[1], José Lull[2] and Maryland Morant[3]
[1]Universitat Politècnica de València, Valencia, Spain
[2]IEPOA – Universitat Autònoma de Barcelona, Barcelona, Spain
[3]Universitat Politècnica de València, Valencia, Spain

ABSTRACT

The continuously increasing annual increments of tourists in Luxor (Egypt), focalized in very few places such as the Valley of the Kings at the West Bank, hardly help the conservation of the ancient monuments and tourist enjoyment. In order to relieve that problem the authors carried out a study of the tourism potential of the Sheikh Abd el-Qurna Necropolis utilizing a methodology to assess both the intrinsic and recreational values of the site. Effective management plans and putting new areas into value with great tourism potential, such as Sheikh Abd el-Qurna, could alleviate to some degree tourist congestion and the very serious preservation problems facing the historic monuments.

1. INTRODUCTION

Archaeological destinations are distinctive tourist products that depend upon a fragile and non-renewable resource. This paper focuses on Egypt, considered to be one of the most significant archaeological tourist destinations in the world (Helmy & Cooper, 2002).

The aim of this paper is to analyze the tourism potential of the Sheikh Abd el-Qurna Necropolis, on the West Bank of the River Nile, close to the city of Luxor. This city is one of the best-known and most visited archaeological sites in the world. The ancient Thebes, including the Valley of the Kings, was designated a World Heritage Site by the United

Nations Education, Scientific and Cultural Organization (UNESCO) in 1979. The area, defined as "antiquities land", is controlled by the Supreme Council of Antiquities.

The West Bank area, especially the Valley of the Kings, recorded more than 5,000 daily tourists in 2009. On the days of cruise tour arrivals (Wednesday and Friday), 9,000 tourists were registered. The Egyptian Ministry of Tourism estimates that daily tourist numbers will double and even triple within the next ten years (Weeks et al., 2006).

The purpose of this work lies in the framework of the guidelines appointed by the Theban Mapping Project (Weeks et al., 2006) as a solution to the problem of tomb degradation in the Valley of the Kings caused by mass tourism and a lack of crowd control. Therefore, we have focused this research on a means to alleviate pressure on the most crowded pharaoh-heritage sites of Valley of the Kings and to improve the tourist experience.

The hill of Sheikh Abd el-Qurna holds about 150 New Kingdom (1539 to 1077 BCE, 18th-20th dynasty) tombs that belonged to the nobility. This paper presents the opportunities to mobilize the Sheikh Abd el-Qurna Necropolis for tourism purposes, due to its proximity to the Valley of the Kings and because this site embodies suitable Egyptian heritage elements. To achieve this goal we have studied its visited and non-visited tombs, assessing them from the point of view of their intrinsic and recreational values. In addition, we have taken into consideration questions related to the psychological comfort of tourists in order to improve their experience in the site. We cite some studies devoted to this topic in the context of carrying capacity studies, for example Stevens & Geoffrey (1980), Cifuentes (1992), Viñals et al., (2004), Manning (2007), Segrado et al., (2008) and Chen & Shian (2010) among others.

2. ANALYSIS OF POTENTIALS OF SHEIKH ABD EL-QURNA TOMBS

The study of the tourism potential of the Sheikh Abd el-Qurna Necropolis was carried out utilizing methodologies to assess both the intrinsic and recreational values of the site. The methodologies employed have been defined and already tested in other sites (Viñals et al., 2005). These two approaches are based on different scientific criteria.

Intrinsic value is related to the ethnological, artistic, archaeological and/or historical potential of the Sheikh Abd el-Qurna Tombs. The criteria used for this analysis are: significance, representativeness, and singularity.

The evaluation of *significance* is based on the artistic, archaeological and historical potential of the tombs as representative elements of West Bank Egyptian tombs. *Representativeness* is assessed on the basis of the degree to which the tomb presents the characteristics or attributes typical of the group to which it belongs. *Singularity* has been established according to the rarity of the tomb in relation to the typical characteristics of the class or type to which it belongs. This criterion takes the spatial scale into consideration.

Recreational value is a measure of the tourists' attachment to the resource; in this case, the Sheikh Abd el-Qurna tombs. Criteria for this assessment are: attractiveness, fragility/vulnerability, accessibility, feasibility and educational and interpretation potential. *Attractiveness* or tourist appeal refers to aesthetic, emotive and perceptual parameters such as the beauty, originality, symbolism and emotions that this necropolis awakens in tourists. *Fragility/vulnerability* is defined as susceptibility to disturbance, usually human-caused (impacts). In this case, we found that the conditions of degradation and/or alteration of the

Sheikh Abd el-Qurna tombs are similar to that of the Valley of the Kings. We have observed that temperature and humidity changes, along with the excessive number of tourists, and degradation/destruction of the fabric and paintings are the main impacts for determining vulnerability. As we can see, tourist impacts are most pronounced where capacity of the tombs is frequently exceeded to potentially dangerous limits (Rivers, 2000). *Accessibility* refers to how easy it is to visit the tombs in terms of their size, shape, trail facilities, recreational facilities and services in general. *Feasibility* is associated with the tombs' recreational carrying capacity and the internal and external repercussions of the tourists' options in terms of viability (costs and benefits, restoration costs, management and maintenance), social benefits, etc. *Educational and interpretation potential* measure the tombs' aptitude for raising public awareness about heritage conservation and bringing knowledge to the tourists on history, art and archaeology.

A tourist satisfaction analysis has been included in order to evaluate possibilities for improving the experience of tourists in relation with their expectations. Therefore, we have carried out the practitioners psychological comfort study, taking into consideration that enclosed and small spaces are not the best places for developing recreational activities, in particular when they usually are overcrowded such as the Valley of the Kings tombs.

Most recent recreational studies take into consideration one or more criteria for the tourism planning and management processes (Cracolici & Nijkamp, 2009; Poria et al., 2009; Van der Ark & Richards, 2006; Kyriakou, 2006; Pedersen, 2002; Bettini & Massa, 1991; Var et al., 1985). However, this study goes one step further by considering a holistic approach which applies a consistent set of criteria.

3. INTRINSIC HERITAGE VALUE ANALYSIS OF THE EL-QURNA TOMBS

Most of the Sheikh Abd el-Qurna Nobles' tombs follow the typical Theban T-shaped rock cut type. The tombs consist of a courtyard which leads to a vestibule, followed by another long corridor that leads into a chapel often with a small niche at the rear (Manniche, 1988). They are decorated with carved and painted raised reliefs, or paintings on a layer of plaster applied to the flat limestone bedrock with scenes and hieroglyphic texts. Normally, the decorations contain the so-called daily life scenes, funerary processions, funerary rituals before the mummy, the ritual travel to Abydos, etc. (Dodson, 1991).

At the present time, the Sheikh Abd el-Qurna Necropolis is an infrequently visited site by tourist groups despite its great potential. The inhabitants of Qurna were recently relocated and their homes destroyed by the Supreme Council of Antiquities (Hawass, 2009); so the site could be totally cleaned of rubble and prepared for adequate tourist use. There are ten tombs open to the tourists, most of them with colorful paintings or high-quality reliefs of unbelievable value, meaning that all of them are representative of the New Kingdom artistic style and contain important archaeological findings for reconstructing the historical evolution of the New Kingdom lifestyle. The TT 55, TT 56, TT 57, TT 96, TT 100, TT 31, TT 343, TT 51, TT 69 and TT 52 are the tombs included in our analysis.

TT 55 is the tomb of the vizier Ramose (Davies, 1941). This is a large private tomb with high quality compositions, many of the scenes are in relief. A stairway with a center ramp leads into a courtyard. Although this tomb is unfinished, it is significant because the artwork shows the transition to the Amarna style. It also provides evidence of the different stages of carving and decorating a tomb and is one of the best pieces of ancient art in the world.

TT 56 is the Userhat tomb, south of the tomb of Ramose. It has been open to the public for many years. For this reason, it is one of the better known non-royal tombs of the West Bank at Luxor. The intrinsic value of this tomb derives from the singularity of its inverted T-shape and from the well-preserved state of its paintings with unusual scenes.

TT 57 is the Khaemhat tomb. This tomb is significant because of the high quality of the reliefs and because of the uniqueness of the variation of the standard T-shaped plane. It also contains a number of agricultural scenes which are somewhat rare.

TT 96 is the tomb of Sennefer (Hornung et al., 2006). This tomb is located high on the hillside above Rekhmire's tomb. It has a courtyard and a decorated chapel which are not open to the public (Angenot, 2007). The entrance leads down a steep, 35 degree staircase directly into an antechamber which precedes the four-pillared burial chamber. Both of these rooms are decorated, unlike other private tombs of the period (Porter & Moss, 1994). The significance of this tomb is based both on the wall paintings of the underground chambers, painted in bright colors which are extremely well-preserved, and on the spectacular decoration of the ceiling in the burial chamber.

TT 100 is the tomb of Rekhmire (Davies, 1935; 1943). It consists of a courtyard leading into a transversal vestibule 20 meters in length and then a longitudinal corridor that is 25 m in length, and ranges in height from three meters at the beginning to eight meters at its rear (James, 2003). The decorative arrangement begins in the vestibule with multiple themes that deal with common elements found in tombs, but also includes unique scenes. In addition, the quality of work in the longitudinal corridor is outstanding as it includes nearly 300 m^2 of colorfully decorated wall surfaces. All these features make this private tomb one of the most interesting and significant of the West Bank at Luxor.

TT 31 tomb belongs to Khonsu. The tomb has the typical inverted T-shape and numerous attractive paintings showing the cult of the god Montu as well as that of Thutmosis III.

TT 343 is the tomb of Benia. The vestibule is located behind the courtyard and is accessed by crossing a very short corridor at which point a transverse vestibule comes into sight. Inside the vestibule a scene portrays Benia apparently performing his duties, including weighing and storing gold, silver, ivory, ebony and turquoises while two scribes meticulously record the event. In the other scene we see musicians playing at Benia's funeral banquet.

TT 51 is the tomb of Userhat. The tomb has a typical T-shape, with a courtyard, followed by a short corridor leading into the vestibule. Only this section of the tomb is open to the public. A singular scene depicting the tree goddess is the earliest known Egyptian art with shading. The Userhat tomb is said to be one of the most beautiful in Thebes.

TT 69 is the tomb of Menna. The tomb is significant because of its well-known wall-paintings of scenes of daily life, depicted in bright colors. In fact it is considered to be one of the finest painted, non-royal Egyptian tombs open to the public.

TT 52 belongs to Nakht (Shedid & Seidel, 1991). Paintings, as usual, represent daily life and the rural lifestyle, but some of them are especially graceful, as is the case of the famous group of three female musicians. Thus, the most significant element of this tomb is the wall paintings of the transverse vestibule because they are very colorful and well-preserved. During the decade of eighties a series of works were undertaken in order to protect the walls and their paintings of TT52. Fluorescent light bulbs and glass panels were inserted reducing the dimensions of the room. Furthermore, the dust accumulated on the glass, the poor illumination system and the limited utilizable area can cause a claustrophobic sensation.

4. RECREATIONAL VALUES ANALYSIS OF THE EL-QURNA TOMBS

Taking into account the aforementioned recreational criteria, we established that the Sheikh Abd el-Qurna tombs have a high tourism potential. Therefore, we began the assessment by using an attractiveness rating to determine the degree to which a tomb has the ability to draw tourists by provoking either interest or pleasure. For this determination we used five components: conservation status, archaeological value, historical value, and artistic value.

Conservation status addresses the state of conservation of the tomb, taking into account the fabric structure, reliefs and paintings. *Archaeological value* is determined by the importance of the tomb from the archaeological point of view, because of its rarity or its findings.

Historical value describes the significance of the tomb's contribution to the knowledge of history, economy and society associated with its age by studying its inscriptions or its findings. *Artistic value* describes the tomb's importance due its architecture and also includes the quality and relevance of the reliefs or paintings found inside the tomb.

Table 1 shows the assessment of the 10 tombs' attractiveness by assigning values ranging from one to five (very low, low, moderate, high to very high).

Table 1. Attractiveness-rating criteria for Sheikh Abd el-Qurna Tombs

	TT 55	TT 56	TT 57	TT 96	TT 100	TT 31	TT 343	TT 51	TT 69	TT 52
Conservation status	4	4	4	4	4	3	4	4	4	4
Archaeological value	4	3	4	4	5	3	3	3	4	3
Historical value	4	3	4	3	5	3	3	3	4	3
Artistic value	5	4	5	5	5	3	3,5	3,5	5	4,5
	4.25	**3.5**	**4.25**	**4.0**	**4.75**	**3.0**	**3.3**	**3.3**	**4.25**	**3.6**

Unit values ranging from 1 to 5 (from very low, low, moderate, high to very high).

Findings from this analysis ranks tombs TT 100 (Rekhmire Tomb), TT 55 (Ramose Tomb), TT 57 (Khaemhat Tomb) and TT 69 (Menna Tomb) as the most attractive among the Sheikh Abd el-Qurna tombs, due to their artistic values and good states of conservation. In addition, tomb TT 100 has remarkable archaeological and historical value.

On other hand, enclosed spaces such as tombs present some user constraints. For this reason is very important to assess their accessibility. Two features of the tombs inform us of the ease of visiting them. One, outside access: defines the difficulty of accessing the tomb for the tourists from the Necropolis entrance to the tomb entrance (distance, slope, etc.). Two, inside access: defines the difficulty of accessing the tomb for the tourists from the tomb entrance to the deepest part of the tomb opened to the public (distance, slope, stairs, narrowing, etc.).

It is important to highlight that practically all the tombs proposed for visitation in this study present good access conditions with the exception of TT 96 (table 2).

Table 2. Accessibility-rating criteria for Sheikh Abd el-Qurna tombs

	TT 55	TT 56	TT 57	TT 96	TT 100	TT 31	TT 343	TT 51	TT 69	TT 52
Outside access	5	5	5	3	4	5	5	5	4	4
Inside access	5	5	5	3	5	5	5	5	5	5
	5	**5**	**5**	**3**	**4.5**	**5**	**5**	**5**	**4.5**	**4.5**

Unit values ranging from 1 to 5 (from very bad, bad, moderate, good to very good).

The feasibility of mobilizing the Sheikh Abd el-Qurna site for tourism purposes is directly related to the recreational carrying capacity of the tombs. This concept can be defined as the number of tourists that could move without problems inside the tomb, without causing unacceptable changes in the physical environment and integrity of the tomb (direct or indirect impacts) or a decline in the quality of the tourist experience (disturbing anybody, uncomfortable feeling of overcrowding, build-up of people that could obstruct the flow of tourists, etc.).

The first factor considered in this analysis was the size of the tombs. In general terms, Sheikh Abd el-Qurna tombs are roughly the same size as most of the tombs of the Valley of the Kings. They vary in size from 18 m^2 to more than 1,000 m^2. It is important to consider the volume of space within the tombs as this capacity impacts air conditions and the air available for tourists to breathe. The plan of the tombs is also important as tombs with steep staircases require greater linear space to hold the same number of tourists.

In this study, we have followed the rule of thumb of allocating each tourist one linear meter of space. This number was established through on-site observations in open trails (Morant, 2007; Morant & Viñals, 2009) and other authors have extrapolated it to closed spaces as well (Weeks et al., 2006). We consider it to be the surface space required to carry out the visit satisfactorily because we have observed that people walking in lines in other heritage sites (Petra World Heritage site, Jordan; Copán World Heritage site, Honduras; Lonja de Mercaderes de Valencia, España; etc.) feel uncomfortable with less separation than this.

This one-meter rule combined with the tomb size gives us the physical carrying capacity, but it is necessary to adjust this number according to the tombs' shape and pathway, some architectural features and protective elements (glass fences, barriers, etc.) and to consider the fragility of the site. Therefore, we have identified vulnerability, or the intrinsic susceptibility or predisposition of the tombs to suffer damage or loss due to visitation.

The main direct impacts from visitation detected are the abrasion of walls and paintings. Other relevant indirect impacts affecting the tombs are related to dramatic changes in temperature/humidity levels that produce microclimate alterations and the degradation of the paintings. This impact is caused by an elevated number of tourists, and it is not visible immediately but becomes apparent in the medium term. Paradise (2005) relates that in the Petra World Heritage Site (Jordan), the rising level of humidity in the interior of the Nabatean tombs is due to the increasing number of tourists in the recent years. It is necessary to point out that tombs must be considered non-elastic cultural resources in that they do not have the ability to repair damage after the disturbances cease.

Table 3. Recreational Carrying Capacity of Sheik Abd el-Qurna Tombs

	TT 55	TT 56	TT 57	TT 96	TT 100	TT 31	TT 343	TT 51	TT 69	TT 52
RCC	5	3	3	2	4	2	2	2	3	1
	5	**3**	**3**	**2**	**4**	**2**	**2**	**2**	**3**	**1**

1- Very low carrying capacity, it does not allow more than 5 visitors; 2- Limited capacity, between 6 and 10 visitors; 3- Groups of 11 to 15 visitors; 4- Groups for 16 to 20 visitors; 5- It allows a higher number of visitors.

Taking into account all these considerations in calculating the tombs' carrying capacity, Table 3 shows us the different possibilities for hosting tourists. The rating ranges from one (very low carrying capacity which does not allow more than five people), two (limited capacity, between six and ten people), three (groups of 11 to 15 people), four (groups for 16 to 20 people) and to five (allows for a higher number of people). The figures show that the most suitable tomb for holding tourists is TT 55 (Ramose tomb) because more than 20 people can visit the site at the same time. This number does not pose a threat to the paintings because the water vapor and CO_2 coming from tourists' breath do not alter inner microclimate conditions.

Educational and/or interpretative potential is another important criterion taken into consideration. It is basically aimed at raising public awareness about heritage conservation, sharing knowledge and provoking emotions in the tourists. From our analysis of all the tombs we concluded that the most valuable tombs from the educational point of view are TT 55 (Ramose Tomb) and TT 100 (Rekhmire Tomb).

To complete this analysis of tourism potential for this Necropolis, and thinking basically of improving the tourist experience, the next step undertaken was the practitioners psychological comfort analysis. This concept refers to the number of people able to carry out an activity in a determined space without feeling perturbed by the presence of other tourists in the same place or by the behavior pattern of tourists in general. It depends on many factors which are very difficult to evaluate because of their subjective components. These psychological factors affect a tomb's carrying capacity. We stress here as the more important components for this analysis: physical comfort, tombs claustrophobic sensation, crowding, and expectations about the visit.

In relation with the physical comfort, it is necessary to take into account that tourists need not submit themselves to extreme temperatures and/or humidity levels both outside and within tombs. Also, it is important to keep in mind that to promote the Sheikh Abd el-Qurna Necropolis for tourism purposes it will be necessary to develop basic facilities regarding first aid, toilets, trails, shaded meeting points, etc.

Claustrophobic sensation is defined as the uncomfortable sensation of claustrophobia or panic, which could be generated, in some tourists, in the interior of the tomb because of the narrowness of its corridors, chambers or low ceilings. According to the ranking showed in Table 4 which ranges from one to five (with one being high potential for a sensation of claustrophobia, two being significant potential, three being slight potential, four very slight potential, and five no claustrophobia problems), most of the tombs do not present problems in this sense. The exceptions are TT 52 (Nakht tomb) and TT 96 (Sennefer tomb) with a significant-to-slight potential for claustrophobia sensations.

Table 4. Claustrophobic Sensation of el-Qurna tombs

	TT 55	TT 56	TT 57	TT 96	TT 100	TT 31	TT 343	TT 51	TT 69	TT 52
CS	5	5	5	3	5	4	5	5	5	2
	5	5	5	3	5	4	5	5	5	2

1-High sensation of claustrophobia; 2- Remarkably sensation of claustrophobia; 3- Slightly sensation; 4- Very slightly sensation; 5- There is absolutely no problem.

Regarding crowding, it must be pointed out that in comparison with the Valley of the Kings, this Necropolis has never recorded these kind of problems. Nevertheless, the risk of becoming overcrowded is high because the size of the tombs and the high potential number of tourists who could visit the site. Associated with this problem is that of congestion, which is more a management problem related to tourist flow (UNTWO, 2004).

Congestion does not currently exist at the Sheikh Abd el-Qurna Necropolis. This congestion can be subjectively detected when the tombs appear too full, when the movement of individuals and groups is hindered, when lines form at the entrance of the tombs, etc. Following figures from the Map Theban Project (Weeks et al., 2006), we must keep in mind that the worst situation appears when more than 1,700 tourists per hour are visiting the Valley of the Kings. No recreational carrying capacity study has addressed the issue thus far. According to some surveys undertaken by said project, tourists feel a sense of crowding. In this sense, it is necessary to point out that tourists perceive crowding differently. Therefore, Doorne (2000) in a case study in the Waitomo Caves in New Zealand, found out that nationals are the tourists least tolerant to crowding.

The last factor analyzed is Sheikh Abd el-Qurna visit expectations which are in direct relation with an experience of quality. It is important to note that experiencing a site can be addressed with a good thematic interpretation program, signage, facilities and some services provided to tourists that allow them to carry out activities in good conditions. All these elements must be provided in order to fulfill tourists' expectations when the site holds exceptional heritage assets, as in this case.

Table 5. Main criteria and average

	TT 55	TT 56	TT 57	TT 96	TT 100	TT 31	TT 343	TT 51	TT 69	TT 52
Attractiveness rating criteria	4.5	3.7	4.3	4.2	4.8	3.2	3.5	3.3	4.5	3.8
Accessibility rating criteria	5	5	5	3	4.5	5	5	5	4.5	4.5
Recreational Carrying Capacity	5	3	3	2	4	2	2	2	3	1
Claustrophobic sensation	5	5	5	3	5	4	5	5	5	2
Average value	**4.9**	**4.2**	**4.3**	**3.1**	**4.6**	**3.6**	**3.9**	**3.8**	**4.3**	**2.8**

Average values ranging from 1 to 5 (from very bad, bad, moderate, good to very good).

At this point is important to highlight that the thematic interpretation program must create emotional and intellectual connections between the tourist and the Egyptian tombs heritage. For this commitment, the participation of good interpreters working on site to provoke the tourist to think, do or/and feel something new will be necessary, as suggested by Ham (1992) and Ham & Krumpe (1996).

CONCLUSION

The Sheikh Abd el-Qurna Necropolis contains a set of tombs with intrinsic and recreational values that allow us to propose this site for developing interpretative tourism activities. As we show in Table 5, five of the ten opened tombs meet the minimum requirements for tourism purposes. In addition to their intrinsic values, they present attractiveness, accessibility, educational and interpretation potential, feasibility (recreational carrying capacity), and the best conditions to guarantee the psychological comfort (absence of claustrophobic sensation) to tourists. These tombs are TT 55 (Ramose Tomb), TT 100 (Rekhmira Tomb), TT 69 (Menna Tomb), TT 57 (Khaemhat Tomb) and TT 56 (Userhat Tomb).

According to the characteristics of the site, we foresee that the potential targeted audience could include both specialized tourists looking to increase their knowledge of the Egyptian New Kingdom noblemen life and also tourists seeking a more comfortable visit because the site is less crowded relative to the Valley of the Kings tombs. Opportunities for other audiences can be explored, experiencing the site by offering a meaningful interpretation program to smaller interested groups.

Some tombs of the New Kingdom's noblemen at Sheikh Abd el-Qurna are beautifully decorated with paintings and reliefs, and unlike the royal tombs of the Valley of the Kings, which are confined to an specific iconography difficult to understand for the non-initiated tourists, the private tombs' decorations often break with these norms and are therefore artistically more pleasing and more understandable to the eyes of the regular tourists.

In addition to the restoration work of the tombs, it is necessary to improve the accessibility of the site and to develop the facilities and services since this would by easy both in technical and economic terms.

The Sheikh Abd el-Qurna Necropolis can be presented as a complementary option of quality, differentiating the product from the Valley of the Kings for tourists who wish to appreciate a more culturally accurate and pleasant offer.

Therefore, this proposal must be considered as a strategy to alleviate pressure over the Valley of the Kings. Finally, we want to stress that promoting this Necropolis for increased visitation will require not only facilities and programs, but it is also essential to develop a good tourism management plan, which includes carrying capacity management, tourists flow control, a ticketing policy, indicators and an environmental system for tomb monitoring, tourist satisfaction surveys, etc.

REFERENCES

Angenot, V. (2007). Les peintures de la chapelle de Sennefer (TT 96A). *Africa & Orient*, 45, 21-32.

Bettini, G. & Massa, S. (1991). Preservation problems, visitors and deterioration on the painted Etruscan tomb. In Baer, N. S.; Sabbioni, C. & Sors, A. I. (Eds.): *Technology, and European cultural heritage: proceedings of the European symposium.* Butterworth-Heinemann. Bologna. 761-769.

Cifuentes, M. (1992). *Determinación de Capacidad de Carga Turística en Áreas Protegidas.* CATIE. Turrialba.

Chen, C. & Shian, F. (2010). Experience quality, perceived value, satisfaction and behavioral intentions for heritage tourists. *Tourism Management*, 31(1), 29-35.

Cracolici, M & Nijkamp, P. (2009). The attractiveness and competitiveness of tourist destinations: A study of Southern Italian regions. *Tourism Management*, 30(3), 336-334.

Davies, N. de. G. (1935). *Paintings from the Tomb of Rekh-mi-Re' at Thebes.* Metropolitan Museum of Art. New York.

Davies, N. de G. (1941). *The Tomb of the Vizier Ramose.* Egypt Exploration Society. London.

Davies, N. de. G. (1943). *The Tombs of Rekh-mi-Re' at Thebes*, vols. 1-2. Metropolitan Museum of Art. New York.

Dodson, A. (1991). *Egyptian Rock-cut tombs.* Shire Egyptology. Haverfordwest.

Doorne, S. (2000). Caves, Cultures and Crowds: Carrying Capacity Meets Consumer Sovereignty. *Journal of Sustainable Tourism*, 8 (2), 116-130.

Ham, S. (1992). *Environmental Interpretation. A Practical Guide for People with Big Ideas and Small Budgets.* Fulcrum Publishing. Golden.

Ham, S. & Krumpe, E. (1996). Identifying Audiences and Messages for Nonformal Environmental Education. A Theoretical Framework for Interpreters. *Journal of Interpretation Research,* 1(1), 11-23.

Hawass, Z. (2009). *The Lost Tombs of Thebes. Life in Paradise.* Thames and Hudson. London.

Helmy, E. & Cooper, C. (2002). An Assessment of Sustainable Tourism Planning for the Archaeological Heritage: The Case of Egypt. *Journal of Sustainable Tourism*, 10(6), 514-535.

Hornung, E.; Krauss, R. & Warburton, D.A. (Eds.) (2006). *Ancient Egyptian Chronology.* E. J. Brill. Leiden.

James, T.G.H. (2003). *Pharaoh´s People. Scenes from life in Imperial Egypt.* The Bodley Head Ltd. London.

Kyriakou, V. (2006). Impact of tourism on cultural heritage sustainable management. The case of Macedonian tombs. *International Conference of trends, impacts and policies on Tourism Development.* Hellenic Open University. Crete.

Manniche, L. (1988). *The Tombs of the Nobles at Luxor.* American University in Cairo. Cairo.

Manning, R. (2007). *Parks and Carrying Capacity. Commons withouth tradegy.* Library of Congress and British. Washington.

Morant, M. (2007). *Desarrollo de un modelo para la determinación de la capacidad de carga recreativa y su aplicación espacios naturales protegidos de la Comunidad Valenciana.* PhD Thesis. Universidad Politécnica de Valencia.

Morant, M. & Viñals, M. J. (2009). Modelo para evaluar la capacidad de carga recreativa en áreas de uso intensivo de espacios protegidos. Casos de estudio de la Comunidad Valenciana (España). In: *Turismo y gestión de espacios protegidos.* Tirant lo Blanc.

Paradise, Th. (2005). Petra revisited: an examination of sandstone weathering research in Petra, Jordan. *GSA Special Papers*, 390, 39-49.

Pedersen, A. (2002). *Managing Tourism at World Heritage Sites: a Practical Manual for World Heritage Site Managers.* UNESCO. Paris.

Poria, Y.; Biran, A. & Reichel, A. (2009). Visitors' Preferences for Interpretation at Heritage Sites. *Journal of Travel Research*, 48 (1), 92-105.

Porter, B. & Moss, L.B.M. (1994). *Topographical Bibliography of Ancient Egyptian Hieroglyphic Texts, Reliefs and Paintings, I: The Theban Necropolis, private tombs.* Griffith Institute, Ashmolean Museum. Oxford.

Rivers, J. (2000). Thebes (Luxor, Egypt). In Shakley, M. (Ed.), *Visitor Management. Case Studies from World Heritage Sites.* Butterworth-Heinemann publications. Oxford, 161-182.

Segrado, R.; Palafox-Muñoz, A. & Arroyo, L. (2008). Medición de la capacidad de carga turística de Cozumel. *El Periplo Sustentable,* 13, 33-61.

Shedid, A. G. & Seidel, M. (1991). *Das Grab des Nacht.* Philip von Zabern. Mainz.

Steven, H. & Geoffrey, P. (1980). Estimating the benefits of recreation under conditions of congestion. *Journal of Environmental Economics and Management*, 7(4), 395-400.

UNTWO (2004). Tourism Congestion Management at Natural and Cultural Sites. Madrid: World Tourism Organization.

Van der Ark, A. & Richards, G. (2006). Attractiveness of cultural activities in European cities: A latent class approach. *Annals of Tourism Research.* 27(6), 1408-1413.

Var, T.; Cesario, F. & Mauser, G. (1985). Convention tourism modelling. *Annals of Tourism Research,* 6 (3), 194-204.

Viñals, M.J.; Morant, M.; Hernández, C.; Ferrer, C.; Quintana, R.D.; Maravall, N.; Cabrelles, G.; Ramis, J. & Bachiller, C. (2004). Albufera de Valencia (Spain): Measuring carrying capacity in a fragile ecosystem. In: *Indicators of sustainable Development for tourism destinations. A guidebook.* UNTWO. Madrid.

Viñals, M.J.; Filiberto, I. & Morant, M. (2005). *Manual para o inventário dos valores culturais das Zonas Húmidas.* Instituto da Conservaçao da Natureza. Lisboa.

Weeks, K.R.; Hetherington, N.J. & Jones, L.T. (2006). *The Valley of the Kings, Luxor, Egypt. Site Management Master Plan.* Theban Mapping Project. Cairo.

In: Methods and Analysis on Tourism and Environment ISBN: 978-1-62417-824-5
Editors: J.M.Jiménez, M.V.Vargas, F.J.O.Rosell et al. © 2013 Nova Science Publishers, Inc.

Chapter 3

LINKING ECOTOURISM'S OPPORTUNITIES AND NATIONAL PARKS PROTECTION THROUGH GEOCACHING

Ángel Peiró-Signes,[1] Blanca de-Miguel-Molina,[1]
María de-Miguel-Molina[1] and María-del-Val Segarra-Oña[1,2]
[1]Management Department, Universitat Politècnica de València, Valencia, Spain
[2]INERTE, International Network of Economic Research on Tourism and Environment,
Oviedo, Spain

ABSTRACT

The practice of geocaching, based on the use of GPS (Global Positioning System) devices, is especially concentrated in the rural environment and its leading members are hikers or campers, highly skilled in the use of technologies that find, in this game, a new reason to involve their friends or relatives. For tourism businesses close to "treasures" it can be an opportunity to attract "ecotourists", advertising on its website or providing geocaching as an additional activity. However, it can also represent a significant environmental impact when these "treasures" are in vulnerable or less traveled sites, such as national parks. Geocaching is relatively new in some countries, such as Spain, but already has a significant online community that has grown exponentially in recent years. We study the potential environmental impact of this practice at Spanish national parks by empirical data analysis.

Keywords: National Parks, ecotourism, geocaching, GPS

INTRODUCTION

Geocaching is an online treasure hunting game anywhere in the world using GPS (Global Positioning System)-enabled devices. The basic idea is to locate containers hidden outdoors called "geocaches", and then to share these experiences online. It is aimed at people of all ages with strong environmental concerns (O'Hara, 2008). All that is needed is knowledge of how to enter a waypoint, that is, the coordinates of where the treasure is hidden. Already, geocaching has over 5 million users around the world. The business idea was conceived in the United States shortly after the removal of Selective Availability from GPS in 2000, which allowed a small container to be placed in a particular place and then located (James, 2009). Geocaches have been placed in more than one hundred countries around the world and on all seven continents, including Antarctica.

After more than 10 years of activity, over 1.5 million active geocaches have been published on the website www.geocaching.com. When coordinates are published, users can view the hidden treasures around their chosen areas. The rules are very simple (Draycott, 2005): the geocachers must take something from the cache and leave something in its place as well as noting in the "logbook" who left it and the successive people who have found it. The place to hide caches depends on the user. The items included in the cache make the activity a fun "treasure hunt" because the items left by the owner or other visitors are unknown.

Except for explosives, ammunition, knives, drugs, alcohol or food, anything can be placed in the cache subject to the container size. The geocacher then marks the day of discovery on the website, providing or not new clues, thus making the geocacher community its own content creator.

The location of the treasure will also show the skills, knowledge and even the courage of the owner. Some treasures may require long days of hiking or may contain clues or riddles that may lead to other caches. The duration of the treasures depends on the situation of the cache and its impact on the environment and surrounding areas. The owner of the treasure must periodically inspect the cache and the area to ensure that the impact is minimal or nonexistent.

The language in geocaching is English, but this has not stopped other countries creating their own communities in various languages, such as the Spanish public through geocachingspain.com, foroware.com or geocaching-Hispanic.com, or even creating local groups.

Thus, this is not a typical online game, but an activity that combines technology with other outdoor leisure activities and is based on an online community or social network that does not charge users for the service because the users generate content. The earnings come from advertising partnerships with companies related to these activities.

As an activity that, in Spain, has thousands of users, with about 2,800 "treasures" hidden in various places, giving special consideration to national parks, we wonder what opportunities it can provide to tourism businesses located in rural areas and at the same time, what threats it may pose to the environment if its practice is widespread.

1. The Concept of Ecotourism

According to the United Nations (UN), "sustainable tourism" is one that takes into account future economic, social and environmental aspects, combining the needs of visitors, industry, the environment and local communities (UNWTO, 2005). As for "ecotourism", the UN also provides a general definition, specifying that it would have the following characteristics (UNWTO, 2001):

1. All nature-based forms of tourism in which the main motivation of the tourists is the observation and appreciation of nature as well as the traditional cultures prevailing in natural areas.
2. It contains educational and interpretation features.
3. It is generally, but not exclusively organized by specialized tour operators for small groups. Service provider partners at the destinations tend to be small and locally owned businesses.
4. It minimizes negative impacts upon the natural and socio-cultural environment.
5. It supports the maintenance of natural areas which are used as ecotourism attractions by:

- Generating economic benefits for host communities, organizations and authorities managing natural areas with conservation purposes.
- Providing alternative employment and income opportunities for local communities.
- Increasing awareness towards the conservation of natural and cultural assets, both among locals and tourists.

Thus, the term ecotourism refers to a segment of tourism that focuses on environmental sustainability, while sustainability principles generally apply to all types of tourism activities, operations, facilities and projects, including both conventional and alternative modes (UNEP, 2011).

Beyond the concept given by the UN, the International Ecotourism Society (TIES, 2011) defines ecotourism as "responsible travel to natural areas that conserves the environment and improves the well-being of local people". Just as nature tourism simply describes tourism in natural places, ecotourism goes beyond and it would be a type of nature tourism that benefits local communities and places environmentally, culturally and economically.

According to the UNEP (2011), worldwide more than one third of visitors agree with ecotourism and are even willing to pay more for it. Thus, while the growth of mass tourism has stagnated, other niche markets, such as ecotourism, nature tourism, cultural tourism or moderate adventure tourism, are taking the lead and are predicted to grow rapidly in the next two decades.

2. RECREATIONAL USE OF NATURE AND NATIONAL PARKS IN SPAIN

In Spain, among those who undertake physical exercise hiking/trekking has increased in recent years (CIS, 2010) up to 8.6% (Figure 1). In addition, 45% of those who play sports prefer to do so outdoors. In the case of mountaineering, Moscoso (2004) pointed out how the municipalities belonging to preferred tourism and sports mountain areas, are particularly benefiting from nature tourism.

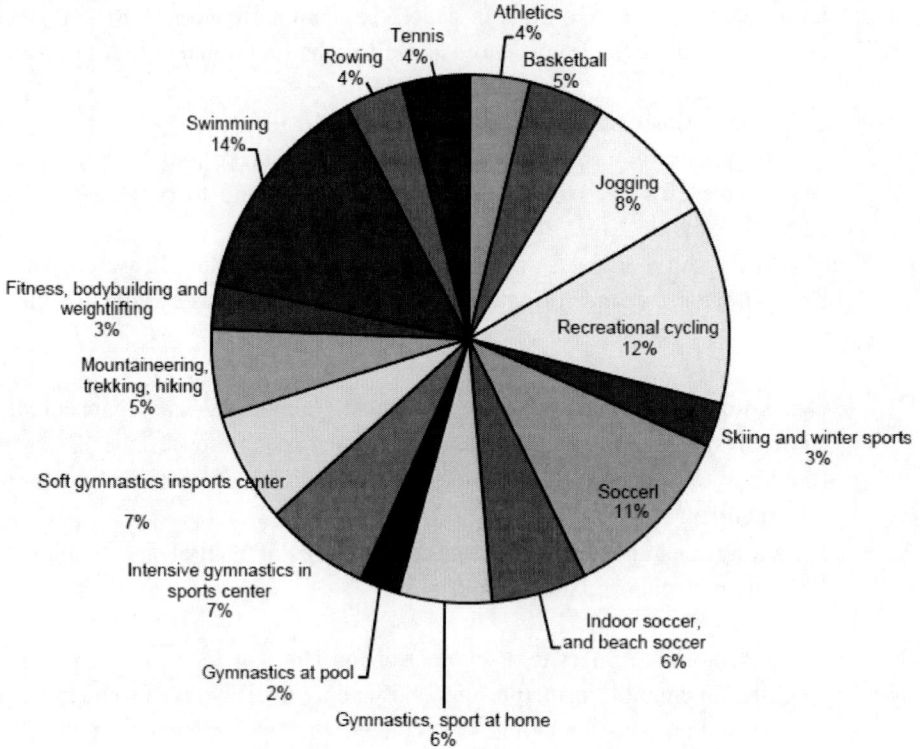

Figure 1. Percentage of the most popular sports in Spain.Source: self-compilation from the CIS[1] (2010), question 17 (People could indicate more than one so that the percentages may change).

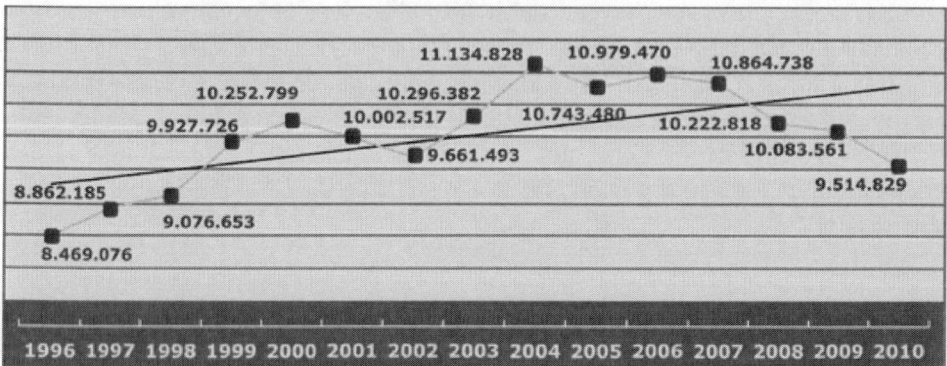

Source: Network of National Parks, Ministry of Environment and Rural and Marine Affairs.

Image 1. Evolution graph of the number of visitors to national parks 1996–2010.

For example some Spanish rural towns previously depopulated, such as Benasque or Vielha, have experienced an unusual growth in population. According to a Eurostat study (2011), in the EU about 20.4 million hectares (equivalent to 13.0% of the total area) of forests

---

[1] Social research center.

are in protected areas, for example in national parks. EU members with the largest protected forest areas are Italy, Germany and Spain.

In Spain, it is mandatory to have some features to be officially considered a national park. The Environment Ministry (National Parks Network, 2011) defines a national park as "a natural area of high natural and cultural value, little altered by human activity, that because of its exceptional natural values, representative character, unique flora, fauna or geomorphologic formations, deserves preferential preservation attention and interest and is declared by the nation to be representative of the Spanish natural heritage".

Thus, for a territory to be declared a national park, according to the Master Plan of the Network of National Parks, it should have the following characteristics:

- Representation: to represent the natural system to which it belongs.
- Extension: have a suitable surface to allow natural evolution, so as to maintain its characteristics and ensure the functioning of ecological processes in the present.
- Condition: far outnumber natural conditions and ecological functionality. Human intervention according to human values should be minimal.
- Territorial continuity: unless otherwise justified, the territory must be continuous, not locked, and there must be no elements of fragmentation to break the harmony of the ecosystems.
- Human settlements: do not include inhabited towns, unless duly justified in exceptional cases.
- External protection: being surrounded by an area susceptible to being declared a peripheral zone of protection.

According to INE[2] (2011), from 2007 to 2009 the number of visitors to national parks has decreased (Image 1). However, this is not seen as negative because the aim is to have a sustainable number of visits.

3. TOURISM AND THE ENVIRONMENTAL IMPACT OF GPS AND GEOCACHING

On the other hand, the development of technologies such as GPS, and especially its use by individuals, has favored various sectors of tourism (such as adventure tourism) by better locating certain places. For anywhere with hiking trails (certified trails), mountain biking, skiing, and sailing, or just contact with nature, this technology allows people to access information on areas in detail (Richardson, 2004; Yasukawa, 2006).

According to recent studies, geolocation services and navigation are becoming increasingly important, linked to the rise of mobile devices. The ICT sector in Spain has resulted in the proliferation of geo-referencing systems on mobile devices (Google Maps, Nokia Maps, etc.) and their increasing use, helped by mobile broadband penetration, makes it easier for advertisers, through layers of information located on maps, to offer users all kinds of information about the products available in the local area.

---

[2] Spanish National Statistics Center

Therefore, the future trend is that location-based services will provide consumers with specific local news and information, and will allow companies to promote advertising to local consumers (PwC, 2010). Likewise, the growth of GPS has been proven to increase sales in tourism enterprises (Hegarty and Chatre, 2008), especially in the niches previously mentioned, and is increasingly being included in more devices, such as mobile phones or cameras, which are often used by hikers (Youngjung, 2009). We could say that most geocaches are located in destinations that promote sustainable tourism and, specifically, in the case of natural environments, in locations that have opted for ecotourism. In addition, the geocacher is usually a hiker, a daily visitor. According to the UNWTO (2005), a visitor is classified as a tourist (or overnight visitor), if the trip includes an overnight stay, or as a day visitor (or hiker) otherwise. Most geocachers are local hikers but some tourists may also engage in hiking. While geocaching started in the United States, currently the most active countries in its use are European countries. The geocaching website is visited, to a greater extent and in descending frequency, in the Czech Republic, Germany, Slovakia, Austria, Denmark, Holland, Switzerland, Sweden, and Finland, and following them, Canada (Google Trends, 2011). In one of the first studies on the use of geocaching in North America (Schneider et al., 2011), results show that geocachers are 40 years old on average, most are college-educated men, and work full time. More than half practice sports or recreational activities, such as: hiking, camping, biking, observation/photography, swimming, picnicking, driving and other relaxing outdoor activities; however, only 19.5% were interested in orientation activities. But 80% of geocachers use GPS both for recreational and non-recreational purposes. Half of geocachers practice geocaching with family members, and groups have an average of three persons. Most geocachers are more likely to look for geocaches than to be the owners of one. Eighty-three percent think that geocaching practice has increased their numbers of visits to parks and recreational areas. Among the benefits of their practice they indicated: enjoying the environment, taking exercise, experiencing new and different activities, and enjoying nature. Also, environmental aspects were found to be very important. Regarding the number of geocaches in Spain included in the geocaching website, most of them are on the east coast, especially in Catalonia (Image 2).

In the case of geocaching, hiking is the sport most related with its practice. According to the Spanish Federation of Mountain Sports and Climbing (FEDME, 2011), walking is a sport that preferably develops on the traditional road network and is aimed at all those people who like walking. It is practiced on the entire Spanish territory and at any time of year, and the practitioner requires little technical or physical preparation and use of low-level specialized materials. According to Luque (2003), among environmental requirements required by hiking we would include:

- Preferably unpaved roads (forest roads, trails, livestock trails, etc.) and minimum widht (less for walking and higher for mountain biking, horseback tours and 4x4 tours).
- Areas that do not have any legal restriction to practice activities.
- Areas that have natural or scenic interest.
- Proximity to population centers.
- Smooth topography.
- Obstacle-free areas.

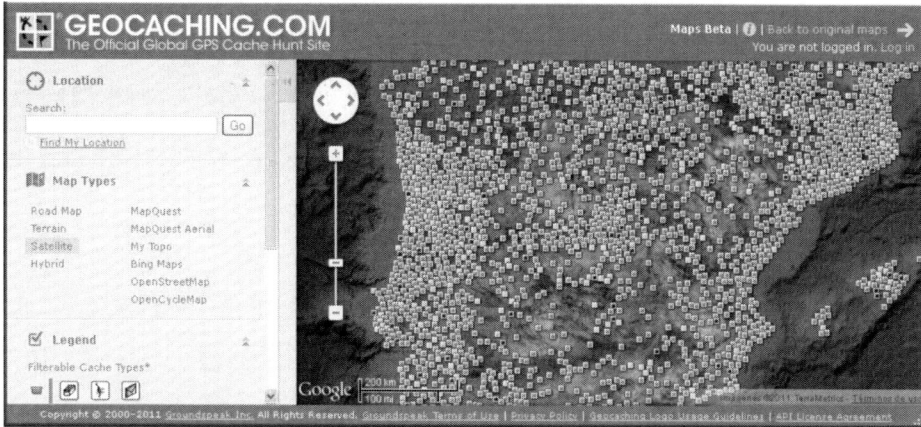

Source: www.geocaching.com

Image 2. Status of geocaches in Spain and Portugal.

Therefore, the impact that GPS ease of access may have on our ecosystems must be taken into account, as in the case of geocaching (Lynn and Brown, 2003). Some parks have expressed their concern about the impact of this practice (Wright, 2003). If undertaken correctly, it is a very good tool for introducing people to ecotourism. However, it may cause alterations to the environment.

Soil compaction, for example, is a direct impact associated with footfall that indirectly can also result in soil erosion. This, in turn, may cause impacts on aquatic organisms. Thus, to avoid eroded and altered trails, some hikers and visitors have contributed to the creation of a secondary trail (Monz et al., 2010). Environmental factors denote whether an area can support outdoor recreation activities, such as hiking and geocaching. The vegetation characteristics, such as resistance and resilience, predict whether recreational traffic can be tolerated.

Also, among the negative impacts of the practice of mountaineering, an activity that can also attract geocachers, one could mention the destruction, alteration or pollution (noise, visual and air pollution) of the mountain's natural environment, and also the soil decompaction and alterations to the ecosystems that occur. However, walking access to certain sites has little impact on the environment if it is properly regulated. We can add that, in Spain, the policies adopted by different public administrations in many cases can lead to confusion because there is never any coordination between them (Moscoso 2004).

In contrast to this threat, geocaching supporters advocate it by linking family, friends and outdoor experience as the best part of this game. That is, this game rather than encouraging individuality does the opposite, generating specific race groups.

Geocaching can even be used in education as it is a stimulus for students to undertake outdoor activities that can contribute to their knowledge of natural sciences, such as biology or geology, or even mathematics (Bragg et al., 2010, Gandy and Stobaugh, 2011, Pettit and Kukulska-Hulme, 2011). As indicated by Weaver (2006), it is a fact that everybody, adults and children, like to seek hidden treasures. Also, the inclusion of activities in nature can serve as an education in environmental protection (Silva et al., 2008).

To educate users to protect the environment, "Cache In Trash Out" is a global environmental clean-up initiative supported by the geocaching community. Since 2002, geocachers around the world have come together to clean up parks and other typical cache locations.

In addition, some impacts may even be positive for the environment (Moscoso, 2004) as the fact that policies for conservation and recovery of the natural environment are arising. Sometimes, these policies focus on restructuring traditional economic activities in the environment, such as farming or ranching.

4. SPANISH NATIONAL PARKS, ENVIRONMENTAL PROTECTION AND GEOCACHING

We have compared the situation of the fourteen Spanish national parks (Table 1) taking into account the possession of a an environmental management certification, their ecotourism promotion through the Michelin "Green Guide", their grade of saturation and the number of geocaches placed in each of them.

We have included the European Charter for Sustainable Tourism (ECST) together with EMAS and ISO 14001 as environmental management certifications in order to be able to classify them as a proposal to effectively advance the principles of sustainable tourism in protected natural areas. This framework has been developed by European representatives of the protected areas and tourism businesses, and establishes the principles of sustainable tourism in these areas and how to apply them in the territory. Achieving certification by the ECST, which is a voluntary agreement, commits the signatories (natural protected area managers, tourism operators and other local stakeholders) to implement a local strategy for sustainable tourism.

Table 1. Situation of Spanish National Parks 2011

National Park	Region	Environmental management certification	3* Michelin	Green Guide Michelín	nº visitors x hectare 2011	nº geocaches
Aigüestortes	Cataluña	ISO 14001 and EMAS	2	sí	21	8
Cabrera	Baleares	ISO 14001	no	no	6	3
Cabañeros	Castilla-La Mancha	ECST	no	no	2	0
C. Taburiente	Canarias	ISO 14001	sí	sí	83	7
Doñana	Andalucía	ECST	sí	sí	6	0
Garajonay	Canarias	ECST	2	sí	153	6
I. Atlánticas	Galicia	no	no	sí	35	0
Monfragüe	Extremadura	no	no	no	19	1
Ordesa	Aragón	no	sí	sí	39	7
Picos de Europa	Cantabria, Castilla-León, Asturias	no	sí	sí	25	28
Sierra Nevada	Andalucía	ECST	2	sí	7	0
T. Daimiel	Castilla-La Mancha	no	no	no	207	0
Teide	Canarias	ISO 14001 and EMAS	sí	sí	127	31
Timanfaya	Canarias	ISO 14000 and EMAS	sí	sí	281	0

* in Cabrera and I. Atlánticas the majority is maritime surface. * all geocaches except virtual caches.
Source: own elaboration from data of National Parks Network, Michelin and Geocaching.

On the other hand, Michelin is known worldwide for its promotion of specific destinations. In the Green Guide (Guía Verde), content focuses on a thorough knowledge of the natural historical and artistic heritage of different destinations, and is particularly aimed at those tourists who give their journeys a cultural approach.

Michelin uses its familiar star rating system, with three stars identifying the most interesting places; two stars those for which it is worth a visit and one star for those that are interesting.

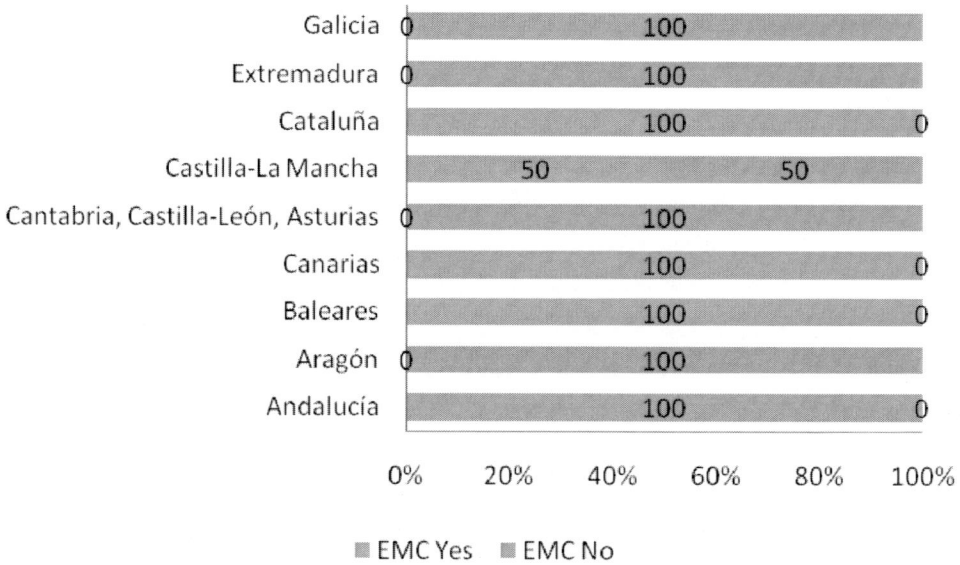

Source: own elaboration from data of National Parks Network (2011).

Figure 2. Spanish national parks with or without environmental management certification by regions 2011.

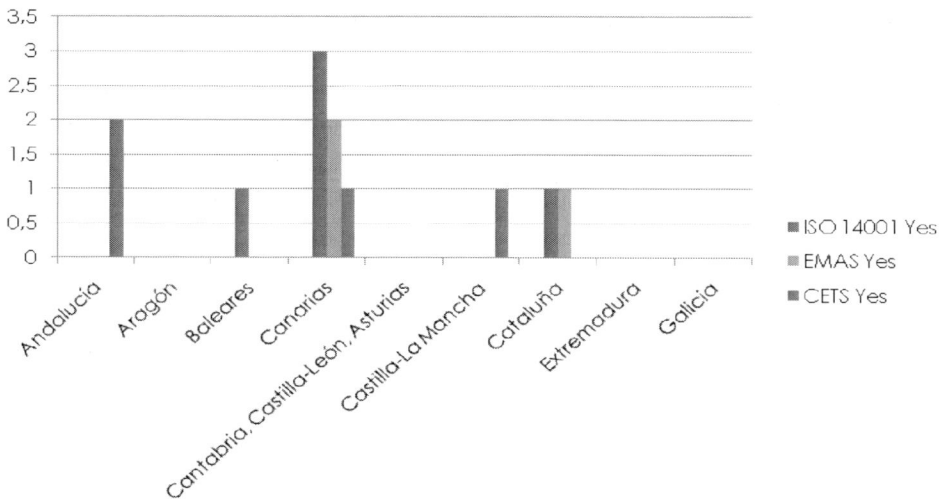

Source: own elaboration from data of National Parks Network (2011).

Figure 3. Spanish national parks with EMC[3]s by regions 2011.

_____

[3] Environmental Management Certification

As we can see, not all the national parks have gained environmental management certification; 64.3% of them have one or more than one, but 35.7% have none. In general, regions with more than one national park have 100% certification (Baleares, Andalucía and Canarias) (Figure 2).

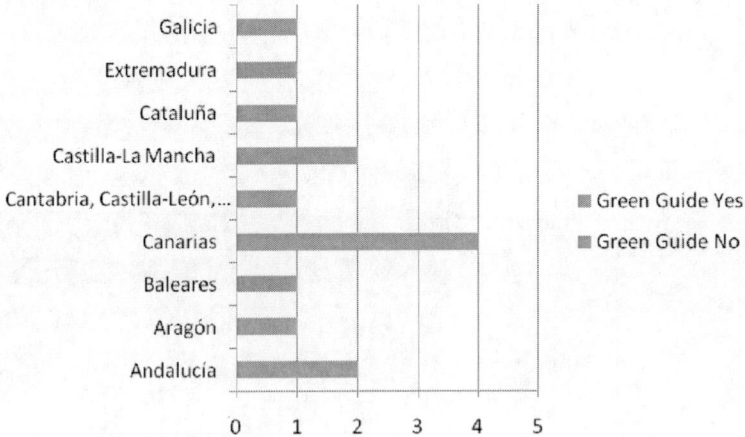

Source: own elaboration from data of Michelin website.

Figure 4. Spanish national parks included in Michelin Green Guide by regions 2011.

Regarding the most chosen certifications, it depends on the regions, although, in general, the most preferred is ISO 14001, followed by ECST and EMAS (Figure 3). Moreover, some of the national parks are not included in the Michelin database or in the Green Guide or do not have the maximum number of stars, despite being supposedly in the "top ten" of the natural parks. Of the Spanish national parks, 64.3% have some Michelin stars but 35.7% have none and 71.4% are included in the Green Guide but 28.6% are not (Figure 4). Star allocation is associated with the regions in which the parks are located, for example, all the national parks of the Canary Islands, Andalucía, Catalonia, Aragón and Cantabria-Castilla León-Asturias have stars while the national parks of Castilla-La Mancha have none (Figure 5).

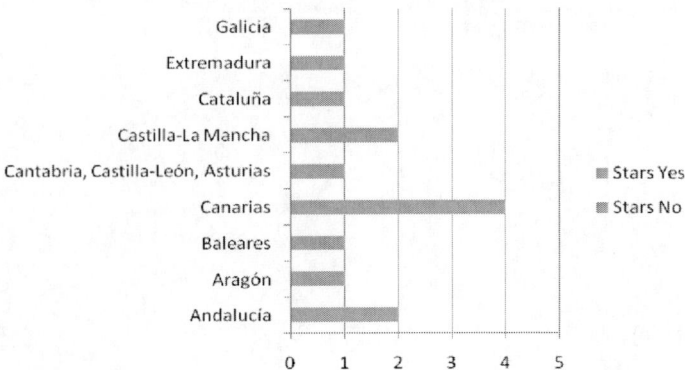

Source: own elaboration from data of Michelin website.

Figure 5. Spanish national parks with Michelin stars by regions 2011.

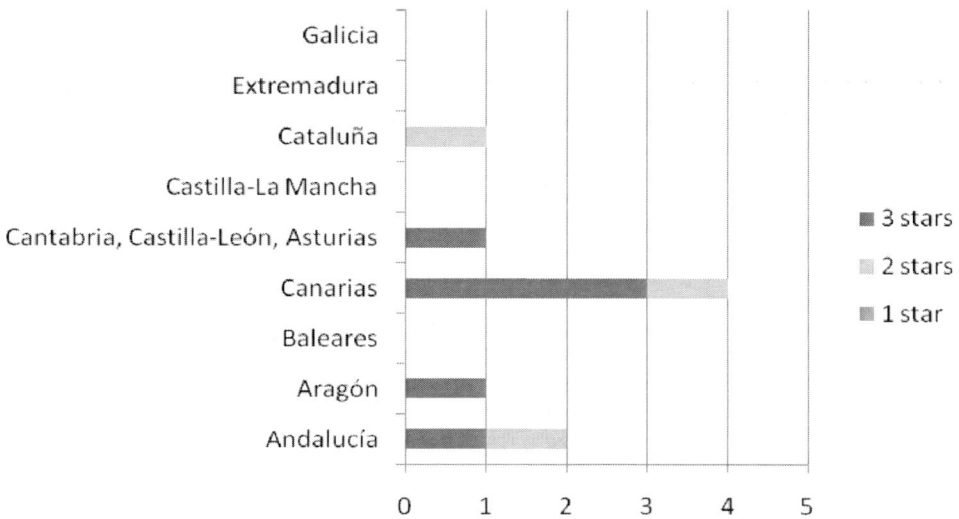

Source: own elaboration from data of Michelin website.

Figure 6. Number of Michelin stars at Spanish national parks by regions 2011.

In relation to the number of stars, the highest three stars category is the most obtained (Figure 6). With all these data we have probed deeply in our analysis using contingency tables (Pérez, 2001), which reflect the number of occurrences of a type regardless of the others (Table 2). Occurrences of certifications, Michelin stars and Green Guide entries show more relation with ISO 14001. That is, there are four national parks with ISO14001 and three or four Michelin stars.

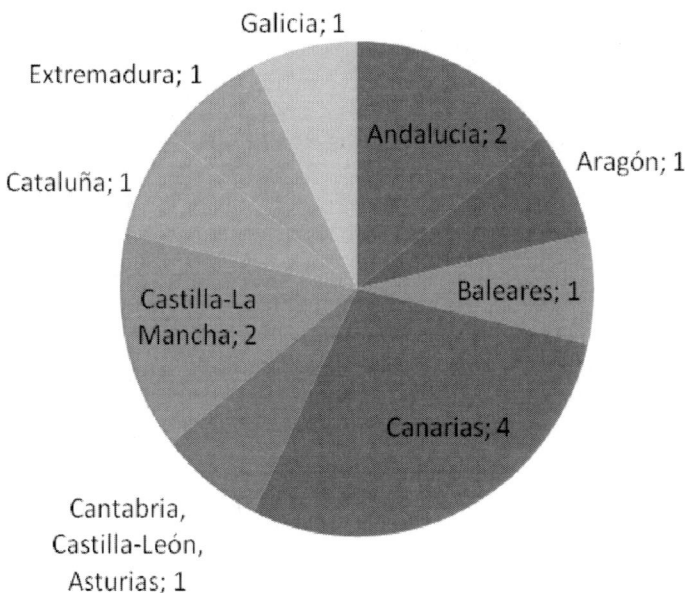

Source: own elaboration from data of National Parks Network (2011).

Figure 7. Regional distribution of Spanish national parks.

Table 2. Contingency tables of EMCs, Michelin stars and Green Guide.

			Michelin stars	Michelin Green Guide	Total
$EnvMangCert	ISO14001	Count	4	4	4
	EMAS	Count	3	3	3
	CETS	Count	3	3	3
	Total	Count	7	7	7

Source: own elaboration from data of National Parks Network and Michelin.

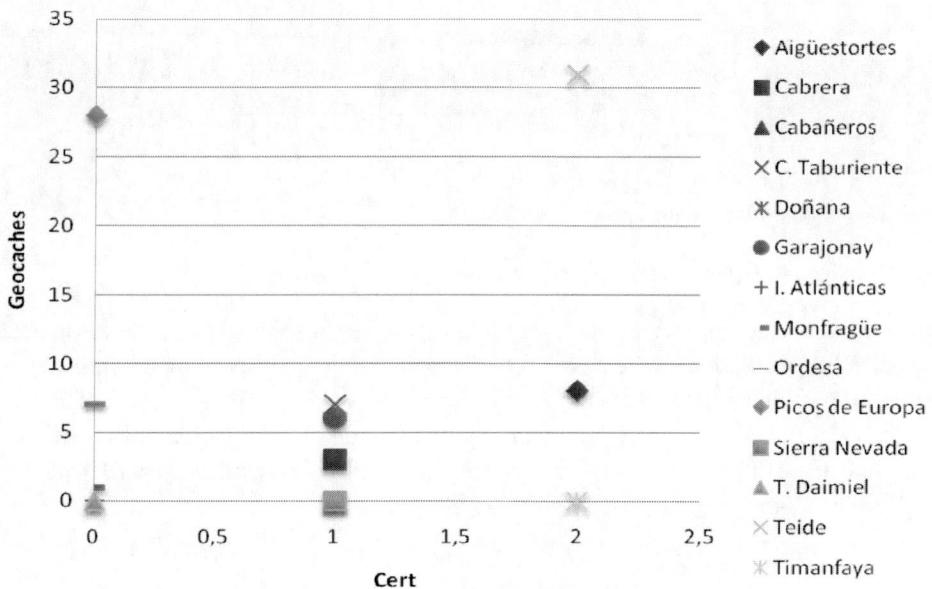

Source: own elaboration from data of National Parks Network and Geocaching website.

Figure 8. Relation between number of EMCs and number of geocaches by Spanish national parks 2011.

Three of them are in the Canary Islands and one in Catalonia. On the other hand, the three national parks with EMAS certification, Michelin stars and included in the Green Guide are also located in the Canary Islands (2) and Catalonia (1). However, the three national parks with ECST, Michelin stars and included in the Green Guide are located in Andalucía (2) and Canary Islands (1). As we can see, the highest visitor saturation is in the Canary Islands national parks (Figure 7) although this is not linked with the number of geocaches, with the exception of Teide National Park.

The Spearman correlation coefficient is 0.1 (Sig. 0.5), meaning that there is no link between the variables "number of visitors" and "number of geocaches", nor between EMCs and geocaches (Figure 8). For example, Teide National Park (Canary Islands) has two EMCs and the highest number of geocaches. However, Picos de Europa National Park has no EMCs and a similar number of geocaches. From the results we can observe that there are regional patterns but no relations among the variables "EMCs" and the number of geocaches or number of visitors. This results show us that some national parks lacked appropriate ecotourism promotion by their regions that could be enhanced through geocaching, taking into account that the geocachers are environmental-friendly people and it seems that they have not overcrowded these spaces with their "treasures".

CONCLUSION

GPS is steadily growing and it is increasingly being used by individuals on more devices, demonstrating the benefits that a company working and providing the location service can achieve, mainly in the tourism sector.

The use of GPS for geocaching is a recreational, sporting or even educational use of this device, which usually brings together groups, such as families, and so, it is also a good tool to introduce children to hiking or trekking. Even its educational use has been tested positively in some schools.

However, the environmental impact caused by geocaching should also be taken into account. As this activity usually takes place in natural sites, possible environmental damage, such as soil erosion, or even private ownership damage, especially when geocaches are placed in unfamiliar or busy places, can occur, although the users' athletic capabilities could enable access to all of them.

According to Schneider, Silverberg and Chavez's (2011) study, 83% of geocachers claimed to have increased their hiking activity to register in geocaching, and this is a factor to be considered.

However, from the data obtained with this empirical study of Spanish national parks, it seems that some of them lacked appropriate regional ecotourism promotion. And, in this case, ecotourism could be enhanced through geocaching, taking into account that the geocachers are environmental-friendly people and have not overcrowded such spaces with their "treasures".

ACKNOWLEDGMENTS

The authors would like to thank the Universitat Politècnica de València for its research funding for the project (PAID-06-2011-1879). With this work we have also participated in the activities of the UPV Research Micro-cluster "Globalization, tourism and heritage: towards a sustainable development".

REFERENCES

Bragg, L.A.; Pullen, Y.; Skinner, M. (2010): Geocaching: a worldwide treasure hunt enhancing the mathematics classroom. *MAV 2010: Proceedings of the 47th Annual Conference of the Mathematical Association of Victoria*, 54-62.

CIS (2010): *Encuesta sobre los hábitos deportivos en España 2010*.

Draycott, D. (2005): Geocaching rules. *New Scientist*, 187, 21.

Eurostat (2011): *Forestry in the EU and the world: A statistical portrait*. Luxembourg.

Federación Española de Deportes de Montaña y Escalada (2011): *Modalidades deportivas: senderismo*, accesible http://www.fedme.es/index.php (16/12/2011).

Gandy, K.; Stobaugh, R. (2011): Avatars, Blabberize, and Cell Phones: ABC's of the Digital Age. *INTED2011 Proceedings*, 4191-4194.

Hegarty, C. J.; Chatre, E. (2008): Evolution of the Global Navigation Satellite System (GNSS). *Proceedings of the IEEE*, 96(12), 1902-1917.

INE (2011). Instituto Nacional de Estadística (INEbase). On-line: www.ine.es

James, R. (2009): A Brief History of GPS. *Time*, 173(22), 18.

Luque, A.M. (2003): La evaluación del medio para la práctica de actividades turístico-deportivas en la naturaleza, *Cuadernos de Turismo*, 12, 131-150.

Lynn, N.A.; Brown, R. D. (2003): Effects of Recreational Use Impacts on Hiking Experiences in Natural Areas. *Landscape and Urban Planning*, 64, 77-87.

Monz, C. A.; Cole, D. N.; Leung, Y.; Marion, J. L. (2010): Sustaining Visitor Use in Protected Areas: Future Opportunities in Recreation Ecology Research Based on the USA Experience. *Journal of Environmental Management*, 45(3), 551-562.

Moscoso, D.J. (2004): El proceso de institucionalización del montañismo en España: una aproximación sociológica. *Acciones e Investigaciones Sociales*, 19, 5-29.

Network of National Parks (2011): http://reddeparquesnacionales.mma.es/.

O'Hara, K. (2008): Understanding Geocaching Practices and Motivations. *CHI 2008: 26th Annual Chi Conference On Human Factors In Computing Systems*, 1-2, 1177-1186.

Pérez, C. (2001): *Técnicas estadísticas con SPSS*. Prentice Hall: Madrid, Spain.

Pettit, J.; Kukulska-Hulme, A. (2011): Mobile 2.0: crossing the border into formal learning? En: Lee, Ma.J.W. and McLoughlin, C. (eds.), *Web 2.0-Based E-Learning: Applying Social Informatics for Tertiary Teaching*. Information Science Reference. Hershey & New York: IGI Global, 192-208.

Richardson, D. (2004): Mapping Opportunities. *Nature*, 427/22 January, 376-377.

Schneider, I.E.; Silverberg, K.E.; Chavez, D. (2011): Geocachers: Benefits Sought and Environmental Attitudes. *LARNet: The Cyber Journal of Applied Leisure and Recreation Research*, 14(1), 1-11.

Silva, A.M.; Inácio, H.L.; Olivera, J. (2008): El crecimiento del ecoturismo y de las actividades físicas de aventura en la naturaleza (AFAN): elementos para comprender la situación actual en España y Brasil. *Apunts*, 94, 45-53.

Tejedor Lorenzo, J.C. (2006): El GPS y sus aplicaciones en las actividades físicas en el medio natural en el ámbito escolar. *Lecturas: Educación física y deportes*, 97.

TIES (2011): *How is ecotourism different from sustainable tourism?* (Frequently Asked Questions), Learning Centre, The International Ecotourism Society, accesible: www.ecotourism.org (17/12/2011).

UNEP (2011): *Towards a Green Economy: Pathways to Sustainable Development and Poverty Eradication*, www.unep.org/greeneconomy (18/12/2011).

UNWTO (2001). *The British Ecotourism Market. Special Report*. United Nations World Tourism Organization.

UNWTO (2005): *Making Tourism More Sustainable: A Guide for Policy Makers*. United Nations World Tourism Organization.

Wright, T. (2003): Geocaching: Trees as Treasure. *American Forests*, 109, (2), pp. 7-9.

Yasukawa, N. (2006): User evaluation of information presentation system for nature observation. *Fourth International Conference on Creating, Connecting and Collaborating through Computing*, 240-245.

Youngjung, S. (2009): A Mobile Phone Guide: Spatial, Personal, and Social Experience for Cultural Heritage. *IEEE Transactions on Consumer Electronics*, 55, (4), 2356-2364.

In: Methods and Analysis on Tourism and Environment   ISBN: 978-1-62417-824-5
Editors: J.M.Jiménez, M.V.Vargas, F.J.O.Rosell et al. © 2013 Nova Science Publishers, Inc.

Chapter 4

"SUSTAINABLE TOURISM" INDICATORS: A MAPPING OF THE ITALIAN DESTINATIONS

Claudio Quintano, Margherita Pagliuca and Monica Rosciano
University of Naples (Parthenope), Naples, Italy

ABSTRACT

Over the last 50 years, tourism has been transformed from a leisure activity into a major business sector worldwide. Particularly, at a local level, it offers opportunities for employment and income, spurring regional and local economic developments, which are often unique chances for many small and distant places with limited options for development. However, it has significantly contributed to environmental degradation, negative social and cultural impacts and habitat fragmentation. As a result, the notion of sustainable tourism emerges in order to conserve and preserve the natural resources, human well-being and long term economic viability of communities. This paper reviews the nature and scope of research into the environmental impact of tourism, the role such research may play in tourist development and conservation and the constraints that may be encountered. The main aim is to explore and illustrate the usefulness of the relationships between tourism and environment of the Italian regions. It may be especially important to be able to isolate key variables which can be consolidated into few indices of environmental conditions as they are related to tourism. Such indices might be used to identify associations among groups of variables, such as specific geographic areas.

1. INTRODUCTION

In the last 50 years, tourism has been transformed from a leisure activity into a major business sector worldwide. At first, it was concentrated in a few world cities and sites, while today it is becoming increasingly global, incorporating new destinations and far distant places. Tourism is a key ingredient in the economic development strategy of many Nations. The attractiveness of tourism as a generator of income, employment, tax collections, and foreign exchange earnings has led many countries to enter the competition of attracting international travelers to their destinations.

The spectacular growth of tourism has brought its potential as an engine for economic growth to the attention of policy-makers, but also its eventual problems if left uncontrolled (EC, 2003).

Tourism as a complex economic activity has multiple linkages to a wide range of other economic sectors and activities, thus having positive multiplier effects and a potential to act as a catalyst for economic development (Vellas, 2002). Particularly, at a local level it offers opportunities for employment and income, spurring regional and local economic developments, which are often unique chances for many small and distant places with limited other options for development.

However, although tourism has economic benefits, it has significantly contributed to environmental degradation, negative social and cultural impacts and habitat fragmentation.

Tourism's unplanned growth has damaged the natural and socio-cultural environments of many destinations. As tourism grows in a destination, major economic, socio-cultural and environmental changes occur and consequently tourism has become a priority field in policy making at local, regional, national, supranational and international level.

As a result, the notion of sustainable tourism emerges in order to conserve and preserve the natural resources, human well-being and long term economic viability of communities.

Three are the dimensions of sustainable tourism: economic, socio-cultural and ecological dimensions. Firstly, there is no doubt that sustainable tourism must be economically feasible, because tourism is an economic activity. Economic sustainability, in this regard, implies optimizing the development growth rate at a manageable level with full consideration of the limits of the destination environment. Moreover, the economic benefits from tourism should be fairly well distributed throughout the community. Secondly, socio-cultural sustainability implies respect for social identity and social capital, for community culture and its assets, and for a strengthening of social cohesiveness and pride that will allow community residents to control their own lives. Thirdly, environmental sustainability recognizes that natural resources of the individual community and the world should be no longer viewed as abundant and are, in fact, constantly being depleted. The natural environment must be protected for its own intrinsic value and as a resource for present and future generations.

This paper reviews the nature and scope of research into the environmental impact of tourism, the role such research may play in tourist development and conservation and the constraints which may be encountered.

Research in this field is characterized by a wide spectrum of generally complex interrelationships and impacts. In recent years, there has been a growing call from policy-makers for environmental guidelines, indicators and other research but as yet few immediate solutions to their problems and answers to their requests are to hand. The complexity of the issues involved and other difficulties have also limited the extent to which research has been fed into the decision-making process. So, there is a challenging need to identify the relationships between environmental quality and tourism.

The aim of this paper is to explore and illustrate the usefulness of the relationships between tourism and environment of the Italian regions. It may be especially important to be able to isolate key variables which can be consolidated into few indices of environmental conditions as they are related to tourism. Such indices might be used to identifying associations among groups of variables, such as specific geographic areas.

2. TOWARDS SUSTAINABLE TOURISM

Tourism is recognised as being one of the world's main economic activities. According to the latest Unwto statistics, in 2008 there were over 900 million international arrivals increased by almost 35% compared to 2000 (Figure 1).

Tourism has grown fast as a result of technological and organizational changes facilitating transport at reduced costs providing opportunities for leisure and travel to a broader segment of modern societies.

As a result of the rapid expansion of the tourism sector, traditional and emerging tourism destinations are facing increasing pressure on their natural, cultural and socio-economic environments. It is now recognized that uncontrolled growth in tourism aiming at short-term benefits often results in negative impacts, harming the environment and societies, and destroying the very basis on which tourism is built and thrives. On the contrary, when tourism is planned, developed and managed using sustainable criteria, its benefits can spread throughout society and the natural and cultural environments.

During '60s tourism was considered like a "smokeless industry", but at the end of the decade the risks linked to its uncontrolled growth were already evident.

Host societies have become progressively aware of the problems of unsustainable tourism, and sustainability concerns are increasingly being addressed in national, regional and local tourism policies, strategies and plans. In addition, more and more tourists are now demanding higher environmental standards from tourist services, as well as a greater commitment to local communities and economies.

Uncontrolled conventional tourism poses potential threats to many natural areas around the world. It can put enormous pressure on an area and lead to impacts such as soil erosion, increased pollution, discharges into the sea, natural habitat loss, increased pressure on endangered species and heightened vulnerability to forest fires. It often puts a strain on water resources, and it can force local populations to compete for the use of critical resources.

In this context, sustainability has become the central issue in tourism development policies throughout the world. A lot of institutions have developed a series of instruments that make it possible to incorporate sustainability criteria in the planning, development and management of tourism (UN, 2005; OECD, 2002; EC, 2002).

A broad perspective is needed to incorporate cross sectorial issues, in a pro-active policy to take the social, economic and environmental tourism into account. In the past, environmental problems had been seen as inevitable outcomes of human activity and economic development. In such a perspective, environmental protection is considered by many as a constraint to development. Hence, the development of tourism is considered as constrained by environmental legislation. Development prospects depend to a great extent on environmental quality, and tourism protection is essential not only on ethical grounds but because the assets (natural and cultural) are the basis for human activities. The resource protection is essential for the long-term development of tourism itself, in addition to other reasons supporting heritage conservation. It is widely recognized not only that uncontrolled tourism expansion is likely to lead to environmental degradation, but also that environmental degradation, in turn, poses a serious threat to tourism activities.

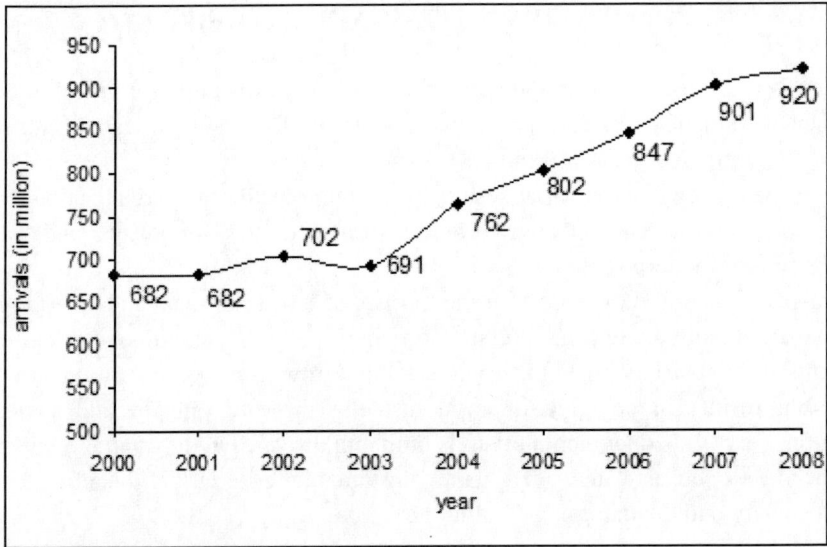

Source: World Tourism Organization.

Figure 1. International tourist arrivals. Years 2000-2008.

This brings to the frontline of public policy the issue of how tourism contributes to sustainable development. Protecting the environment was conceived as intricately linked to social and economic development (WCED, 1987). The approach towards sustainable tourism -as developed by the World Tourism Organization (WTO)- was already emphasized in the International Conferences of Manila (1980), Acapulco (1982), Aja Declaration (1989), Rio de Janeiro (1992).

The World Conference on Sustainable Tourism (Lanzarote, 1995) recognized the need to develop a tourism that meets economic expectations and environmental requirements, and respects not only the social and physical structure of destinations, but also the local population. Since the mid-1990s, the sustainable development of tourism has become a priority also for European Institutions (EC2003; 1995; EEA 2001).

Pressures on existing tourist destinations which can remain competitive are likely to intensify further requiring uniting effective tourism management to cope with increasing pressures. In parallel, new destinations are likely to emerge, not always ready to cope with the pressures of tourism. This would require careful assessment of strengths, weaknesses, opportunities and threats from tourism growth and development in the context of sustainable development. Destinations would have to become competitive realizing a coherent strategy.

It would assist the keeping of the level of development and use without serious environmental deterioration, social and economic problems or decreasing the perceived tourist enjoyment of the area (WTO, 1998). The notion of sustainable development emerged as an alternative to the traditional neo-classical model of economic development.

Sustainable tourism development guidelines and management practices are applicable to all forms of tourism in all types of destinations, including mass tourism and the various tourism segments niches.

Thus, sustainable tourism should:

1. Make optimal use of environmental resources that constitute a key element in tourism development, maintaining essential ecological processes and helping to preserve natural heritage and biodiversity,
2. Respect the socio-cultural authenticity of host communities, preserving their built and living cultural heritage and traditional values, and contributing to inter-cultural understanding and tolerance
3. Ensure viable, long-term economic operations, providing socio-economic benefits to all stakeholders that are fairly distributed, including stable employment and income-earning opportunities and social services to host communities, and contributing to poverty alleviation.

Sustainable tourism development requires the informed participation of all relevant stakeholders, as well as strong political leadership to ensure wide participation and consensus building. Achieving sustainable tourism is a continuous process and it requires constant monitoring of impacts, introducing the necessary preventive and/or corrective measures whenever necessary. Sustainable tourism should also maintain a high level of tourist satisfaction and ensure a meaningful experience to the tourists, raising their awareness about sustainability issues and promoting sustainable tourism practices amongst them (UNWTO, 2004).

3. TOURISM AND ENVIRONMENT IN ITALY: A SPECIAL RELATIONSHIP

In Italy, there were 95 million arrivals and 370 million bed nights (Istat, 2008). Although Italy is losing market share in the international tourism industry, tourism is still a key sector of the Italian economy. Tourism comprises a wide variety of products and destinations and involves many different stakeholders, both public and private, with very decentralised, areas of competence, often at regional and local level. In 2008 the tourism industry generates about 53 billion euro more than 3% of the Italian GDP with more than 6% of the total labour force (AA.VV., 2009).

The tourism industry, for the positive economic effects, has become a prominent economic sector increasing competition on tourism market. Such competition has to seek a balance between short-term revenues at the cost of long-term sustainable development and long-term balanced growth strategies seeking to reconcile local interests with tourism objectives. While tourism provides considerable economic benefits for many areas, its expansion can also be responsible for adverse environmental as well as socio-cultural impact.

In the light of the above exposition, the aim of this study is to describe the relationship between tourism and environment, the effects of environmental factors on tourism, the impact of the tourism industry on the environment and the responses required for the promotion and safeguard of a more sustainable development of tourism and recreational activities in Italy.

The management of tourist destinations is often fragmented among various local, regional and national agencies which have the responsibility to control the various functions such as services, infrastructure, improvements (Bryon and Russo, 2003). The analysis was carried out at regional level for the following motivations:

- firstly, the regions cover a fundamental and a strategic role in accordance with the article 117 of the Italian Constitution;
- -secondly, more and more sustainable tourism strategies are focusing at a local destination level (Dredge, 1999). This orientation reflects not only a broad decentralisation of decision-making by transferring a range of responsibilities to local and regional authorities but also a necessity to adopt an integrated approach to policy making. This is in recognition that policy responses are more effective in addressing to concrete problems and their many cross-sectoral issues are mostly supported at a regional level. Furthermore, managing destination is easier at a regional level where land-use competencies of regional authorities exist (i.e. infrastructure development, land-use regulation, environmental impact assessment) and tourism becomes increasingly integrated in local area management (Haywood, 1989). Therefore it is at this level that attention is being paid on sustainable tourism (Westlake, 1995; WTO, 1998) as evidenced by a growing number of relevant initiatives, such as Local Agenda 21.

Regions, therefore, may significantly affect the rise of a new, sustainable and competitive tourism of many of Italian tourist destinations:

- either those already well established, that's why they are vulnerable to uncontrolled development
- or in those who still have many potentialities to be expressed.

4. AN OVERVIEW OF THE DATA

In order to measure the interaction between tourism and environment there is the need to collect and organize statistical information.

The complexity of the phenomena needs to dispose a wide range of statistical information, especially quantitative indicators. Thus, the role of data and information is central to both the implementation and assessment of sustainable tourism which requires constant monitoring of impacts and the introduction of required preventive and/or corrective measures whenever necessary (Gismondi, 2006; Laimer et al., 2004).

However, common standards to monitor performance and delivery of information in sustainable tourism development is still elusive and comprehensive indicators are not available. In this paper, in order to assess the relationship between environment and tourism, we follow the criteria adopted and suggested by national and international agencies who worked to develop guidelines for sustainable practices in tourism (e.g. Andriola, Interdonato, 2002; EEA, 2005; UN, 2005 and 1999; WTO, 2005).

The most commonly issues used to relate to environment are:

- land and natural resources use/conservation;
- pollution;
- transport and mobility.

Whereas, the aspects like tourism supply and demand, pressure on the local communities or economic linkages are used to measure tourism impact. Each one of the macro-categories above can be represented by more than one indicator. The choice of indicators is central because the success of any indicator-based assessment is reliant on data quality and availability. The study revealed that data were not always available. In many cases, the absence of data is for the proposed regional level, while in other cases there are problems relating to temporal scale and to timeliness. Hence, sometimes it is not possible to insert some relevant aspects or it has to fall back on variables that are partially different from the desired information. The used set of indicators (table 1) contains information with a range of time from 2005 to 2008 and the sources of data are Istat, Ispra and Aci. Obviously, the list of indicators is neither exhaustive nor mandatory. In short, in order to investigate the relationships between environmental and touristic variables, a total of 32 indicators has been analyzed.

5. METHODOLOGY TO MEASURE TOURISM –ENVIRONMENT INTERACTION

Our aim is to identify the associations among groups of variables, such as environmental and touristic measures. The multidimensionality of both environment and tourism suggests the use of a technique that can relate two sets of variables: the canonical correlation analysis (Hotelling, 1936; Alpert et al., 1972; Lambert et al., 1975; Levine, 1977). It is a method that analyses the number, magnitude, and composition of independent dimensions of this relationship. The underlying logic involves the derivation of a linear combination of variables from each of the two sets of variables, called canonical variates so that the correlation between the two linear combinations is maximized (Thompson, 1984). Unlike the multiple linear regression analysis, which is used to predict the value of a single criterion variable from a linear function of a set of predictor variables, the purpose of canonical correlation analysis is to analyze the relationships between sets of variables. Canonical correlation analysis is also different from:

- factor analysis, because no particular variable is signed out as a criterion or dependent variables
- linear discriminatory analysis, where the criterion variable is categorical, while the predicator variables are continuous measurements
- multivariate analysis of variance, where the response criterion is multidimensional rather than unidimensional, as is the case with conventional analysis of variance procedures.

In canonical analysis, the analyst is not concerned with a single criterion, but, rather, as defined by Kendall, with relationships among sets of criterion variables and predictor variables (Kendall, 1957).

Table 1. Environmental and touristic indicators

Macro cateogories	Indicator	Source	year
Environment			
Use / conservation of natural resources	- Bathing coast	Istat	2007
	- Decrease water (million m^3)		
	- Nature 2000	Istat	2008
	- Consumption of electricity per capita	Istat	2007
	- Consumption of electricity industry	Istat	2007
	- Agricultural land company	Istat	2006
	- New buildings	Istat	2006
	- Roads		
Pollution	- Emissions of carbon dioxide (CO_2)	Ispra	2005
	- Water service problems	Istat	2008
	- Wastewater	Istat	2008
	- Wastewater of hotels	Istat	2008
	- Recovery of special waste	Istat	2006
	- Collection of municipal waste	Istat	2007
	- Noise exposure	Istat	2007
Transport and mobility systems	- Total vehicles	Aci	2008
	- Euro 4 and Euro 5 cars	Aci	2008
	- Transport of goods (by rail, air, sea)	Istat	2005-08
	- Transport of passenger (by rail, air, sea)	Istat	2005-08
Tourism			
Tourism offer	- Tourist accomodation	Istat	2008
	- Number of beds in tourist accomodation		
	- Average size of tourist accommodation		
Tourism demand	- Arrivals in tourist accomodation	Istat	2008
	- Nights spent in tourist accomodation		
	- Average stay		
Social pressure of tourism	- Density of accommodation	Istat	2008
	- Density of beds		
	- Tourist nights spent per resident		
	- Tourist nights spent per Km^2		
	- Net tourist pressure		
Economic tourism	- Value added of tourism	Istat	2007
	- Unit of work of the tourism sector		

His objectives are to:

- determine the maximum correlation between a set (of more than one element) of criterion variables and predictor variables

- derive weights for each set of criterion and predictor variables, in such a way that the weighted sums are maximally correlated
- derive additional linear functions which maximize the remaining correlation, subject to being independent of the preceding set/sets of linear compound
- test statistical significance of correlation measures.

As it can be observed from the above description, canonical analysis is a technique for dealing mainly with composite association between sets of variables.

6. RESULTS AND DISCUSSION

Our aim is to determine the overall correlation between the two sets of variables: a set for environmental variables and a set for touristic variables. The initial number of variables had been reduced to 9 (5 about environment and 4 about tourism) through principal component analysis (PCA), because it was higher than the number of statistical units observed (20 regions). In detail, the PCA was performed on each group of tourism and environmental macro-categories (table 2). Essentially, two sets of weighting coefficients were sought, such that if linear combinations of each set were formed (so arriving at a composite variable representing each set) and correlated in a two-variable linear correlation, a higher correlation for this particular set of composite variables would be obtained than any other set of combinations which could be formed (Green et al., 1966). The maximum number of canonical variates that can be extracted from the sets of variables equals the number of variables in the smallest set of variables. Canonical correlation analysis of both tourism and environment resulted in two canonical functions significant (table 3). The first set of canonical coefficients will be related to the highest canonical correlation index. It is 0.91 (table 4). This index is interpreted as a measure of the overall correlation between the two sets of variables.

Table 2. Main results of PCA on the seven macro-categories

Macro-categories	Factors	% of variance	% of cumulate variance
Use / conservation of natural resources	Natural resource use	36.4	63.8
	Resourse use conflict	27.4	
Pollution	Pollution	52.2	72.1
	Noise and irregulatory water	19.9	
Transport and mobility systems	Transport	59.50	59.50
Tourism offer	Accomodation capacity	69.68	69.68
Tourism demand	Arrivals and nights spent	60.80	60.80
Social pressure of tourism	Density of tourism	60.82	60.82
Economic tourism	Economic linkage	98.76	98.76

Table 3. Test of significance of canonical correlation

	Likelihood ratio	F value	Pr > F
1	0.037	3.20	0.0011
2	0.211	2.14	0.0429
3	0.504	1.77	0.1443
4	0.969	0.23	0.8005

Table 4. Canonical variate

	Canonical correlation	Eigenvalues	% of variance	% of cumulate variance
1	0.908710	4.7390	0.6691	0.6691
2	0.762430	1.3883	0.1960	0.8651
3	0.692788	0.9229	0.1303	0.9954
4	0.176874	0.0323	0.0046	1.0000

Each new canonical correlation index, however, will be smaller than preceding value.

To determine which variables were most important in a given pair of canonical variates, the canonical loadings are used (table 5).

Table 5. Canonical loadings for touristic and environmental variables

Variables	Variates	
	V_1	V_2
Environment		
Natural resource use	0.243	0.016
Resourse use conflict	0.472	0.156
Pollution	0.372	0.004
Noise and irregulatory water	0.502	0.006
Transport	0.594	0.064
Tourism		
Accomodation capacity	0.000	0.009
Arrivals and nights spent	0.012	0.397
Density of tourism	0.190	0.139
Economic linkage	0.490	0.376

Table 6. Proportion of variance of V_1, V_2, W_1 e W_2 explained by its variables set

Canonical variate		Proportion of total variance
Environment	V_1	0.44
	V_2	0.05
Tourism	W_1	0.17
	W_2	0.23

The first variate is related to Transport, Noise and irregulatory water, Resource use conflict and Economic linkage. The second variate is matched with Arrivals and nights spent and Economic linkage.

Besides the proportion of total variance explained, environment variables set by the first canonical varied (V_1) is about 44%, which together with the second reach 48%. The proportion of total variance of the set of variables of tourism explained by the first canonical varied (W_1) is about 17%, which together with the second reach 40% (table 6).

In order to show how much of the shared variance in a set can be accounted for by a variate from the other set it is useful the redundancy coefficient (table 7). The first two touristic variate accounted for 39% of variance in the environmental variable set. Similarly, the variance of the touristic variables accounted by the first two variates of the environmental set was 28%.

These results suggest that the touristic variables (at least those considered in this paper) were able to explain much of the regional variation in environmental variables.

7. THE MAPPING OF ITALIAN REGIONS

For many regional economies tourism can bring about an encouraging response to such a sensitive question considering its positive influence on regional employment and income; though, the magnitude of the regional multiplier varies in accordance with the characteristics of each region (and locality).

Moreover, the multipliers are not simply region-specific but also project-specific (Armstrong and Taylor, 2000). Therefore, a special attention must be paid to supporting those tourism projects able to generate the most important benefits to the region and their correlation with other economic and social activities within territorialized networks.

The outputs from a tourism sustainability assessment, using scales of sustainability levels, can be presented in graph form to display the system quality of a tourist destination.

Their purpose can be summarized as follows: to help to identify the current situation in a community; to generate possible future scenarios from the situation; to clarify the trade-offs that are implicit in indicator selection; to make tourism issues or concerns more accessible to stakeholders; to assist stakeholders to define their goals and objectives; to make all parts of the sustainability assessment process clear and explicit; and to serve as an educational tool (Clayton and Radcliffe, 1996).

Table 7. Variance of the original variables accounted for by a variate from the other set

Number	Environmental Variables		Touristic Variables	
	Proportion of variance	Proportion of cumulative variance	Proportion of variance	Proportion of cumulative variance
1	0.3606	0.3606	0.1431	0.1431
2	0.0275	0.3881	0.1339	0.2770
3	0.1494	0.5375	0.2509	0.5279
4	0.0030	0.5405	0.0023	0.5302

In relation to the findings of the analysis a graphical representation of the Italian regions has been done in a plane where the horizontal dimension refers to the first environment canonical variate and the vertical dimension at the first touristic variate.

Recalling that canonical variate are influenced by transport, environmental disturbances, resources use conflict (about environment) economic aspects and level of crowding (about tourism), the graph has revealed four different scenarios for Italian regions.

The first situation - the top-right of the graph- is an area with an already compromised environment, where additional pressures due to increasing tourist numbers may not be sustainable. In this part of the map there are Lombardia, Lazio, Sicilia, Campania, Piemonte, Calabria, and Puglia (whose position near the center makes it less affected by the considerations just made).

The top left graph shows a situation where against a poor contaminated environment there is not an important role of tourism in the local economy. In this scenario there is only Emilia Romagna, characterized by a very young mass tourism.

These regions should think about a strategy to increase the benefits of tourism development in the area more than an increase in tourist flows.

In the left bottom of the chart there are regions where the environment is preserved and where there is tourism that generates wealth. These areas can certainly be regarded as emblematic for the development of sustainable tourism, as they are regions (Valle d'Aosta, Trentino Alto Adige, Liguria, Toscana, Friuli Venezia Giulia), which combine the conservation of key factors of tourism with its economic and social competitiveness.

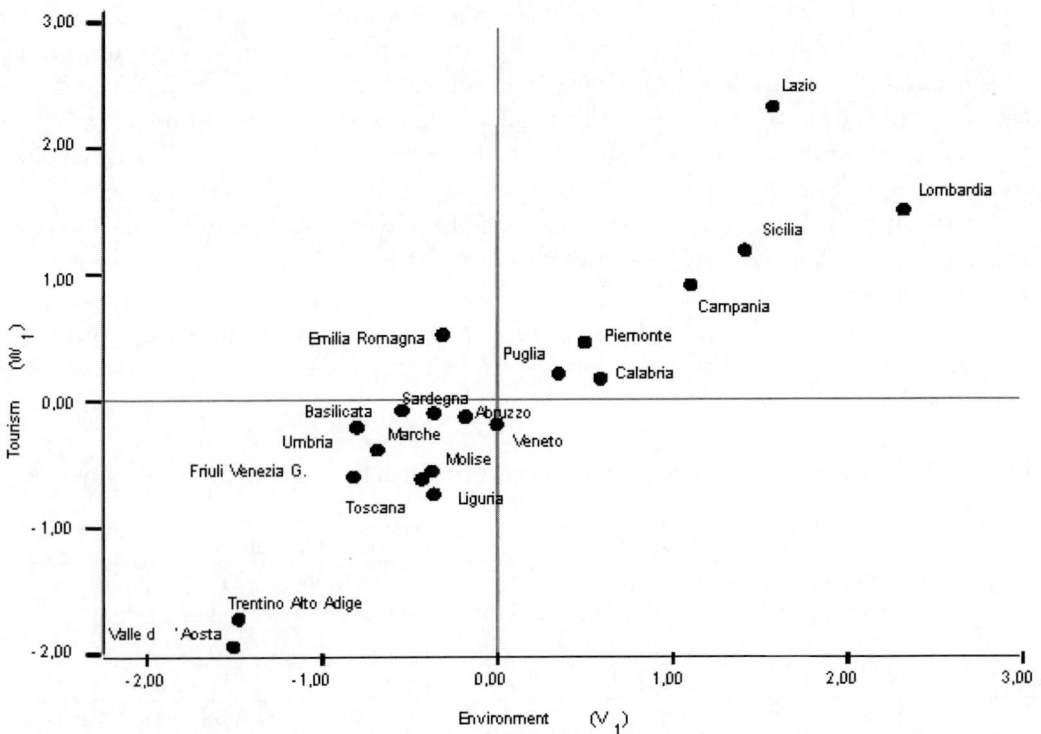

Figure 2. Mapping of Italian regions on the I canonical variate.

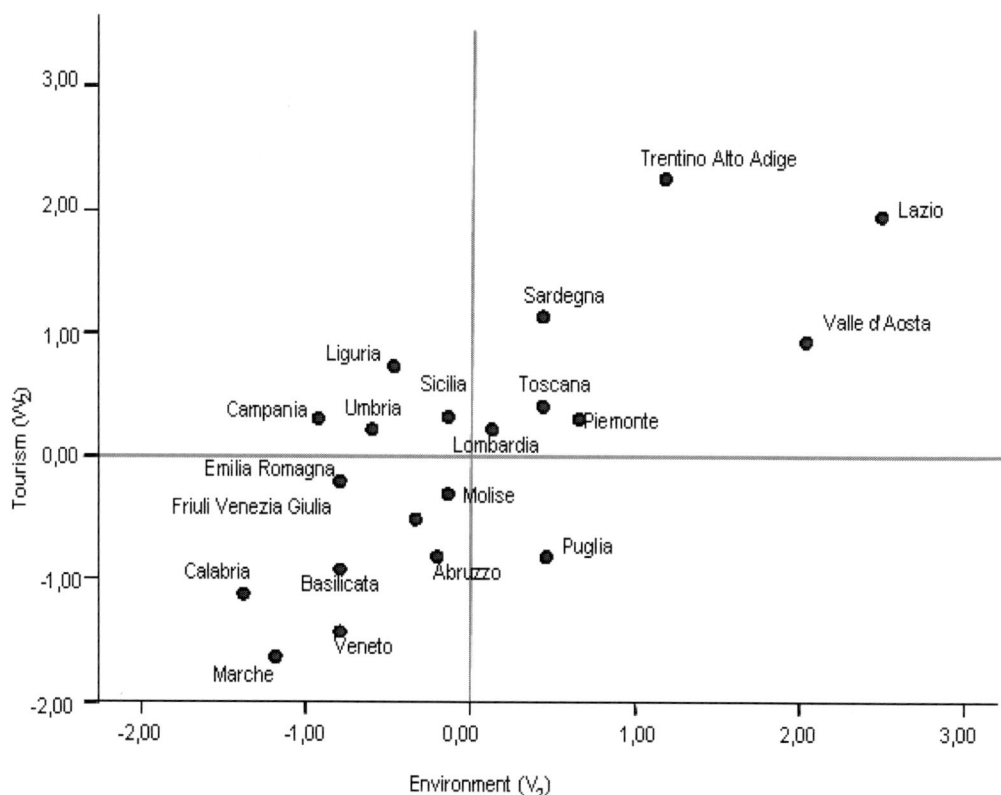

Figure 3. Mapping of Italian regions on the II canonical variate.

Finally, the right bottom of the graph is characterized by a worrying state of the environment despite the economic benefits of touristic activities.

If we can consider that there are bi-univocal relationships between environment and tourism (more from tourism to environment than from environment to tourism), they do not express uniformly throughout the country.

In fact there are areas where the environment becomes more damaged than others, but only in some cases (mainly for the lower right of the figure) we may suggest a key role of tourism in the environmental impact. For the other areas of the country the environmental impact is perhaps to be found in other variables rather than in touristic variables. Then there are the areas where the touristic implications on the environment seems do not compromise its integrity and therefore can be specified as a benchmark for touristic, environmental, social and economic sustainability.

Some more observations are possible looking at the graph built on the second tourism and environmental canonical variate (Figure 3)

The figure shows that Trentino Alto Adige, Lazio, Sardegna, Vallle d'Aosta principally oppose Marche, Veneto, Calabria, Basilicata, Abruzzo, Puglia.

Reminding that the second canonical variate is essentially explained by tourism aspects, like arrivals, nights spent and economic linkage; tourism development plays a central role for local economies in the regions positioned on the high side of the figure. In the other areas there is a need to recognize and increase the awareness on the potentiality of the "resource tourism".

CONCLUSION

As regards the Italian territory, the relationship between tourism and environment is extremely complex. There are some regions that certainly seem to be oriented towards sustainable tourism which are contrasted with areas where a growth of the tourism would determine problems to the environment.

They require a review of both environmental and touristic policies, using the performance of the other regions like benchmark.

In fact, the quality of the environment both natural and man-made is essential for tourism, but the pressure of millions of visitors on natural resources and on the landscape can have devastating impacts. Making tourism more sustainable means creating the right balance among environmental conservation, quality of life of host communities and the profitability of companies, recognizing the interdependence between tourism and the environment through a planned and systematic approach to the management of tourist destinations. While tourism development can generate strong benefits, also triggering processes of exploitation and protection of resources, other touristic activities can have very adverse effects.

It is not unusual, in fact, that the tourism is produced in extensive territories, but sparsely populated, so its expansion can not be supported by a valuable contribution of local labor; the opposite scale, a high population density in small areas causes an enormous tension in terms of carrying capacity of the environment. This situation is even worse if the location becomes a touristic destination, so the already existing problems of environmental pressure grow larger.

Both measures provide the opportunity:

- to investigate important aspects of the issue of tourism on the environment and therefore they will read together in order to make judgments about tourism in various locations
- to offer a tool to analyze and identify critical points and assess the potential of your location to policy makers, taking into account the expectations and needs of local people, tourists and the physical characteristics of the territory
- to provide local administrators the needed knowledge to outline a governance of the tourism in a sustainability vision.

But in order to investigate the limits beyond which tourism begins its pathological stage, it is necessary to have a wide range of information which, as already observed, sometimes are absent. The availability of a good basis of statistical information can generate a competitive advantage because it provides a tool to identify, analyze and evaluate timely and responsible manner the critical points and potential of its territory to policy makers.

REFERENCES

Alpert, M.I. & Peterson, R.A. (1972). On the interpretation of canonical analysis. *Journal of marketing research,* IX.

Andriola, L. & Interdonato, M. (2002). *Il turismo sostenibile: obiettivi, principi e principali esperienze in atto.* ENEA.

Armstrong, H. & Taylor, J. (2000). *Regional Economics and Policy,* third edition. Blackwell.

Automobile Club Italia (ACI) (2009). *Annuario Statistico.*

AA.VV. (2009). *Rapporto sul turismo italiano* (a cura di) E. Becheri, Franco Angeli.

Bryon, J. & Russo, A.P. (2003). The tourist historic city. *Annals of Tourism Research,* 30(2), 492-494.

Clayton, A.M.H. & Redcliffe, N.J. (1996). *Sustainability: A systems approach.* Earthscan. London.

Coccossis, H. (2008). Cultural heritage, local resources and sustainable tourism. *International Journal of Services Technology and Management,* 10(1).

Commission of the European Communities (2003). *Basic orientations for the sustainability of European tourism.* Communication from the Commission to the Council, the European Parliament, the European Economic and Social Committee and the Committee of the Regions

Dredge, D. (1999). Destination place planning and design. *Annals of Tourism Research,* 26(4), 772-791.

European Environment Agency (2001). *Environmental signals 2001,* EEA.

European Environment Agency (2005). *EEA core set of indicators – Guide.* EEA Technical report, 1/2005.

European Commission (2002). *Sistema di rilevamento tempestivo per identificare le destinazioni turistiche in declino e le migliori pratiche di prevenzione.*

European Community (1995). *The role of the Union in the field of tourism.* Commission Green Paper. Commission of the European Community 4/4/95. Brussels.

Gismondi, R. (2006). Indicatori di competitività turistica: il quadro teorico e la realtà italiana. *Rivista di Statistica Ufficiale,* 1.

Green, P.E.; Halbert, H. & Robinson, P.J. (1966). Canonical Analysis: An Exposition and illustrative application. *Journal of marketing research,* III.

Haywood, K.M. (1989). Responsible and responsive approach to tourism planning in the community. *Tourism Management,* 9(2), 105-118.

Hotelling, H. (1936). Relationship between two sets of variates. *Biometrika,* 321-377.

Istituto Superiore per la Protezione e la Ricerca Ambientale (ISPRA) (2009). *Annuario dei dati ambientali.*

Istituto Nazionale di Statistica (ISTAT) (2009). *Statistiche ambientali.* Annuario, 10.

Laimer, P. & Ohlbock, P. (2004). Indicators measuring the sustainability of tourism. *7th International Forum on Tourism Statistics.*

Lambert, V.Z. & Durand, R.M. (1975). Some precautions in using canonical analysis. *Journal of marketing research,* XII.

Levine, M.S. (1977). *Canonical Analysis and factor comparison.* Sage Publications.

Kendall, M.G. (1957). *A Course in Multivariate Analysis.* Hafner. New York.

Organization for Economic Cooperation and Development (OECD) (2002). *Indicators for the integration of environmental concerns into tourism policies.* Working Group on Environmental Information and Outlooks, ENV/EPOC/SE(2001)3/REV1. Paris.

Thompson, B. (1984). *Canonical correlation analysis.* Sage Publications.

United Nations (1999). *Tourism and sustainable development. Sustainable tourism: a local authority perspective.* Department of Economic and social affairs.

United Nations (2005). *Indicators of sustainable development*. Available on http://www.un.org.

Vellas, F. (2002). *Economie et Politique du Tourisme International*. Economica. Paris.

Westlake, J. (1995). Planning for tourism at local level: maintaining the balance with the environment. In Coccossis, H.; Nijkamp, P. (Eds): *Sustainable Tourism Development*. Avebury. Aldershot, UK.

World Commission on Environment and Development (WCED) (1987). *Our Common Future*. Oxford University Press. Oxford.

World Tourism Organization (WTO) (1998). *Guide for Local Planner Authorities in Developing Sustainable Tourism*.

World Tourism Organization (WTO) (2004). *Making Tourism More Sustainable: a Guide for Policy Makers*.

World Tourism Organization (2005). *Tourism's Potential as a Sustainable Development Strategy*.

In: Methods and Analysis on Tourism and Environment   ISBN: 978-1-62417-824-5
Editors: J.M.Jiménez, M.V.Vargas, F.J.O.Rosell et al. © 2013 Nova Science Publishers, Inc.

Chapter 5

A CASE STUDY OF THE METHODOLOGY IMPLEMENTED TO DEVELOP THE GEOGRAPHIC INFORMATION SYSTEM OF TOURISM OFFER IN THE ALENTEJO REGION

*Maria do Rosário Borges[1], Jaime Serra[2]
and Noémi Marujo[3]*
[1]University of Évora, School of Social Sciences, GOVCOOP, Portugal
[2]University of Évora, School of Social Sciences, CEFAGE-UE, Portugal
[3]University of Évora, School of Social Sciences, IGOT-CEG, Portugal

ABTRACT

A Geographic Information System (GIS) is a powerful tool to make an integrated study of the overall spatial expression of tourism resources in the territory, as well as the facilities and the infrastructures required for its development. Tourism policies and strategies are becoming more complex to define due to the diversity of variables and constraints that underlie them. The availability of accurate and update information about tourism offer is thus crucial for the public sector to guide and ground their planning initiatives and for professionals to guide their business management. This chapter focuses on the methodological aspects of the project GIS of Tourism Offer in the Alentejo Regional Area, developed in the context of Regional Observatory for Tourism in the Alentejo (Portugal). Its main purpose is to make an inventory, systematize existing information and gather basic information when missing, about the tourism resources of the Alentejo and represent them in a GIS environment, providing an important tool for decision support of the business sector and tourism planning in the region. The illustrative case study method will be used to describe how the methodological structure of the project was conceived and implemented to achieve the established goals, considering both the existing scientific studies in this field and the reality of the region itself as far as the regional development of sustainable tourism is concerned.

1. INTRODUCTION

When tourism agents are involved in defining a framework for policies, planning and management activities, either alone or within a project network, they need to have appropriate data and information to support their decisions. These tasks fall into the decision-making process regarding the future. The availability of accurate and updated information about tourism offer is thus crucial for the public sector to guide and ground their planning initiatives and for professionals to guide their business management, all in tune toward the development of sustainable tourism. Considering the multifaceted field of action of tourism activities and diversity of services that support them, it becomes clear that a diverse package of information sources is needed. Some of the strongest concepts mentioned in tourist literature (e.g. development, planning, policy and management) are appealing, more and more, for an integrated approach to economic, cultural, social and environmental issues. Sustainable development of the destinations cannot be addressed without a systemic view of its context, and even then the approach can only focus on one of its components. Combining this coverage with the volatile nature of information it becomes clear that there must be an exhaustive work to gather all the necessary information. Usually, the first step is to make an inventory of the resources that are going to be analysed. The inventory of tourism resources, if well planned, managed and updated, is an essential tool to support the decisions of tourist agents, regardless of the specificity of their work. This powerful information framework has to be supported by an information system that allows the storage, handling and use of information tailored to the needs of its users. The inventory will be supported by a geographic information system (GIS), which is considered one of the best tools to assist planner and managers. In the value chain of tourism, where many actors interact, it has usually been the responsibility of state bodies to assume the coordination of such a huge task. In the specific case presented in this chapter, the organisation responsible for the inventory of tourism resources in the Alentejo region is the regional government agency that has competence for promoting the sustainable development of the destination. To support that inventory, a GIS technological tool was designed and structured to suit the needs of information collection, storage, examination, analysis and interpretation. In this context, this chapter presents an illustrative case study on the planning and construction of a GIS designed to meet the information needs of the regional tourism body that manages the sustainable tourism development of the Alentejo region in Portugal. First the main findings which have resulted from the literature review on the issues under review are presented. Then the institutional context in which the GIS emerged to support the decisions is presented. The methodology implemented to develop the GIS of tourism offer in the Alentejo region will be presented and the focus will be given to phases that have been developed to date by all four partners. The conclusions presents some reflections about this case study.

2. BRIEF CONCEPTUAL APPROACH TO THE GIS

A GIS is a system of hardware, software, spatial information and computational procedures, which enables and facilitates the analysis, management and representation of space and phenomena that occur in it. According to Chancellor and Cole (2008: 343), "GIS are to map making what word processors are to writing". Due to its versatility and multifunctions, it can be widely applicable to the easier achievement of sustainable tourism development. "Spatial (environmental) data can be used to explore conflicts, examine impacts and assist decision-making" (Bahaire and Elliott-White, 1999: 159). It is applied in the following main areas: biology, forestry, geology, marketing, urban planning, civil protection, hydrological network, telecommunications, transport, health and tourism. Celikyay (2006: 221) refers that "throughout the world, spatial planning strategies which focus on sustainable development adapt an ecological approach and both the regional and urban planning processes are based upon ecological bases". "A functional GIS turns data, through analysis, into useful information" (Tomlinson, 2007: 1). GIS provides answers to many questions, some already standard, applicable in many areas and domains of analysis. According to Bahaire and Elliott-White (1999: 160) those key questions are: What exists in...? (location); Where is ... located? (condition); What has changed in a given period? (trend); What is the best way to ...? (route); What is the spatial pattern of...? (pattern); What can happen if ...? (modelling). Many other specific questions can be put to the GIS, from simple to complex questions and issues. It depends on the objectives with which it was designed and its technological capability as a proportion of investment made in hardware and software. The five components necessary for carrying out GIS tasks are people, data, hardware, software and procedures. The core functions performed by a GIS for data are: the collection, storage, examination, analysis and interpretation, and presentation and output. As mentioned above, GIS are technologies that allow players to explore the geographical dimension of the data, based on a wide range of data, aggregating several different bases, but with common characteristics or fields. According to Bahaire and Elliott-White (1999: 160), it normally operates with two types of data: geographical or spatial data and alpha-numeric or attributes. The first are elements that have a geographic location like full address, location, civil parish, municipality, region type (e.g. district) and a coordinate system (using a standard geographical frame of reference such as latitude and longitude). The second includes descriptive and statistical data associated with an entity or with a spatial entity. The geographical elements can be represented in vector format, raster / matrix or 3D. In the first model, the representations are made based on a coordinate system and focus on the accuracy of the location of elements in space, using three spatial forms: point, line and polygon. The inventory data is one of the first steps to consider in defining the means to have implementation of a GIS project. The geographic database is the most expensive component, but also the longest-lasting. Thus, the way data are collected and entered are two crucial moments to ensure the best utility and functionality of the system. This step involves identifying the sources of information and data format, defining the treatment to which they are subject for the effects of storage and indicating the destination of the processed information. Along with the collection, it is also necessary to categorize the information according to specific characteristics of thematic analysis, in order to better define the relationship between the layers. A GIS organizes and stores, independently, the information as a collection of thematic layers or levels. Each level contains elements that share similar attributes that are located in the same geographical extent. This capability makes GIS a very attractive tool, given its speed and easy use, enabling the users to relate the information through the existing position and topology of objects, in order to generate new information. The geographical analysis is usually divided into three types: proximity analysis, overlay, and networks. Regarding the presentation of information a map or chart is often chosen (as they are very efficient at storing and communicating geographic information) that can be integrated into reports, three-dimensional views, photographic images and other outputs such as multimedia. The potential of these systems goes far beyond the drawing of maps. In fact, GIS is an analytical tool, which is of particular relevance for the possibility it offers to identify spatial relationships between geographic features represented on maps. Its main advantage is associated with the fact that it integrates diverse databases, enables research, inquiry and data manipulation and spatial modelling to communicate spatial information analysed, with customized maps and graphics, to meet the specific needs of each type of user.

3. APPLICATIONS OF GIS

GIS systems in tourism can be used for public or management use. For the first purpose tourists search for geographic information in order to find the location of services and amenities, as well as other searches about place-specific information. For example, web-based GIS or information kiosks can satisfy this need. For management use, GIS can be used by both the private and public sector. Management users can query the GIS with several questions depending on the scope of contents contained in the databases that support it. The private sector uses the tool to intervene in the short term, while the public sector uses it to look at the medium- and long-term effects of their actions. Developing GIS and other information technology has proved to be one of the most powerful policy-making devices for local government managers (O'Looney, 2000). Public managers use it in a way that is unique due the scope of its responsibilities. The author presented a wide range of areas in which the public sector applied GIS to plan and manage (e.g. land-use and urban growth, infrastructure and transportation management, educational planning, public health, public information services, security and tourism services). Worrall (1994: 232) refers that "local government is a heterogeneous business which (potentially) has a profusion of roles to play ranging from "routine" asset-management functions through to assisting in the strategic management of the local authority as a whole". Improvements in usability, power, versatility, capability and diversity of users of GIS technology are registering an exponential increase. Today desktop GIS software exists (second-wave GIS) designed to be used by non-technical user (managers and decision makers). O'Looney (2000) says that public administrators have a special responsibility in using GIS as an instrument, and as such they should integrate and implement public values and contemplate social issues when using it.

4. GIS AND TOURISM

The origin of the recent interest in GIS in the tourism field is mostly based on the relevance of its application in the area of planning and tourism management in a variety of scenarios (Bahaire and Elliott-White, 1999). Considering its potential, there is not yet wide use by different stakeholders in tourism as they are in other economic areas, perhaps because of its complexity (Farsari, 2003). Initially, its use began with planning professionals concerned with environmental issues and resource management, although more recently several authors have manifested a growing interest in its use (Bahaire and Elliott-White,

1999). The reason is because they are facing new challenges related to the process of decision making that sustainable development of tourism currently requires. As already emphasized, the construction of a GIS makes it possible to group and question the information in an integrated and dynamic way and thus effectively increase the capacity of decision and action. In a certain moment of reference, it will be possible to examine responses to certain situations, such as those listed here (Borges et al., 2007): to identify and inventory existing resources and tourist attractions in the territory under study; to provide information about the tourist objects in a geo-referenced base; to identify areas with tourism potential to have an integrated vision about measures already taken and that will be taken, according to several variables; to update information quickly that is relevant to (re) think the strategies defined; to analyse the characteristics of tourism by type and by land area, among other variables; To analyse the characteristics of tourism demand by type and by geographical area limits, among other variables; to identify the current spatial pattern of land use for tourism services; to determine the suitability of a region to develop certain forms of tourism; to analyse the trends of spatial location of a particular task; to analyse, through scenarios, alternative forms of exploitation of a given area; to analyse scenarios to find the most cost-effective use of space; to analyse the impacts caused by the activity; and to show the territory as if the user were flying over. Other conditions of analysis may be triggered in a GIS applicable to the area of tourism, which depend on the technical ability, creativity and imagination of its users in exploring the full potential of the tool. The importance of GIS in tourism is based on the fact that it is a powerful aid in the planning and management of resources and tourist attractions, a key tool in assessing and determining the suitability of the tourist area, providing information for decision support systems ; it is a tool that enables constant innovation to satisfy different classes of potential users, including tourists and tourism professionals in the many areas in which they operate; and that it is an aid to carrying out research work either by professionals or academics.

Gunn (2002:184) lists several projects that were developed based on this technological tool, highlighting the main advantages associated with their use, with special focus on speed, which requires the analysis phase, especially in the stage that involves the determination of areas with potential interest. The multi-level analysis done using a GIS allows the combination of the variables under consideration, contributing to the reduction of costs associated with projects, facilitating the visualization of data and information and thus making the analysis phase faster and more effective. Pearce (1995) also emphasises the usefulness of the GIS and its role in decision-making process of geographers in activities related to planning. As examples of the successful application of this tool in the field of tourism planning, Bahaire and Elliott-White (1999) refer to the Tourism and Recreation Information Package (TRIP) as one of the first developed in the United Kingdom to support the planning and formulation of tourism policy Scotland. Christodoulakis et al., (1998) point out the sites of the cities of Chania (Greece) and Venice (Italy) by having a GIS that facilitates the capture of information for the traveller who wants to organize their trip in a particular geographic area. From a different perspective, Zhang, Xu and Zhuang (2011) investigated the spatial dependence and mechanisms of international and domestic tourist distributions in 299 cities in mainland China through a set of Geographical Information Systems (GIS)-based spatial statistical tools. Although at a different rhythm of development, in Portugal there are also already some companies using GIS in the management of tourism enterprises to anticipate, plan, coordinate and optimize the maintenance of, for example, networks of water and sanitation, roads, collection circuits of municipal solid waste, green spaces, commercial management and environmental management. Quinta do Lago and Costa Terra projects are references in the application of GIS software in the private tourism sector. As for public sector tourism in Portugal, Turismo de Portugal, I.P. recently developed a GIS as a tool to support the implementation of policy for the sector and to support business strategies. This GIS allows for greater efficiency and effectiveness in carrying out functions that are committed to Turismo de Portugal IP and, above all, to provide relevant geographical information, harmonized and with quality, which constitutes a decisive contribution to: overseeing and monitoring the implementation of the strategic guidelines of the National Strategic Plan for Tourism with a territorial impact; support for monitoring and advice on instruments of territorial management, as well as analysis and decision on the location of tourist enterprises; and the promotion of sustainable tourism development. The use of this tool is restricted and is not yet accessible to the general public.

5. THE CASE STUDY: THE METHODOLOGY IMPLEMENTED TO DEVELOP THE GEOGRAPHIC INFORMATION SYSTEM OF TOURISM OFFER IN THE ALENTEJO REGION

5.1. Institutional Background of the GIS-TOAR Activity

In the period of April 2010 to April 2012 the Regional Tourism Observatory of Alentejo (RTO-A) project is being constructed, with the coordination of Turismo do Alentejo (TAERT) and funded by the INAlentejo 2007-2013. TAERT is the main body of tourism in the Alentejo region and its priority mission is the development of tourism of its geographical area, aiming at the balanced exploitation of its historical, cultural and natural tourism potential, within the guidelines and directives of the tourism policy defined by the government and multi-annual plans of State and municipalities that form the area (Ministério da Economia e da Inovação, 2008). The overall objective of the RTO-A is the production, analysis, dissemination and follow up of information about tourism in the Alentejo in order to contribute to the sustainable development of this sector in the region. To this end, several main activities were planned within the project: an Information System; a Geographic Information System of Tourism Offer for the Alentejo Region (GIS-TOAR); a Tourism Barometer; a Tourism Satellite Account of the Alentejo Region; a Visitor Profile Study; Outbound markets for the Alentejo Region. Other activities related to institutional management have been defined which are not relevant to this investigation. The strategic partners of the RTO-A project are the three public higher education institutions in the region that offer courses in tourism fields: the University of Évora (UÉ), the Polytechnic Institute of Portalegre (IPP) and the Polytechnic Institute of Beja (IPB). Each activity of the RTO-A has a coordinator who manages the development of actions associated with each activity. In each activity all partners are involved in proportion to their budgets, organized in a formal network. In the case of GIS-TOAR activity, IPP is the coordinating body. The UÉ and IPB are cooperating entities. TAERT also belongs to the team which was constituted for GIS-TOAR activity, since it is the coordinator of the RTO-A.

5.2. Aims of the GIS-TOAR Activity

One of the several specific goals of RTO-A is precisely the definition of the starting point situation, with the completion of the portrait of the tourism sector in the region. The achievement of this goal is grounded in the Geographic Information System of Tourism Offer for the Alentejo Region (GIS-TOAR). The main goal of GIS-TOAR is to identify and characterize the tourism resources of the Alentejo Region in a GIS environment. It will specifically look into the supply side, namely the inventory of resources that are able to motivate the flow of visitors to tourist destinations and to occupy their time with an enjoyable and unique experience (OMT, 1998; DGT, 1996). This survey and evaluation of resources is essential to know the Alentejo territory's tourist potential. With this basic work, the different users have at their disposal an informational tool to support their decisions (e.g. set investment priorities and definition of products to be developed). Policy definition and processes of tourism development of the territory will be more realistic and certainly more effective. The main reason for developing the GIS lies in the fact there is still no tourist inventory for the region that is properly designed, coordinated, managed and updated regularly by an official entity. According to Inskeep (1991), an inventory of tourism resources should include the characterization of a territory that portrays its physical, economic, social and cultural dimensions. In the tourism field, an inventory which is housed in a GIS is the most effective solution to manage the different categories or themes of the territory's resources, due to the need to make a systemic approach to understand its operational context.

5.3. Chronogram of the GIS-TOAR Activity

The activity planning includes seven distinct phases of work as shown in Figure 1. The responsibilities associated with the phases P1, P5 and P6 are carried out almost exclusively by the commitment of the coordinator body. Under his general coordination, all four partners have formed a team and together focused their efforts in phases 2, 3, 4 and 7. In the following sections will the steps undertaken so far by all four partners (P2, P3 and P4) be described in detail by the time this chapter appears.

Description of P2 - Definition of Tables of Tourism Resources and Collection of Geo-referenced Data

The second phase began in September of 2011 and was divided into two domains. First a resource table theme was defined, with main categories and subcategories. This work was conducted according to the methodological guidelines presented by Inskeep (1991), the criteria defined by the Directorate General of Tourism (a national public body, established in 1986 and dissolved in 2006) and based upon the establishment of the Inventory of Tourist Resources at national level (1996), the set of tourism characteristic products considered in the Tourism Satellite Account (2003), and the National Registry of Tourism (2008) edited by the tourism national authority of tourism activity - Turismo de Portugal. In table 1 all six main categories are presented and the two levels of sub-category that were defined to identify and organize resources in the data base.

Table 1. Category and sub-category of tourism resources

6 Main Category	Sub-category Level I	Sub-category Level II
Natural Attractions	Classified Areas	At international, national, regional and local level
	Others	Waterfalls, capes, caves, rivers and ocean beaches, mountains and valleys
Cultural Attractions	Monumental	Archeological sites, cathedrals, churches, chapels, convents, monasteries, castles, forts, palaces, mansions, public art, pillories, crosses, obelisks, world heritage, shrines, chapels, towers, historic houses, monuments, gazebos, fountains, aqueducts, historic bridges
	Artistic	Museums, religious art, painting, sculpture, jewelry, collections, carving, tiles, furniture, bands, choirs, theater and dance companies
	Ethnographic	Crafts, folklore, folk theater / puppetry, regular festivals, popular games
	Complementary	Parks and public gardens, lakes and dams, preserved villages, viewpoints, industrial (mills, oil mills, dams, mines), urban architectural value, planetariums and botanical gardens, buildings of special interest, zoos and aquariums, theme parks, activities with economic interest, urban areas of interest
Activities	Land sports	Nature trail, skiing, climbing, motorized sports
	Water sports	Diving, rowing, canoeing, fishing from a boat, fishing in rivers and lakes, deep-sea fishing, water skiing, windsurfing
	Air sports	Parachuting, balloon flights, parasailing, gliding and paragliding
	Gastronomy & wine	--
	Routes and tours	Themed
Events	Cultural	Religion, performing arts, traditional folk activities, gastronomy, celebrations
	Sports	Air sports, land sports, water sports
	Business	Fairs and specialized exhibition
	Mega-events	--
Equipment	Cultural	Exhibition space, gallery, auditorium, hall, cultural center, library
	Sport	Tourist hunting area, equestrian center, golf, multi-sports pavilions, playground, tennis court, shooting range, swimming pools, fitness circuits, local motorsports, adventure and nautical
	Recreational	Multi-purpose facility, bullring, theater, concert hall, casino, bingo, fairs, markets, dance hall
	Tourist services	Food and beverage establishments, rent-a-car, travel agencies and tour operators, tourist animation companies, tourist offices, city tour and coach, train tours and spas

6 Main Category	Sub-category Level I	Sub-category Level II
Infrastructure	Transport services	Roads, railways, ports, marinas, piers, ferry ports, taxi ranks, airports, airfields, helipads, train stations, bus stops, bus stations
	Other services	Hospitals, health centers, pharmacies, post offices, shopping centers, banks, public security authorities, fire departments, institutions of higher education in tourism

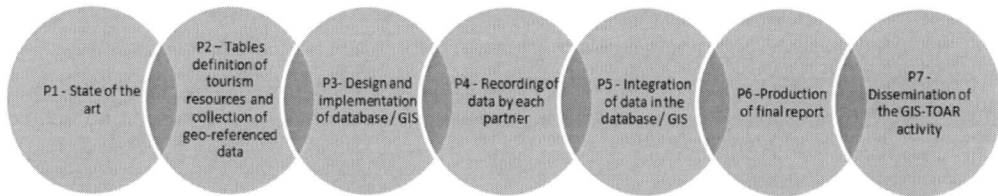

Figure 1. Phases of the GIS-TOAR activity.

Three basic criteria of mandatory application in identifying all the resources have been identified: be legal, be open to visitors and be guided by signs. The specific criteria were identified for each resource in Sub-category Level II. For example, only the museums included in the Alentejo Museum Guide (2010 edition) could be identified. As for tourist accommodation, only those that are already in a database that was created by Turismo do Alentejo could be characterized. With regard to travel agencies and entertainment companies, only those that are identified in the National Register of Tourists Activity it can be characterized. Also only the walking routes approved by the Federation could be part of the list. Other criteria have been established to identify and characterize the resources for the purposes set out in GIS-TOAR activity. After this step, several thematic sheets for the characterization of these resources were created. Attributes were defined for the characterization of each main Category and Sub-category at Level I of resources. For all resources common attributes have been identified – code in the data base, name of the resource, spatial location (line or polygon), responsible entity, description, URL and sources of information used. Subsequently, specific attributes were defined according to the type of resource and the level of detail set took into account the project objectives and the aims of the several activities. These include descriptive and statistical data. To identify the most appropriate attributes by resource category (for each thematic sheet) some characteristics of existing records were also taken into account. For example, the surveys/records used by the Institute for Management of Architectural and Archaeological Heritage (IGESPAR) regarding classified heritage and by the National Institute of Statistics (INE) regarding tourist accommodation were used. Not all attributes that were desirable were included on the list of resources characterization because their collection would make the process of gathering information much more lengthy and complex. So the level of facility access to data was taken into account. The second main task within this phase was the identification and collection of secondary data. It was important to know what information was available and if it could be used, in order not to duplicate efforts. The research was conducted in three areas: (i) official databases at national, regional and local levels, (ii) non-official data bases (enterprises, associations for development and others), and (iii) other sources (official documentation, thematic studies and reports, regional and local private agents and local population).Official public entities that regularly edit data on tourism were identified. At this phase, some of the secondary data were obtained only from those authorities at national, regional and local levels. To this end, the TAERT body established several formal requests for their collaboration in this study, although some information is freely accessible. According to the attributes of the available information, the sheets for characterization of tourism resources were reviewed. In addition to the previous tasks a request was also made to gather secondary data published by official bodies (e.g. Army Geographic Institute, Meteorological Institute) related to different resources areas, but without the need for additional characterization research by the teams. Specifically, to gather information on administrative boundaries of the territory, military charts (with information on roads, railways, airports and aerodromes, hydrology), REN and RAN charts, letters of land use, climate data, relief, population centres, urban boundaries, and population. This set of information was already available in GIS format. Some had to be purchased and some was provided for free. This information, combined with that presented in table 1, enables Turismo do Alentejo, and also other users, to do a comprehensive analysis of information associated with the operation of the economic, social, cultural and environmental systems where tourism development occurs. At the end of this second phase, a report was concluded containing the details of the methodology that should be followed by partners or entities to contract in data collection phase (P4). This report identifies the premises to carry out the fieldwork, and contains the procedure for validation of information, through quality control.

Description of P3 - Design and Implementation of Database / GIS

The design of the structure of the geodatabase was made according to the previous tables and their attributes, by type of resource. It was combined the spatial data (geo) with data repository (database) to create a central data repository for spatial data storage and management. The first draft of the geodatabase was conceived in proper software – ArcGIS. Since the various partners do not have this software or skills to use it, an Excel file to record all the information compiled was designed in accordance with the requirements defined in the previous phases. Another reason to use Excel was to facilitate the information request to the municipal councils and the process of exchanging information in a more universally used format. In the fifth stage all information will be integrated into the GIS database software by the coordinator.

Description of P4 - Recording of Data by Each Partner

Each partner has seven months to complete their task in the geographical area of influence (from March to October 2011). The administrative boundary of the district was established. At this stage the compilation of secondary data identified in the second phase was concluded. After that the question was: what additional information must still be obtained? And how to access that information? In order to achieve the desired outcomes, alternative methods were considered and used conjointly to gather the information needed. A mixed-method approach was used in order to understand complex relationships and interactions among multiple sources of information that, when compared, reveal no consistency or accurate data. The teams tried to find and nullify the differences. Desk research was made to extract secondary data from several sources. After, that information was compared with primary data obtained in this phase. To collect primary data, several approaches were used.

First of all, according to the methodological procedures defined for the activity, each team had to make contact with all municipalities at the district level. Local councils were asked to provide a list of all the resources of their territory, in accordance with the general and specific criteria. To this end, meetings were held. Only after having this list would contact be made with each resource identified in order to make a detailed characterization of it. Meanwhile the working sheet was transformed into a basic questionnaire to send by e-mail to the various private agents to gather information. Due to the lack of adherence in participating on the first contact, other initiatives were taken to increase the response rate (survey by telephone, self-completion questionnaires and face-to-face interviews). Participant observation was made primarily to confirm some of data provided by local towns (e.g. characterization of the surrounding built heritage). Photographic recording was also made.

Constraints of P4

Some of the constraints encountered during P4 were previously forecast, but the teams have created the expectation to overcome them with some extra effort. However, it was not possible to counter some of these obstacles. The constraints related to the timeliness of official data were as follows: a major limiting factor in this research is that the few existing official databases are not updated; currently, national bodies are being restructured (organisms that generate important resources for the activity became extinct, making its reference in the DB difficult in the following weeks); the various official bodies that have jurisdiction over the same kind of resources do not have the exactly same lists of organisms and data do not coincide; and in the space of seven months time there were changes in the number of resources available. The constraints related to communication with private agents were: it was very difficult to obtain the cooperation of private actors (the reasons they presented were: they are tired of answering so many requests for information, they thought the teams were working for the tax authorities'); and the information available does not always match the records contained in the official entities (e.g. number of rooms and facilities). The constraints related to communication with public agents were: the main partners in every town (the town council) do not meet the institutional requirements made for the project, delaying and complicating the identification of certain categories of resources; sometimes, they listed resources that are not legal; they never managed to meet deadlines set by mutual agreement, in turn delaying the achievement of objectives for weeks and in some cases months; and some town councils identified features that are not legal, while others listed a lower number of resources than actually exist in their geographic area. The constraints within the working groups were: there was no regular meeting between the partners to clarify doubts and the specificities of resources of each geographical area; contacts made by phone and e-mail did not prove effective; certain criteria had to be cancelled, but this information only came after some lists were ready (e.g. the criterion "have signs" marginalized many important resources, because in Portugal theft and vandalism of signs is an issue of concern); the specific services available in some locations determine an increase of the inventory list of resources, sometimes leaving it in doubt as to the thematic group to be allocated, and thus the level of detail to implement in its characterization.

CONCLUSION

Market dynamics are becoming more complex, so the planning and management activities are more complicated. If, in parallel, decision support systems are not properly constituted and updated (such as GIS) sustainable development will be even more of a utopia. This illustrative case study explained how a regional authority engaged in directing an activity that would allow an inventory of the tourism resources that it has to manage, as an obligation, and from there on, started building a geodatabase to analyse the context of the tourism operation.

All the partners of the SIG-TOAR activity combined their efforts to respond accurately to the defined methodology. As in any other planned activity, it was necessary to adjust the rhythm of work and review some operational criteria. In an initial phase possible problems in collecting information for the geodatabase were identified. The teams expected to overcome obstacles, but found the real scenario was not the best. The work required for characterization of stakeholders' activities and services was difficult to do. Without their contribution, data consistency is lost. The teams tried to compensate with the use of alternative methods of information collection, focusing on those that involve personal contact. In this case the success rate of response was increased. Also, the official authorities still do not have the organizational capacity to have their databases updated, despite successive changes in legislation regarding the creation of information systems for tourism. The private sector also does not cooperate in this task. It is clear that even with the most expensive GIS technology and all the money available to support the costs of an activity like this, if there are no changes in the legal procedures for the registration of activities and changes in the mentality of the stakeholders, in order to contribute to building a tool that can also help them, it becomes almost impossible to obtain a high rate of success in achieving the scope of these objectives and analyses. Informal discussions between the working groups evidenced that during fieldwork, the way the constraints were felt were similar in the different districts under review. In this reduced perspective comparative analysis, the authors hazard the opinion that the problem was not based in the methods of approach, but in the political, legal and institutional context that prevails in stakeholders' context of operation.

Some limitations to this chapter can be referenced. The fourth phase ends at the end of October 2011 and the last phase at the end of April 2012. And as such, the reflections on the activity and final balance are not yet fully possible. It was not possible to compare this study with another study of a similar case, in Portugal or any other country. The literature review gave only few results for studies with this framework focus. A comparison among the methods chosen by different bodies in similar study cases might evidence, for a future project, improvements to increase the rate of adherence within private agents. The triangulation was made to cross-checked the quality of information, but the large volume of information accumulated with this methodological option resulted in a more complex process for information gathering and management. The structure of the teams did not remained stable during this period hindering the rhythm of work required. So, maybe it is important for a future investigation, to verify if the profile and motivation of human resources influence the level of success in compiling the data. GIS assume an increasing role in supporting decision-making and spatial expression in the study of tourism in the territory, and may be a significant contribution to promoting sustainable development in tourism destinations. But, given the complexity of obtaining accurate data and information for tourism planning, efforts must continue to keep inventory data as updated as possible.

ACKNOWLEDGMENTS

This work was developed in the context of Regional Tourism Observatory of Alentejo (RTO-A) project, coordinated by Turismo do Alentejo, ERT and funded by the INAlentejo 2007-2013 [Operação n.º ALENT-01-0428-FEDER-000312].

REFERENCES

Bahaire, T. & Elliott-White, M. (1999). The Application of Geographical Information Systems (GIS) in Sustainable Tourism Planning: a review. *Journal of Sustainable Tourism, 7*(2), 159-174.

Borges, M. R.; Cravo, P.; Devile, E. & Lima, S. (2007). Os Sistemas de Informação Geográfica no Planeamento de Itinerários Turísticos. In Muñoz, M., Freitas, A. & Cravo, P. (Eds.): *Livro de Actas da Conferência Ibero-Americana InterTIC 2007.* International Association for the Scientific Knowledg (IASK). Porto. 120-126.

Celikyay, S. (2006). Research on New Residential Areas Using GIS: A case study. In Jos P. van Leeuwen & Harry J. P. Timmermans (Eds.): *Innovations in Design & Decision Support in Systems in Architecture and Urban Planning.* Springer. Dordrecht. 221-233.

Chancellor, C. & Cole, S. (2008). Using Geographic Information System to Visualize Travel Patterns and Market Research Data. *Journal of Travel & Tourism Marketing, 25*(3–4), 341-354.

Christodoulakis, S., Anastasiadis, M., Margazas, T., Moumoutzis, N., Kontogiannis, P., Terezakis, G. & Tsinaraki, C. (1998). A Modular Approach to Support GIS Functionality in Tourism Applications. In *Conference Proceedings on Information and Communication Technologies in Tourism.* Springer-Verlag. 63-72.

Direcção-Geral do Turismo (1996). *Inventário dos Recursos Turísticos.* DGT. Lisboa.

Farsari, Y. (2003). GIS based support for sustainable tourism planning and policy making [CD-ROM]. In *Proceedings of 12th International Leisure and Tourism Symposium.* ESADE. Barcelona.

Giles, W. (2003). GIS Applications in Tourism Planning. In *GIS 340 – GIS Seminar of GIS Advanced Diploma Program.* College of New Caledonia.

Gunn, C. A. & Var, T. (2002). *Tourism Planning: basics, concepts and cases.* 4.ª Ed. Routledge. London.

Inskeep, E. (1991). *Tourism Planning – An Integrated and Sustainable Development Approach.* Van Nostrand Reinhold. New York.

Ministério da Economia e da Inovação (2008). *Decreto-Lei n.º 67/2008, de 15 de Outubro,* Diário da República, I.ª Série, N.º 200.

O´Looney, J. (2000). *Beyond maps: GIS and decision making in local government.* Environmental Systems Research Institute, Inc (ESRI). Redlands, CA.

Pearce, D. (1995). *Tourism Today: a geographical analysis.* 2.ª Ed. Longman. England.

Tomlinson, R. (2007). *Thinking about Geographic Information System Planning for Managers*. 3rd Ed. ESRI Press.

Zhang, Y. & Xu, J.; Zhuang, P. (2011). The Spatial Relationship of Tourist Distribution in Chinese Cities, *Tourism Geographies*, *13*(1), 75–90.

Worrall, L. (1994). The role of GIS-based Spatial Analysis in Strategic Management in Local Government. *Computer, Environment and Urban Systems*, *18*(5), 323-332.

In: Methods and Analysis on Tourism and Environment   ISBN: 978-1-62417-824-5
Editors: J.M.Jiménez, M.V.Vargas, F.J.O.Rosell et al. © 2013 Nova Science Publishers, Inc.

Chapter 6

TOURISM IMPACT AT LOCAL SCALE: THE CASE OF TUSCANY

Stefano Rosignoli[1], Enrico Conti[1] and Alessandro Viviani[2]

[1]Regional Institute Economic Planning of Tuscany (IRPET), Italy
[2]University of Florence, Italy

ABSTRACT

The chapter has two basic objectives: to construct suitable statistical measures for the agreed requirements and to assess the economic and environmental impact of the presence of tourists on a sub-regional scale (local economic system). The first goal is pursued through two different methodological tools. For the first tool, the number of nights spent by tourists in houses (not recorded by official statistics) is estimated by mean of a statistical model, on a municipal scale,.. The second tool is represented by the estimate of the tourists' average daily spending in Tuscany through the integration of different statistical sources. The second goal - assessment of the economic and environmental impact of tourism spending - is pursued through the use of a multi-regional input-output model integrated with an array of satellite environmental accounting. The results of the assessment exercise confirm the importance of tourism for the region's economy and the consequent environmental impacts. Therefore, the tool we have put together constitute a valid back-up for monitoring regional tourism development at the local level and for planning processes.

1. INTRODUCTION

The measure of the territorial distribution of the positive and negative effects of tourism is a fundamental step in any planning activity for sustainable and competitive development (Giljum, Behrens, Hinterberger, Lutz and Meyer, 2008; Rotmans et al., 2000). In spite of the many limitations that have been pinpointed (Dwyer et al., 2003), input-output models are still a valid tool for assessing the impacts of tourism, in particular at local level (Loveridge, 2004).

Furthermore, in many cases the results are in line with those obtained from general economic equilibrium models (CGE or AGE) (Polo and Valle, 2008).

The interest is focused on Tuscany, which is one of the regions with the highest numbers of tourists in Europe: in the last 15 years the ratio between tourist numbers and inhabitants has grown by 47% and at present the region comes in 32nd out of 273 in the European tourism intensity classification.

Among the Italian regions, it is second only to Trentino Alto Adige and Valle d'Aosta (two small regions with low populations) and Veneto.

The goal of this chapter is twofold: on one hand, to address the problem of constructing suitable statistical measures for the agreed requirements, on the other hand to assess the economic and environmental impact of tourism as a driver of regional economic development.

Standing out among the main issues to be dealt with in regard to tourism analysis are: the lack of information on tourist numbers in non-official accommodations (which is difficult to retrieve from administrative sources); the lack of a reliable estimate of overall tourist spending (a particularly extensive investigation would be needed to find this out); and the construction of input-output tables at local level to assess the economic and environmental impact. This chapter deals with these three problems using the following approaches:

1) The lack of information with relation to numbers of tourists in non-official accommodation is dealt with using an econometric model which is focused on water consumption for domestic use. This model produces estimates at municipal level which are then aggregated at local economic system (LES) level.
2) The lack of information on tourist spending is dealt with by integrating existing statistical sources in order to estimate the average daily spending per capita of overnight tourists and day trippers in Tuscany.
3) The economic and environmental effects of this spending are then calculated by applying a multi-regional input-output model with sub-regional details to the overall tourism spending (the IRPET multi-LES model) which is integrated with a module that also measures the environmental outfall of the tourist spending and the production activated by this spending. The result of knowledge accumulated within IRPET, it is almost the only approach of its kind at local level and hence is a particularly informative assessment tool.

The chapter is set out as follows. In paragraph 2 we describe the process of estimate of the number of tourist in private houses at municipal level (2.1) and the procedure to estimate the daily tourist spending per capita by type of accommodation and type of tourist destination (2.2).

We then describe the multi-LES input-output model used to assess the economic and environmental impact (2.3). In paragraph 3 we assess the impact of tourism in economic and environmental terms and comment on the results obtained. In paragraph 4 we discuss the strengths and weaknesses of the methodology adopted and draw short conclusions.

2. The Estimation Procedure for Local Variables

2.1. The Number of Tourists in Houses at Municipal Level

The annual official data available at municipal and provincial level relating to tourist numbers in the Italian regions exclusively concern overnight stays in commercial accommodation such as hotels, residences, holiday farms, camp sites, etc., but exclude those staying in houses.

A "proxy" of the total number of non-official tourists at regional scale can be obtained by overlapping two surveys. The sample survey carried out by the UIC (Italian Foreign Exchange Office) relating to foreign tourists staying in Italy and the ISTAT sample survey "Italians' Holidays and Travel" which produces estimates on the Italian component of tourists staying in non-official accommodation. By reading the two inquiries at once, it results that the number of tourists in houses counts the same as the total official tourist flow, and that it constitutes the great majority of non-official tourism. Hence, the importance of putting together reliable information on the number of tourists in houses becomes immediately clear. In addition, this information must be sufficiently divided into different territories as to take account of the pressure that the tourist flow exercises on numerous economic, social and environmental ambits.

A step in the direction of estimating numbers of tourists in houses was made by Gismondi (Gismondi; 2000, 2001), who used UIC statistics and elaborated individual data from the ISTAT-domanda survey to obtain a regional estimate. The methodology that we are presenting attempts to fill in the lack of information on tourist flows in private accommodation with greater territorial detail than can be found in the quoted sources. This operation is done using a statistical model that allows us to estimate the numbers of tourists in private accommodation at municipal level on a yearly basis.[1].

The number of tourists in houses was estimated using a model that relates a type of consumption – water for domestic use – with some determinant variables that can account for the population's propensity to consume and the share consumed by tourists in accommodation. This way we were able to estimate the number of people which we are interested[2].

The Model
The proposed model uses the following information:

1) Annual data relating to cubic metres of water for domestic consumption billed by the water service companies to the domestic users in each municipality. The data was supplied by the local authority water boards.

---

[1] The proposed model makes use of a critical reading of a previous attempt by Fabrizio Cipollini to build a method to estimate tourists in houses using electrical consumption as the variable; Cipollini F. (2004), Un modello statistico per la stima del turismo in alloggi privati in Toscana, Firenze: Dipartimento di Statistica dell'Università di Firenze, *MIMEO.*

[2] The procedure we will describe allows to estimate the total amount of tourist night spent in houses in each municipality of Tuscany using the inversion of the regression model specification. There are other old and new approaches to make this estimation using for instance Structural equation models, latent variable models or Confirmatory Factor Analisys.

2) Data relating to the number of wells for domestic and drinking water use present in each municipality in Tuscany).

3) Data relating to the resident population as at 1 January of each year for each municipality, supplied by IRPET.

4) Data relating to the number of houses available for use by tourists for each municipality as at 2006. The variable was built from the Census data.

The model assumes that the variable of water consumption for domestic use is interesting because, owing to how it is measured, besides the present resident population, it only reflects the presence of non-residents in houses, the very great majority of whom are tourists. Starting from the piece of data relating to the cubic metres billed to users for domestic uses, available on a yearly basis and at municipal level, the model proposed below breaks water consumption down into two components:

1) Water consumed by the resident population.
2) Water consumed by the population of tourists staying in houses.

Therefore, Considering a linear relation between the two components and respectively the resident population and equivalent tourist population in the year y and municipality m we can write:

$$CM_{ym} = CMRESPOP_{ym} + CMTOURHOU_{ym} \qquad [2.1]$$

where

$$CMRESPOP_{ym} = \alpha_0 + \alpha_1 \, t \cdot RESPOP_{ym} + \varepsilon \qquad [2.2]$$

$$CMTOURHOU_{ym} = \beta_0 + \beta_1 t \cdot HOUSTAY_{ym} + \varepsilon \qquad [2.3]$$

and

CM_{ym} = Water consumed for domestic use in cubic metres in the year y in municipality m
$CMRESPOP_{ym}$ = Water consumed by the resident population in the year y in municipality m
$CMTOURHOU_{ym}$ = Water consumed by tourists in houses in the year y in municipality m
$RESPOP_{ym}$ = resident population in the year y in municipality m
$t \cdot HOUSTAY_{ym}$ = equivalent tourist population in the year y in municipality (t = time, is a coefficient introduced in the hypothesis that, in addition to the propensity to consume, the consumption of water also depends on the time for which people are present in the house, either as a resident (RESPOP) or as a tourist staying in a house (HOUSTAY). With respect to the time present in a house, we make a very simplifying hypothesis, according to which in a year, which is the interval at which the water consumption figures are made available to us, the average time the resident population is present is 352 days. The value "352" is an average value coming from ISTAT surveys).

Now we introduce the second element, the equivalent number of tourists in houses *TOURHOU*, which we will consider for simplicity = *t·HOUSTAY*.

TOURHOU is linked to the number of houses available for tourism (*HOLHOME*). Hence, we can hypothesise a proportion like

$$TOURHOU_{ym} = \gamma_1 \, HOLHOME_{ym} \tag{2.4}$$

so forth

$$CMTOURHOU_{ym} = \beta_0 + \beta_1 \gamma_1 \, HOLHOME_{ym} \tag{2.5}$$

and therefore

$$CM_{ym} = \alpha_0 + \beta_0 + \alpha_1 \, tRESPOP_{ym} + \beta_1 \gamma_1 \, HOLHOME_{ym} + \varepsilon \tag{2.6}$$

In the end we estimate the following model

$$\frac{CMnew_{ym}}{RESPOP_{ym}} = \alpha^{**} + \frac{\beta_1 \gamma_1 \, HOLHOME_{ym}}{RESPOP_{ym}} + \beta_2 \, COAST + \beta_3 \, MOUNTAINS \tag{2.7}$$

where:

$$CMnew_{ym} = CMP_{ym} + CMwells_{ym}$$

and

CMP$_{ym}$ = consumption of water distributed by pipelines in the year y and municipality m
CMwells$_{ym}$ = consumption of water drawn from wells in the year y and municipality m
COAST = dummy variable that takes the value of 1 if the municipality has access to the coast
MOUNTAINS = dummy variable that takes the value of 1 if the municipality falls among those classified by ISTAT as "inner mountains"

In the model α^{**} the new intercept, represents the consumption per capita that can be attributed to residents, that is, the propensity to consume, which we assume = β_1. This means that we suppose the same quantity of water is consumed in relation to the same time t of length of stay in a house by a resident and a tourist. In this way, by estimating the two parameters α^{**} and β_1 and the coefficients of the COAST and MOUNTAINS dummies, we can obtain

$$\gamma_1 = \frac{\alpha^{**}}{\beta_1 + \beta_2 \, COAST + \beta_3 \, MOUNTAINS} \tag{2.12}$$

As a consequence we calculate

$$TOURHOU_{ym} = \gamma_1 HOLHOME_{ym} \hspace{4cm} [2.13]$$

$TOURHOU_{ym}$ represents the number of tourists equivalent to residents. As a consequence, to obtain the number of tourists in terms of length of stay in days, we multiply $TOURHOU_{ym}$ by 352, which is the average number of days on which it is assumed residents are present yearly hometown.

Table 1. Regression statistics

Variance-weighted least-squares regression				Number of jobs = 260		
Goodness-of-fit chi2(260) = 24198.49				Model chi2(3) = 35503.95		
Prob > chi2: < 1.00E-08						
	Coef.	Standard error	z	P>|z|	[95% Conf. Interval]	
holhome	24.6	0.26	96.09	0	24.14325	25.14868
coast	13. 9	0.18	77.81	0	13.51927	14.2179
mountains	-7.2	0.12	-59.17	0	-7.3887	-6.91493
_cons	53.3	0.06	779.9	0	53.16794	53.43585

Table 2. Number of nights spent by tourists in houses at provincial scale. Year 2006

	Absolute Values	Distribution
Prato	300,766	1.00%
Massa Carrara	4,190,295	10.00%
Lucca	7,937,783	19.00%
Pistoia	2,096,936	5.00%
Firenze	2,064,702	5.00%
Livorno	9,821,173	23.00%
Pisa	1,250,149	3.00%
Siena	1,840,781	4.00%
Arezzo	1,470,469	3.00%
Grosseto	11,416,351	27.00%
Toscana	42,389,404	100.00%

The Estimates

We made a check using a cross-sectional regression of the relation shown above with the OLS method. To face the problem of heteroscedasticity (that often occurs when, as in this case there is a large difference among the sizes of the observations) we decided to apply a weighted least squares estimation method: a particular case of GLS estimation in which the diagonal of the Var-Cov matrix of residuals is proportional to a function of a known size variable (in this case we used a power of population variable). We could have also used a different specification (such as logarithmic transformation) but in this case we would have faced problems in the estimation of the target variable (number of tourist nights) inverting a non linear equation.

$$\frac{CMnew_{ym}}{RESPOP_{ym}} = \alpha^{**} + \frac{\beta_1 \gamma_1 HOLHOME_{ym}}{RESPOP_{ym}} + \beta_2 COAST + \beta_3 MOUNTAINS \hspace{2cm} [2.14]$$

The model, the constant, the explicative variable and the dummies turn out to be statistically significant, the coefficients have the expected signs, and the fit is good (Goodness-of-fit chi2(260) = 24198.49.The estimated numbers of tourists in houses in Tuscany in 2006 amount to around 42.4 million.

2.2. Estimate of Tourist Spending

In order to make an assessment of the economic and environmental impact of tourists it was necessary to indirectly assess the amount of the tourists' consumption in the local economic systems (LES). In the previous paragraph we showed the method used by IRPET to estimate the numbers of non-official tourists within the local economic systems. In this paragraph we describe the method that we used to make the estimate of the tourists' average daily spending per capita by type of accommodation and type of tourist destination. By combining the previous result with the result we obtain in this paragraph, we get to an estimate of the overall amount of spending for tourism by official and non-official tourists.

In table 3 we list the sources of information used to estimate the average daily spending per capita:

Below we list the steps that used the sources described in order to come to the estimate of the tourists' average daily spending per capita.

1. From the "Statistics on tourism" source we took the ISTAT matrix of official tourist numbers by region of origin (including abroad) and destination region and added a column representing the numbers of Italians abroad by region of residence (data taken from the Bank of Italy survey on international tourism).
2. The "Italians' travel and holidays" inquiry estimates the overall numbers of (official and non-official) tourists, dividing them by origin (North, Centre, South) and destination region. We used this data to reassess the official numbers recorded in the matrix created in point 1.
3. The Bank of Italy border crossing survey estimates foreign tourists' average daily spending per capita by destination region. In the first approximation we estimated the tourist expense matrix by multiplying this average spending by all the columns in the matrix of overall tourist numbers calculated in point 2.
4. We added the internal non-tourist consumption of residents calculated as the difference between families' internal consumption (known from regional accounting) and the column total of this matrix to the diagonal of the spending matrix. When modified in this manner, the column total of matrix S indicates the total internal consumption per region of presence and the row total indicates an approximate estimate of consumption by region of residence.
5. By using resident families' consumption (from the ISTAT sample survey), opportunely corrected make it coherent with the national accounting data, we got a good estimate of the row total of the consumption matrix and carried out a so-called biproportional balancing (usually called RAS balancing), that is, an iterative procedure that proportionally adjusts the matrix cells until the row and column totals are coherent with the known restrictions. Thus we obtain an origin/destination spending matrix that is coherent with the regional accounting data. From the matrix

cells we can get the residents and non-residents' consumption for each region and the internal and external consumption. At the end of this procedure we have the origin-destination consumption matrix from and for the Italian regions and abroad. The row total of this matrix indicates the residents' consumption by region of residence, the column total indicates the regional internal consumption in coherence with the ISTAT regional accounting data. The elements outside the diagonal of this matrix are the regions' incoming (by column) and outgoing (by row) tourist consumption.

6. From the survey on tourist consumption in the Tuscan provinces we found the average daily spending per capita for the different types of tourist destination (coast, mountains, hills and cities of art), for different types of accommodation (hotels, other accommodation) and for spending functions. Then to make them fit with the estimates in the different local economic systems these average spending figures were readjusted on the basis of the average prices of 3-star hotels in the single municipal territories. Hence we obtained the average daily spending per capita by spending function in each LES in Tuscany.

7. The average spending previously found and updated as at 2008 (using the ISTAT price variations for the different spending functions) was multiplied by the number of tourists in hotels and other accommodation, and in houses. Therefore, we obtained an overall spending which was then linked to the Tuscan total estimated in points 1 to 6 deemed most reliable. Finally, by using the bridge matrix that connects 12 tourist spending functions to 30 branches of production (data information available from the regional accounting matrix produced yearly by IRPET) we found the total spending for tourism per LES and for the thirty production branches of the demanded goods.

The average spending varies with relation to the type of accommodation where the tourists stay. It goes from 116 euros per day in hotels to 74 euros on average per day for tourists in houses. The composition of the spending also varies with relation to the accommodation type: we go from tourists in a hotel, for whom the spending for hotels and restaurants exceeds 60% to those in houses for whom it goes down to 11%. Housing expenses are only present for tourists in houses and are nil for the other types of accommodation. The other tourist spending items are in order: recreation and culture, clothes and footwear, food and sundry goods and services.

2.3. Input-output Model with Environmental Accounts

We assessed the economic and environmental impact of tourist spending using a multi-regional input-output model in which the single regions (the model's territorial entities) are the LESs (local economic systems)[3] in Tuscany. The model is closed within Tuscany and open with respect to the rest of Italy and the world, in the sense that the trade flows are not calculated endogenously with the latter two economic entities (with the exception of the import flows coming from the two areas).

---

[3] The LESs in Tuscany are 42 groups of municipalities in the region. The logic behind them is to join adjacent municipalities that "contain" the movements of commuters. They do not have any institutional value but cover an important role in economic and local development analysis.

Table 3. Sources to estimate tourist consumption

Sources/Surveys	Information
Statistics on tourism - ISTAT	Matrix of official tourist numbers per region of origin and destination region
Italians' travel and holidays – ISTAT	Matrix of official and non-official tourist numbers divided by origin and destination region
International tourism – Bank of Italy	Numbers and consumption of Italian tourists abroad by region of residence and foreign tourists by region of destination
National accounting – ISTAT	Non-residents' spending in Italy and residents' spending abroad
Regional accounting – ISTAT	Families' internal consumption (including non-residents' consumption) by region of spending
Inquiry on resident families' consumption – ISTAT	Resident families' consumption by region of residence
Families institutional sector regional accounts – ISTAT	Families' net disposable income by region of residence
IRPET surveys on tourist consumption in the Tuscan provinces	Average spending per capita by type of accommodation, type of tourist destination and spending function
Tourism prices in Tuscany by the CST (Tourist Studies Centre), 2008, Florence.	Average daily spending per capita of tourists for overnight stays distinguished by destination and accommodation type.

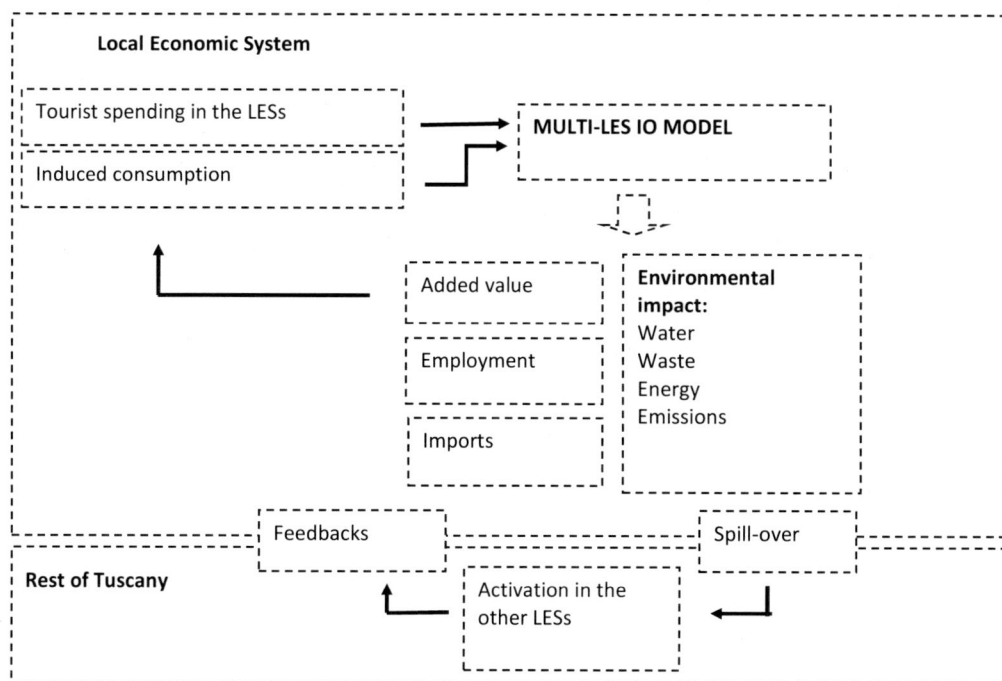

Figure 1. Diagram summing up the input-output models.

The input-output models are assessment tools built from input-output matrices (Miller R. E. Blair P. D). They can indicate the production total, added value and employment activated by a certain amount of final demand (consisting of household consumption, public administration consumption, investments and exports). In particular, tourist spending vectors can be inserted in the multi-regional IO models for each local economic system where the spending is done and for the sector producing the demanded goods.[4] The disaggregated results obtained from the model relate to: the amount of added value production; Tuscan, Italian and foreign imports; and employment activated by the demand vector in each LES and each production sector.

Inside the multi-LES IO model, there is a module to assess the effects of the final demand on the environment. With this module the direct, indirect and induced environmental effects of tourist spending can be calculated in terms of water consumed, waste produced, energy consumed and CO_2 emitted into the atmosphere.

3. APPLICATION TO THE TUSCAN CASE

We inserted tourist spending from 2008 divided into local economic systems and thirty sectors producing assets and services (demanded by tourists) as the exogenous variable in the multi-LES IO model. The impact results obtained are available for the same separate areas and sectors. In economic terms, they concern production, added value, labour units and activated imports. In environmental terms, they concern water and energy consumption, waste production and CO_2 emissions into the atmosphere. The model was applied simultaneously to the spending vector in all the LESs. This means that it is not possible to decompose the effect of direct spending in the LES from the spill-over effects from spending in other LESs in Tuscany. The effect of tourism spending at regional level are shown in table 4.

Totalling around 83 million in 2008, tourists in Tuscany (both official and tourists staying in houses) spent around 7.56 billion euros (around 12% of families' final internal consumption). The numbers staying in official accommodation count around half of the total tourist numbers and make up around 60% of the total tourist spending.

The GDP activated by tourist spending is over 6.0 billion (5.7% of the Tuscan gross domestic product), and regional and foreign imports exceed 3.7 billion and respectively make up 4.6% and 4.4% of the overall regional and foreign imports in Tuscany. The labour units activated amount to around 113 thousand (6.7% of the labour units in Tuscany), 71.4% of whom are activated by the official tourists (a higher share than the GDP activated owing to the greater intensity of work possessed by the sectors linked to tourism).

As far as the effects on the environment are concerned, the environmental impact of the spending on the regional total is lower than the impact on the GDP (which is 5.7%) for water (3.8%) and electrical energy (4.5%) and higher for the production of waste (5.9%) and CO_2 emissions (6.5%). From the impact results we can find the characteristic assessment parameters called impact multipliers and elasticity shown in table 5.

---

[4] The IRPET model divides goods into thirty branches of production which correspond to the subsections of the ATECO 2002 economic activity classification, with subsection K divided into K72 73 74 (25th branch) and K70 71 (30th branch).

**Table 4. Economic and environmental impact of tourist spending
on the regional territory**

	Tourist numbers in hotels	Tourist numbers in other accommo-dation	Tourist numbers in houses	**Overall impact**	Share of regional total
Tourist numbers (units)	21,774,275	19,725,650	41,429,524	**82,929,449**	
Tourist spending (millions of euros)	2,525	1,957	3,076	**7,557**	11.70%
GDP (millions of euros)	2,147	1,506	2,375	**6,027**	5.70%
Italian imports (millions of euros)	800	690	1,026	**2,515**	4.60%
Foreign imports (millions of euros)	379	300	532	**1,210**	4.40%
Labour units (units)	44,973	33,531	34,468	**112,972**	6.70%
M^3 of water consumed annually (thousands of m³)	8,124	6,504	14,007	**28,635**	3.82%
Municipal, similar and special waste (in tonnes)	197,210	161,227	251,759	**610,196**	5.96%
Electricity consumed (in millions of kwh)	312	218	402	**932**	4.47%
CO_2 emissions (tonnes)	16,625	13,559	35,344	**65,527**	6.48%

In Tuscany, average daily tourist spending in all the accommodation amounted to 913 euros in 2008. This number was higher for tourists staying in hotels (116 euros) and lower for tourists staying in houses (74 euros). The spending multiplier on GDP measures the intensity of the economic effects of tourist spending and overall amounts to 79.80 euros. In terms of employment, for every million euros spent by tourists, around 15 labour units (LU) are activated and every thousand tourists activates around 1.4 labour units. The semi-elasticity is an index of reactivity that measures the effects of a 1% variation in tourist numbers on the GDP and LU levels. In particular, this variation would lead to an increase in GDP of around 60.3 million euros and an increase of 1,129 in annual labour units. The environmental multiplayers (on the bottom side of the table) show the overall direct and indirect effect per tourist nights on water consumption (with an average of 345 litres consumed per tourist night in all accomodation), waste produced (7.36 kg per tourist night), electricity consumed (11.24 kwh per tourist night) and CO_2 emissions (0.79 kg per touristi night).

Table 5. Impact multipliers and elasticity

	Tourist numbers in hotels	Tourist numbers in other accommodation	Tourist numbers in houses	**Overall impact**
Average daily spending per capita (euros)	115.94	99.2	74.24	91.13
Tourist spending multiplier on GDP (every 100 euros of spending)	85.00%	76.90%	77.20%	79.80%
Tourist numbers multiplier on GDP (euros)	98.58	76.33	57.32	72.68
Spending multiplier on LUs (per million of spending)	17.81	17.13	11.21	14.95
Tourist numbers multiplier on LUs (per thousands of tourists)	2.07	1.7	0.83	1.36
Tourist numbers semi-elasticity on GDP (extra millions of GDP per 1% of tourists)	21.5	15.1	23.7	60.3
Tourist numbers semi-elasticity on LUs (extra LUs per 1% of tourists)	449.7	335.3	344.7	1129.7
Water consumed annually (litres per tourist nights)	373.1	329.72	338.09	345.29
Municipal, similar and special waste (kg per tourist nights)	9.06	8.17	6.08	7.36
Electricity consumed (kwh per tourist nights)	14.33	11.05	9.7	11.24
CO_2 emissions (kg per tourist nights)	0.76	0.69	0.85	0.79

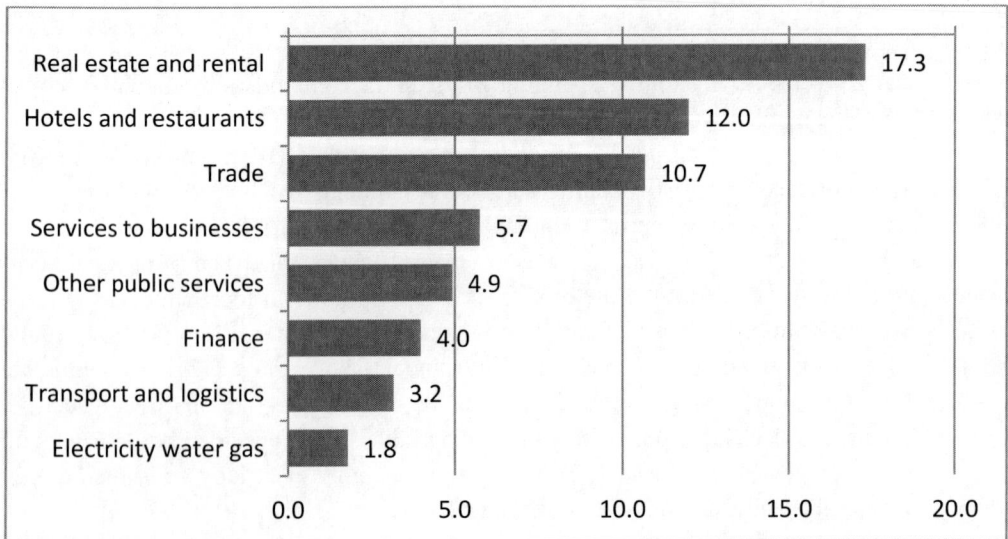

Figure 2.Sectorial added value multipliers.

Table 6. Economic and environmental impact on the provinces in millions of euros (labour units in units)

Province	Tourist spending	GDP activated by direct indirect internal	GDP activated by spill-over	GDP activated by induced effect	Labour units (units)	Direct and indirect impact on water consumption (thousand of m³ per year)	Direct and indirect impact on waste produced (tonnes)	Impact on kwh consumed (millions of kwh)	Direct and indirect impact on CO_2 emissions (tonnes)
Massa Carrara	392	206	13	50	4,176	1,520	25,832	40	2,776
Lucca	992	538	35	139	11,981	3,732	71,845	113	7,930
Pistoia	335	197	38	65	6,133	1,622	36,743	55	3,361
Florence	1,513	928	123	319	24,836	5,340	132,446	209	13,311
Livorno	1,502	872	59	240	20,156	5,459	89,872	144	10,841
Pisa	310	170	68	65	6,482	1,213	28,532	41	2,260
Arezzo	213	112	32	34	3,387	1,038	22,415	34	2,687
Siena	721	405	50	112	14,350	2,466	62,197	93	7,768
Grosseto	1,516	797	40	189	18,901	5,799	128,728	186	13,406
Prato	63	35	66	29	2,571	447	11,588	17	1,185
Tuscany	7,557	4,261	525	1,242	112,972	28,636	610,196	932	65,527

From the sectorial point of view, Figure 2 shows the added value activated per 100 euros of spending (also called sectorial added value multiplier).

The first sector in order of activation is real estate and rental. This is understandable if we think that for tourists in houses the actual (and imputed) rent is part of the added value of this sector (17.3 euros activated per 100 euros of tourist spending). This is followed by the "hotels and restaurants" sector with 12 euros activated for every 100 euros of spending and trade (10.7 euros). These first three sectors are mainly activated directly by tourists who rent houses, stay in hotels and shop. The following sectors, such as services to businesses, other public services, finance, transport and electricity are mainly activated indirectly through intermediate purchases by the undertakings directly involved in tourism. Besides these first eight sectors, the activation in the remaining ones is very low (less than 1%).

The multi-LES IO model has the advantage of calculating the economic (and also environmental) effects at sub-regional level. This means we can observe what effect tourists have on the single local systems and, by grouping them together, on the Tuscan provinces. Hence we can plan operations to strengthen facilities as a result of the economic results obtained. Table 6 shows the economic and environmental results at provincial level:

In terms of level (both in terms of spending and GDP activated), Florence is the top province for activation, followed by Livorno, Grosseto and Lucca, with Siena, Massa, Carrara Pistoia, Pisa, Arezzo and Prato a long way behind. The order of activation owing to the spill-over effect is different: in this case the provinces that receive most activation are Florence, Pisa and Prato (high levels of exportation activated towards the Tuscan LESs), followed at an intermediate level by Livorno, Siena and Grosseto, with Pistoia, Lucca and Massa following at a low level of activation from spill-over. The order of induced activation usually follows the economic and demographic size of the provinces themselves.

If we are to look at the effect of internal tourist spending on the GDP only (what we called the direct indirect internal effect), the share of GDP activated out of the provincial GDP results higher in the provinces of Grosseto and Livorno by 13.3% and 9.5% respectively, mainly due to coastal tourism. They are followed by Siena (5%), Lucca (4.7%) and Massa Carrara (4.4%). Tourism accounts for less than 3.0% in the remaining provinces. If we are to add the spill-over effect, all the Tuscan provinces tend to increase their activation with differences that range from 0.7% in Arezzo to 3.9% in Grosseto.

CONCLUSION

In this chapter we used technical tools that allowed us to achieve a good estimate of the official and non-official tourist numbers as well as the tourists' average daily and overall spending, then we made an assessment of the economic and environmental impact of this spending. Below we describe some possible shortcomings and limits of the tools used for the assessment.

The model used to estimate the numbers of tourists in houses produces estimates at municipal level and at local economic system level.. The main shortcoming of this model concerns the way in which the variable relating to the number of houses available for tourism is constructed. The hypothesis that there is a constancy – from 1991 to nowadays - in the ratio between the number of houses available for tourism and the number of houses not occupied by residents in each municipality is very "strong". Then there are the problems relating to the quality of the measurement of annual consumption, which are in part attributed and not measured. Finally, there is the aforementioned population that is not officially resident but present on a permanent basis. By way of logic these people should be added to the resident population as a component that causes non-tourism-linked consumption of water in houses, but this data is not available.

The average daily spending per capita is assessed in two phases. In the first we calculated the average daily spending at regional scale. This phase uses all the statistical information available and builds the estimate of spending in perfect coherence with the data available from the regional accounts. The second phase to build the estimates at regional level makes use of the few surveys carried out by IRPET at local level in Tuscany, while attributing the same estimates of daily tourist spending to reasonably similar territories. Of course this generalisation could be improved and this will be done as soon as new sources of information are available from local-scale investigations.

The multi-regional input-output model is particularly suited to assessing the short-term impact of a shock in final demand and measuring the effects of tourist spending, and it is part of the products that have been consolidated and repeatedly tested out in IRPET's research activity.

Alongside these sources of imprecision which require our attention in the phase of presenting and interpreting the results, we consider that the assessment carried out in this chapter covers an extremely important field of analysis for the local economy.

Building and using indirect methods to estimate tourist numbers and spending at sub-regional level is certainly new to the Italian and Tuscan panorama of sector studies. Thanks to using the IRPET IO models, integrated with an environmental accounting matrix, we can go onto assess the economic and environmental impact of tourism at the sub-regional level. This is an important back-up – not available before – for local-level regional tourist development planning and monitoring processes.

The economic and environmental impact exercise performed highlights the importance of tourism in the Tuscan economy. The tourist spending impact multipliers on the GDP appear higher than the demand multipliers of the main Tuscan manufacturing sectors and just lower than the public spending multipliers.

The analysis also confirms the relative concentration of the effects of tourism in particular areas of the region and the different impact that tourism has on the local economies.

The assessment of the environmental effects of tourism highlights the environmental costs linked to the presence of tourists in different areas. It is another important tool for planning and monitoring local-level tourism development, also in view of preparing tax instruments to deal with cost increases for local institutions caused by tourism.

REFERENCES

Cipollini F. (2004). Un modello statistico per la stima del turismo in alloggi privati in Toscana. Dipartimento di Statistica dell'Università di Firenze, *MIMEO*.

Cline S. & Seidl A. (2010). Combining non-market valuation and Input-Output analysis for community tourism planning: open space and water quality values in Colorado, Usa. *Economic System Research*, 22, 4, 385-405.

Dwyer L.; Forsyth P. & Spurr R. (2004). Evaluating tourism economics effect: new and old approaches. *Tourism management,* 25, 3, 307-317.

Gelan, A. (2003). Local economic impacts. The British Open. *Annals of Tourism Research,* 30, 2, 406-425.

Giljum, S.; Behrens, A. & Hinterberger, F.; Lutz, C.; Meyer B. (2008). Modelling scenarios towards a sustainable use of natural resources in Europe. *Environmental Science and Policy*, 11, SERI WP, 4, 204-216.

Gismondi R. (2000). Le presenze turistiche in Italia nel 1997: problemi di integrazione tra fonti. *Turistica*, 1, 13-60.

Gismondi R. (2001). Le potenzialità di crescita dell'industria turistica italiana. In Touring Club Italiano. *Decimo rapporto sul turismo italiano*. Milano. 197-217.

Gismondi R. & Mirto A.P. (2002); Tourism in Collective and Private Accommodations in Italiy: Definitions, Classifications and Estimation Techniques. *Tourism Statistics*, September, Budapest.

Loveridge S. (2004). A typology and assessment of multisector regional economic impact models. *Regional Studies*, 38, 305-317.

Madsen B. & Zhang J.(2010). Towards a new framework for accounting and modelling the regional and local impact of tourism. *Economic System Research*, 22, 4, 313-339.

Manente M. & Zanette M. (2010). Macroeconomic effects of a VAT Reduction in the Italian Hotels & Restaurant Industry. *Economic System Research*, 22, 4, 407-425.

Miller R. & Blair P. D. (2009). *Input Output Analysis. Foundations and Extensions.* Cambridge University Press. New York.

Polo C. & Valle E. (2008). A general equilibrium assessment of the impact of a fall in tourism under alternative closure rules: the case of the balearic islands. *International Regional Science Review*, 31, 1, 3-34.

Rotmans J.; Van Asselt M; Anastasi C.; Greeuw S.; Mellors J.; Peters S.; Rothman D. & Rijkens N. (2000). *Visions for a sustainable Europe. Futures*, 32, 809-93.

Sun Y. Y. (2007). Adjusting Input Output models for capacity utilization in services industries, *Tourism Management*, 28, 6, 1507-1517.

In: Methods and Analysis on Tourism and Environment   ISBN: 978-1-62417-824-5
Editors: J.M.Jiménez, M.V.Vargas, F.J.O.Rosell et al. © 2013 Nova Science Publishers, Inc.

Chapter 7

VISITOR PROFILES AT WORLD CULTURAL HERITAGE SITES: AN EMPIRICAL STUDY OF ÉVORA, PORTUGAL

Maria do Rosário Borges[1], Jaime Serra[2] and Noémi Marujo[3]

[1]University of Évora, School of Social Sciences, GOVCOOP, Portugal
[2]University of Évora, School of Social Sciences,
CEFAGE-UE, Portugal
[3]University of Évora, School of Social Sciences, IGOT-CEG, Portugal

ABSTRACT

Some of the most important historic cities are faced with a complex relationship between heritage conservation and tourism development. These sites are of unquestionable importance in strengthening a country's tourism destinations. Every world heritage place, as recognised by The United Nations Educational, Scientific and Cultural Organization (UNESCO) has outstanding universal value. Some studies confirm that visits to these sites are almost justified by this prestigious classification and that motivations are closely associated with their cultural aspects and quality of the overall environment. The main purpose of the chapter is to define the tourist profile of the world heritage city of Évora and to determine the main motivations for visits to the destination. Based on visitor characteristics, the market segmentation was made. The methodology used is based on explanatory research to assess who the visitors are and why they choose Évora heritage site for their trips. The central findings provide evidence that the fact that Évora is classified as a world heritage city is an important factor in destination choice. However, an analysis of the population means evidenced differences among the visitors in the degree of influence of the fact that it is classified as World Heritage by UNESCO on the decision to visit Évora. For some markets this classification does not influence the decision to visit the city of Évora, but for others it greatly influences it. The most important motivations for visitors in selecting Évora are leisure, heritage, gastronomy and wines and to have a new cultural experience.

1. INTRODUCTION

Tourism in Évora is considered by many as a key strategic activity for local development. Due to its economic and socio-cultural contribution, tourism is an important factor in the economic development of this city. According to a macroeconomic view, it is one of the activities with more weight in the municipality's economy bringing a set of highly relevant activities because of its multiplier effect. Évora is a historic town that presents an interesting tourism potential as far as cultural tourism in concerned because of its monumentality and cultural heritage. Its history acts as one of the main tourist attractions in our days (Fortuna, 1995). On the other hand, heritage is the core of historic towns' identity and, in parallel, the basis of its main tourist attraction. The classification of Évora by UNESCO in 1986 as "World Heritage" has fostered not only the preservation of heritage but also the tourist promotion of the town. This fact led the city to think of a process of a globalization of its own culture, attracting national and international visitors with several cultural reasons. It should be noted that visitors look at all aspects and attributes of a destination that they are visiting and compare it with their own city, which means that the singularities of places leverage the distinctive aspects of cultural sites, and allow visitors to make comparisons that would never occur to residents, for whom the city is part of their ordinary life. Évora is a historic town that appeals to a different way of looking called the tourist gaze. Cultural Tourists' motivations to travel arise when they seek for something different than what exists in their area of origin. They move in search of icons which somehow characterize the local identity and collective memory. Mckercher & Cross (2003) point out that some cultural tourists are motivated to consume the cultural output of a region and are looking for a cross-cultural experience. Others may also be highly motivated for such visits, but have a very different experience in terms of quality. Specifically the main objectives of this chapter are to (1) define the profile of visitors to the world heritage city of Évora, (2) determine the level of influence that classification of World Heritage (WH) has on the visitor's decision to travel to the city of Évora, and (3) to define homogeneous groups according to the country of residence, level of WH influence on their decision and main motivations.

2. LITERATURE REVIEW: CULTURAL TOURISTS AND MOTIVATIONS

The tourism system is made up of three main elements: origin, destination and linkage, thus "the understanding of the consumer is relevant in the tourism system and, in particular, tourist motivations (…)" (Andreu et al., 2006: 3). Tourism is a complex economic and social phenomenon, hence the study of the behaviour aspects of its main actors (tourists) has wide dimensions for understanding their needs, motives, motivations and attitudes during the pre-decision and decision stages before they travel. Motivation is a starting point in studying tourist behaviour (Mill & Morrison 1985; Gunn 1988; Pearce & Lee 2005). The concept of tourist motivation is discussed in the literature according to the adoption of general theories of motivations in the context of tourism research. Several reputable authors have developed researches in the field of tourism motivations issue since the 60s and 70s of the last century, among whom, Cohen (1972); Plog (1974); MacCannell (1976); Dann (1977); Crompton (1979); Mayo & Jarvis (1981); Ross & Iso-Ahola (1991); Witt & Wright (1992); Uysal &

Hagan (1993); Pearce (1988, 1993); Rojek (1995); Ryan & Gledon (1998); Hanqin and Lam (1999); Wang (2000); Kozak (2002); Correia et al., (2008); Law et al., (2011). In tourism research there are two disciplines besides tourist motivation that present the greatest discussion on motivation: those of psychology and sociology. Nevertheless, other disciplines, as well as anthropology by MacCannell (1976) and from the socio-psychological point of view by Iso-Ahola (1982) produced knowledge relevant to this issue. Looking for the main researchers in the field of tourist motivations through their theoretical approach and also for their focus of discussion it is possible to understand their scope approach.

Prebensen (2006) presented the main theoretical contributions of tourist motivations, as is highlighted in the following paragraphs. Pearce (1988) based on Maslow (1943; 1954) and Rapoport & Rapoport (1975) proposed the travel career leader describing tourist motivation integrated in five distinct levels, which were based on the Maslow's (1943, 1954) needs-hierarchy theory of motivation. Motivations for travel change over time and are influenced by past holiday experiences. A distinction must be made between internally (self) and externally (other) directed motives. People have a range of touristic motives. Dann (1977, 1981) brought to us the Pull and Push Theory of Tourist Motivation, which discussed and explained the factors that predispose a person to travel and those that attract the tourist to a given destination. Iso-Ahola (1980, 1989) through the theoretical approach of Optimal Arousal Theory explains why people avoid overstimulation (mental or physical exhaustion) or boredom (too little stimulation). Travel is based on seeking intrinsic awards and escaping everyday problems, troubles and routines. Mayo & Jarvis (1981), starting with the theoretical approach of Need for Consistency Versus Complexity stated that as far as the need for consistency is concerned, individuals are expected to seek things that are predictable and consistent in order to reduce psychological tension. On the other hand complexity needs are viewed as the result of tourists seeking novelty, change and unpredictability because they are inherently satisfying. Witt & Wright (1992) according to their Expectancy Theory applied to tourist motivations, reviewed content theories of motivation and applied conceptual/review expectancy theories of motivation to explain tourist motivations. Motivations may be understood as strength to practice a specific action and contain results of situation-person interactions (Gnoth, 1997). From a general perspective, every human being has needs that will give rise to a certain behaviour to accomplish and satisfy those needs. These needs are structurally ranked according to the priorities of each one of us. According to this idea Ryan & Deci (2000) assume that motivation thus implies that the individual "is moved to something". Research approaches in tourism are always related to human nature and relations. In this way the question of why people travel and what they want to apprize is the key starting point to investigate tourist motivations and also understand what could differentiate between several tourist profiles. As far as research about cultural visitor's profiles is concerned, it is clearly a consentaneous statement that traditional cultural motivations as well as a search for knowledge and learning are among the important issues for these visitors. In this way a large proportion of cultural visitors are stimulated to gather information about the destination in advance, and the use of the internet appears as an information source with very high importance among cultural visitors (Richards, 2002). The concept of motivation is considered as an element in defining visitor profiles (market segmentation) in tourism, as is noted in several empirical investigations (Crompton, 1979; Card & Kestel, 1988; Ryan & Glendon, 1998; Yavuz, Baloglu, Uysal, 1998; Bieger & Laesser, 2002; Andreu et al., 2006). According to several authors, there are studies that reveal differences in motivation. Thus, if it is consentaneous in the literature that tourist motivations are a heterogeneous and a dynamic construct, the importance of motivations in determining the tourist profile emphasizes the need to conduct the present research.

3. METHODOLOGY

3.1. Questionnaire Design

The main purpose of the chapter is to define the profile of visitors to the historic centre of the world heritage city of Évora and to determine the main motivations for the destination. Based on the results it is intended to identify the main market segment of visitors to the historic centre of Évora. A visitor survey was designed to define the tourist profile of the heritage site of Évora, in Portugal. The questionnaire was divided into 3 sections. Dimensions of analysis considered 3 main sections: socio-demographic data, background behaviour before visiting the destination and behaviour during the stay. The first section comprised six questions in total. The second section was based on the evaluation of the sources of information used before travelling to the destination, how visitors acquired the services and measured if the fact that Évora is classified as world heritage site by UNESCO influenced the decision for travelling to the destination; the motivations for visiting Évora. The last section was based on the behaviour of tourists during the visit. In order to understand the behaviour during the visit respondents were asked the length of stay in Évora; the average spending per day during the visit; the form of transport used to get to Évora; the chosen visit itinerary in the historic city centre; the most valuable attraction; the importance of the visit for their personal enrichment; the degree of evaluation of the tourist attributes of Évora and evaluation of the degree of expectations after visiting Évora. In every question where the main proposal was the evaluation of attributes, the degree of influence in the decision to visit, or resources of information and expectations, a five point Likert-type scale ranging from *very bad (1)* to *very good (5)*; *not influenced (1) to very influenced (5); very unsatisfied (1)* to *very satisfied (5)*; *far below expectations (1) to far above expectations (5)*, was adopted.

3.2. Data Collection

The first step in conducting the present research was an applied pre-test survey of 50 questionnaires, between April and May of 2009. Analysis of the data allowed adjustments to the questions to meet the objectives set. After that, a personal survey was used to collect the data in this study during the spring and summer of 2010 and 2011 (April-August). That is when the greatest number of visitors to Évora is registered, according to the statistical record of the tourist information office. The target of our research was visitors to the historic centre (downtown). The inquiry points were selected according to the most visited monuments that are located in the historic city centre. Points of inquiry were near S. Francisco Church / Chapel of Bones, Giraldo Square, the Cathedral of Santa Maria; the Roman Temple and the University de Évora. A total of 451 usable questionnaires were obtained. This sample was provided from a universe of 148362 visitors registered at the tourism office in 2009. Based on this visitor registration a stratified sampling plan, by residence, was adopted. Dividing the number of visitors by nationality, the sample was defined according to the weight percentage of each nationality (Table 1).

Table 1. Visitor registration by country of residence (stratified sample definition)

Country of Residence	2009	Total (%)	Sample
Portugal	36282	24.5%	110
Spain	31438	21.2%	96
France	17515	11.8%	53
Germany	9295	6.3%	28
Brazil	8366	5.6%	25
Japan	6835	4.6%	21
USA	5920	4.0%	18
Italy	5762	3.9%	18
Netherlands	5624	3.8%	17
United Kingdom	3686	2.5%	11
Sub-Total	130723	88.1%	397
Others	17639	11.9%	54
TOTAL	**148362**	100.0%	**451**

Source: Évora Tourism Office, 2010.

Table 2. Exploratory profile of Évora visitors

Education Level	Higher Education (60%)
Professional Status	Employee (57%)
	Retired (17%)
Travelling with	With partner (46%)
	Family (20%)
Motivation for Travelling	Leisure (32.6%)
	Gastronomy & Wines (26.1%)
	Heritage, Monuments and Buildings (14.1%)
Sources of Information	Travel Agent
	Internet (64%)
	Travel Guide (Lonely Planet) (34.1%)
	Family / Friends
Services Acquired	Individual Reservation (62.1%)
	All-inclusive package (27.2%)
	Invitation from family / friend (10.6%)

Source: Own data - SPSS output (2011).

The sampling adopted method was a probabilistic method, by a random sample which was organised upon a stratified sample by place of residence.

3.3. Data Analysis and Results

The collected data were analysed through the Statistical Package for the Social Sciences (SPSS 17.0) computer program. An exploratory descriptive statistic was employed to understand the general information and characteristics from the sample. According to Table 2 it was possible to find out the percentages of responses in each field of questions and understand the visitor profile in two dimensions: before the visit and during the visit.

3.3.1. Visitor Profile of Évora

According with Table 2, it is possible to fulfil the first objective of the current research, which is defining the visitor profile of the world heritage city of Évora.

Table 3. Visitor profiles in Évora (during the visit)

Length of stay (Portugal)	9 nights (40.5%)
Length of stay (Évora)	half a day / day (16.7%)
	1 night (26.7%)
	2 nights (27.5%)
	3 nights (14.2)
	> 3 nights (15.0%)
Average spending per day during the visit	< 50€ (43.0%)
	51€-100€ (35.9%)
	> 101€ (21.1%)
Form of transport	Own vehicle (42.3%)
	Rent-a-car (19.7%)
Itinerary at the historic centre	1. Giraldo Square
	2. Sé - Cathedral St.ª Maria
	3. Roman Temple
	4. Chapel of Bones
	5. University of Évora
Most valuable attraction	Sé - Cathedral St.ª Maria (28.6%)
	Roman Temple (44.3%)
	Chapel of Bones (12.9%)
Degree of importance for personal enrichment (education and learning)	Important (75.9%)
Expectations met?	Neither below or above expectations (44.3%)
	Above expectations (28.0%)
Intend to come back?	Yes (79.2%)
Will recommend?	Yes (98.1%)

Source: Own data - SPSS output (2011).

The main motivations identified by visitors to visit Évora were leisure, gastronomy and wines, and heritage, monuments and building. The sources of information gathered by visitors before the visit were internet (64%) and secondly travel guides, namely Lonely Planet (34%). For planning their stay in Évora they seek out tourist services mainly by individual reservations (62%).

Starting with the socio-demographic characteristics of Évora visitors, they have a high level of education (60%) with an employee and retired professional status that corresponds all together to 74% of all visitors to Évora. These visitors normally travel with their partners (46%) as well with their families (with their children - 20%).

Data presented in Table 3 show the visitors' behaviour during their visit to Évora. According to this, 40% of international visitors stay on average 9 days in Portugal and 68% spend 1 to 3 nights in Évora. The average visitor spending per day is situated at 43% less than 50€ and 27.5% between 50€ and 100€. Visitors to Évora travel by their own vehicle (42.3%) and also rent-a-car (19.7%). A framework for spatial dispersion concerning their itinerary was identified, by ranking their itinerary in the historic centre in Évora. Thus the five major points of visit and consequently the ranking of their itinerary is first visiting Giraldo square, secondly the Cathedral, thirdly the Roman Temple, fourth the Chapel of Bones and fifth the University of Évora. As it is possible to observe, visitors considered that the visit to Évora is important for self education and learning.

3.3.2. Determining the Level of Influence That the Classification of World Heritage (WH) Has on the Visitor's Decision to Travel to the City of Évora

To accomplish the second objective of the chapter, another field of analysis was conducted. To determine the level of influence that the classification of World Heritage (WH) has on the visitor's decision to travel to the city of Évora, this was applied using an analysis of variance (ANOVA), mainly to understand if differences existed among the visitors (by place of residence) in the degree of influence on the decision to visit Évora due to the fact that Évora is classified as World Heritage by UNESCO. Before the applied analysis of variance (ANOVA), the means of responses concerning to the degree of influence in the decision to visit Évora caused by the fact of its heritage classification were explored through a descriptive statistics. Analysis of Table 4 shows that the mean of responses was 3.36. According to this, on average visitors considered that the fact Évora is classified as World Heritage by UNESCO as of neither little nor great influence on their decision to visit.

However further analyses based on comparing the means of responses between all the visitors (by place of residence), results in evidence, by using a one-sample T test, that there are significant differences between the means of all responses (Table 5).

Analysis of the data (Table 5) indicates that the significance value is <.000 which confirms that there is a significant difference between the mean (3.36) and all of responses of those in the sample.

According to these results, it was possible to identify if there is differences in the population. In this way using variance analysis allow to compare the means of several populations that were defined by place of residence. A simple random sample was drawn from each place of residence, mainly for the markets identified according to the 2009 statistics data provided by tourism office. Therefore this draw sample was used to test the null hypothesis that the population means are equal. ANOVA allowed compares the variation among groups with the variation within groups. Therefore it was considered the following hypothesis test:

- *The question*: Is there a difference in the population means of the degree of influence of the fact of the Heritage classification by UNESCO on the decision to visit Évora?
- *The Research Hypothesis*: There is a difference in the population means of the degree of influence of the fact of the Heritage classification by UNESCO on the decision to visit Évora.
- *The Null Hypothesis*: There is no difference in the population means of the degree of influence of the fact of the Heritage classification by UNESCO on the decision to visit Évora.

According to ANOVA test (Table 6) the p-value is .001. So it can be concluded that data means (3.36) is not all the same between visitors.

Table 4. Descriptive statistics

			Statistic	Std. Error
World Heritage by UNESCO influenced the decision to visit Évora?	Mean		**3.36**	.058
	95% Confidence Interval for Mean	Lower Bound	3.24	
		Upper Bound	3.47	
	5% Trimmed Mean		3.40	
	Median		4.00	
	Variance		1.524	
	Std. Deviation		1.235	
	Minimum		1	
	Maximum		5	
	Range		4	
	Interquartile Range		2	
	Skewness		-.589	.116
	Kurtosis		-.693	.231

Source: Own data - SPSS output (2011).

Table 5. One-Sample Test

World Heritage by UNESCO influenced the decision to visit Évora?	Test Value = 3.36					
	t	df	Sig. (2-tailed)	Mean Difference	95% Confidence Interval of the Difference	
					Lower	Upper
	6.098	445	.000	.357	.24	.47

Source: Own data - SPSS output (2011).

Table 6. ANOVA. World Heritage by UNESCO influenced the decision to visit Evora

	Sum of Squares	df	Mean Square	F	Sig.
Between Groups	56.080	15	3.739	2.577	.001
Within Groups	619.568	427	1.451		
Total	675.648	442			

Source: Own data - SPSS output (2011).

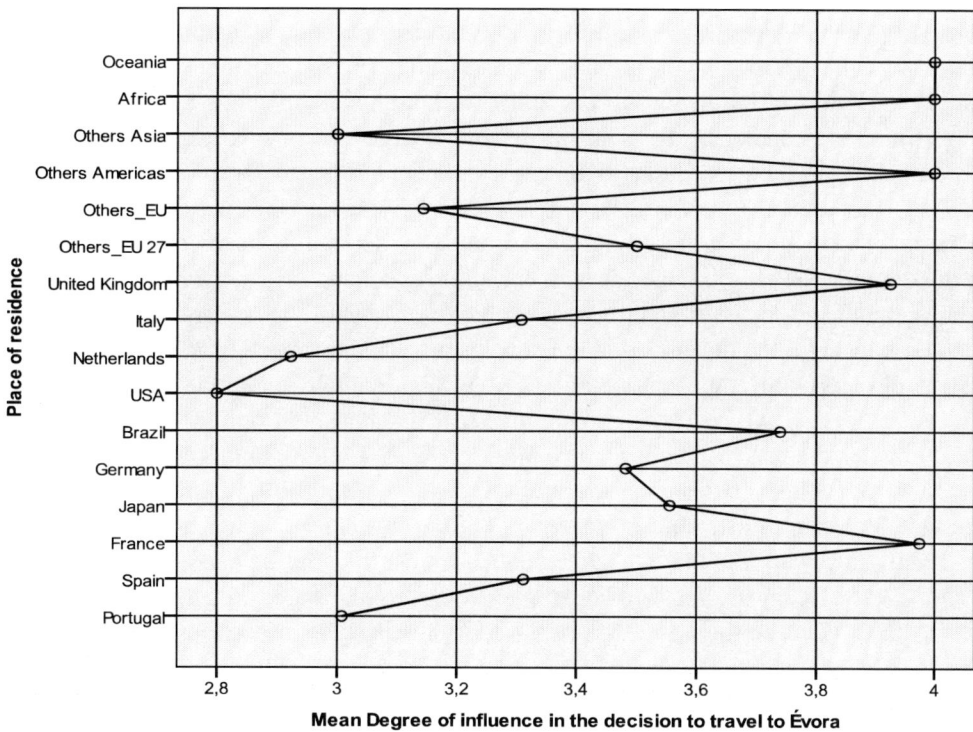

Source: Own data - SPSS output (2011).

Figure 1. Means Plot.

Figure 1 summarized that there are differences in the means of degree of influence of the fact of awareness of Évora's World Heritage status concerning the decision to visit the town. In fact the results of the present research support the suggested findings provided by Pizam and Sussmann (1995) that stated an existence of differences in the tourism behaviour and motivations between different tourist nationalities.

3.3.3. Exploring Homogeneous Groups According to the Country of Residence, Level of WH Influence on Their Decision and Main Motivations

A cluster analysis was adopted to fulfil the above objective. According to Reis (2000) cluster analysis aims to organize a set of cases into homogeneous groups in such a way that individuals belonging a group are as similar as possible. This analysis seeks to classify a set of objects (people, products...) in groups or categories using the observed values of the variables without it being necessary to define criteria to classify the data that comprise a particular group (Aaker, Kumar & Day, 2001). Hierarchical methods can be used, requiring the calculation of a matrix similarity / distance or hierarchy that does not apply directly to the original data and departing from an initial allocation of individuals to a number of groups defined by the researcher. On the other hand an example of a non-hierarchical K-means is when an individual is transferred to the cluster for which the centroid is the shortest distance. Proposed by J. MacQueen in 1967, the k-means algorithm (or algorithm of k-means) is one of the best known and used, in addition to being the one with the largest number of variations. The meaning of K-means algorithm is to provide a classification of information according to the data itself. This classification is based on the analysis and comparisons between numerical values of the data. Thus, the algorithm will automatically provide an automatic classification without any human supervision, in other words without any pre-existing classification (Hair et al., 1998; Reis, 2001; Janssens et al., 2008). According to the above-mentioned k-means potentialities, and concerning the primary exploratory purpose of this research, five clusters were defined according to four attributes, these being influence on the decision to travel caused by the fact that Évora is WH; nights spent in Évora and the first and second chosen motivation. The reason that those four dimensions were defined to conduct cluster analysis is supported by the lowest missing values in each dimension and also supported by the various statements gathered in the literature review about tourist motivations and visitors' cultural behaviour which will be developed in the conclusion. Data presented in Table 7 showed five different clusters with some particularities. It is important to underline that a criteria of convergence was fulfilled because it was found that five clusters from the centroids changed in verifying that the maximum absolute coordinate change for any centre is .000.

ANOVA (Table 8) indicates that with the exception of the *WH influence on the decision to travel to Évora* dimension (p-value = .008), four other homogenous groups score significantly different, and that the same conclusion can be applied to the other dimensions (p-value <.001). It may also be said here that the cluster groups are formed in such a way that the differences between them in terms of the four dimensions are maximum, and that the p-values in principle may not be linked to the fact of whether the null hypothesis is rejected or not (H_0: The five clusters have identical scores for the four dimensions). As is visible in the p-values, which are here less than .05, we may thus conclude that particular dimensions are a good basis for the formation of clusters.

Table 7. Final Cluster Centres

	Cluster				
	1	2	3	4	5
WH influence on the decision to travel	Influenced	Very little influenced	Neither little nor very influenced	Influenced	Neither little nor very influenced
Nights spent in Évora	2 nights	+ 3 nights	2 nights	< 1 - 1 night	2 nights
1st Motivation to visit Évora	Leisure	Study Trip/ Education/ Training	Business and Incentives	Heritage/Monuments and Buildings	Finding and having a new cultural experience
2nd Motivation to visit Évora	Business and Incentives	Finding and having a new cultural experience	Finding and having a new cultural experience	Natural Heritage / Landscape	Business and Incentives

Source: Own data - SPSS output (2011).

Table 8. ANOVA

Dimensions	Cluster		Error		F	Sig.
	Mean Square	df	Mean Square	df		
WH influence on the decision to travel	4.377	4	1.254	286	3.489	.008
Nights spent in Évora	17.378	4	1.414	286	12.288	.000
1st Motivation to visit Évora	540.445	4	1.295	286	417.293	.000
2nd Motivation to visit Évora	480.593	4	1.282	286	375.010	.000

The F tests should be used only for descriptive purposes because the clusters have been chosen to maximize the differences among cases in different clusters. The observed significance levels are not corrected for this and thus cannot be interpreted as tests of the hypothesis that the cluster means are equal.

Source: Own data - SPSS output (2011).

Table 9. Number of Cases in each Cluster

Cluster	1	118.000
	2	3.000
	3	23.000
	4	94.000
	5	53.000
Valid		291.000
Missing		160.000

Source: Own data - SPSS output (2011).

Finally, Table 9 provides insight into the number of visitors per cluster group, and then it appears that the clusters 1, 4 and 5 are the best represented. Cluster 1, who spent 2 nights in Évora during their visit, assumed that the fact that Évora is classified WH by UNESCO influenced their decision to visit Évora and their first motivation is leisure and secondly business and incentives. They are represented by visitors from Portugal, Spain, United Kingdom and Brazil. Cluster 4 assumed that they are influenced by the fact that Évora is WH. They stay more between less than 1 and 1 night and their first motivation is visiting heritage, monuments and buildings and the second one is visiting the natural heritage and landscape. Visitors belonging to this cluster come mainly from France, Japan and Germany. Concluding, Cluster 5 is represented by the fact that they are neither little nor very influenced by the fact that Évora is WH in their decision to visit; they spend 2 nights during their visit and the main motivation for visiting Évora is seeking and having a new cultural experience.

CONCLUSION

In general the research findings show that the traditional motivation for Évora prevails. The proposed research fulfils the necessity of identify tourist motivations to better understand visitors choices, preferences and needs (Kozak, 2002; Bansal & Eiselt, 2004 and Andreu et al., 2006) considering this dimension in a process of visitor profiling. As an exploratory research it allows an understanding that, besides visitors' motivations to visit Évora for leisure, learning about and tasting the local gastronomy and wines and visiting heritage, monuments and buildings, according to cluster analysis a new motivational dimension was identified named by the visitors as finding and having a new cultural experience. As Krippendorf (1986) stated, people are motivated to travel by the desire to escape from the monotony of daily routine. Corresponding to this it is possible to suggest that the main motivation to visit Évora is linked firstly to spending leisure time associated with the experience of gastronomy and wines and the contemplation of monuments and local heritage. The experience evidence identified in Cluster 5 confirms what Mayo & Jarvis (1981) stated, which is crucial for an understanding of the factors that influence tourist behaviour and which particular elements are seen by tourists as important. This information also confirms what Pine & Gilmore (1999) assessed about the emerging *experience economy*. The authors referred that consumers seek unique experiences beyond merely consuming products and services because the consistent, high level of product and service quality can no longer be used to differentiate choices for consumers. This new demand, for unique and memorable experiences requires firms to develop a distinct value-added provision for products and services that have already achieved a consistent, high level of functional quality. Another theoretical contribution is endowed by the findings proposed by Richards (2002). Therefore the results provide some support for exploring the relationship between geographical origin of tourists and factors such as motivations, age, education, etc. in Évora. Motivations could differ from one individual (or group) to another (Andreu et al., 2006), and also as Pizam & Sussmann (1995) stated there are differences in the tourism behaviour between different tourist nationalities. The findings of the present research also support both statements showing an existence of differences in motivations to visit Évora according to the place of residence and also differences in the population means of the degree of influence of the fact of their Heritage classification by UNESCO on the decision to visit Évora. Finally it was proved that tourist motivations are not homogenous but a dynamic concept as Pearce (1993) argued, and they are an important dimension for understanding the visitor profile. Some managerial implications are provided from this research, namely for local trade and local/regional tourism authorities. Thus this research shows the necessity of enhancing a thorough behaviour analysis of visitors who are influenced by the fact that Évora is considered a World Heritage Site. It also suggests the development of stronger partnership policies between the regional and local tourism and culture authorities, promoting synergies between them in order to implement actions that promote the sustainability of cultural heritage. Finally it suggests the need to reinforce promotional plans in the markets of visitors who assume a weaker influence of Évora's classification as World Heritage Site on their decision to visit. A brief discussion about the methodology used for an efficient tourist profile study is necessary. As an exploratory research, cluster analysis was used on the basis of K-means and five clusters were found. However the study requires a confirmatory analysis to establish the main markets segments in Évora. As for the discussion of limitations of the study, plenty of points can be raised. Hence future directions for future research are proposed at the same time. Although the study was based on several dimensions of tourist behaviour, the need to emphasize the difference between the motives and travel motivations may lead to a more complete understanding of tourist behaviour in Évora. Another limitation was the extent of the survey applied to the visitor, which caused a lot of non-answers and caused missing values in some questions. Above limitation could provide more dimensions to integrate into a cluster analysis. In future researches the survey should be restricted to a smaller number of questions. Insofar as tourist motivations are dynamic and differ from one visitor to another, this dimension should be adjusted to the specificities of the destination. The application of this study in other world heritage sites is also proposed, and with those results competitiveness analysis between these awarded destinations could be established and cultural tourist behaviour could also be explored.

REFERENCES

Aaker, D.A., Kumar, V. & Day, D.S. (2001). *Marketing Research.* 7th Edition. John Wiley. NY.

Andreu, L.; Kozak, M; Avci N. & Cifter, N. (2006). Market Segmentation by Motivations to Travel. *Journal of Travel & Tourism Marketing*, 19 (1), 1-14.

Bansal, H. & Eiselt, H. A. (2004). Exploratory research of tourist motivations and planning. *Tourism Management*, 25 (3), 387-396.

Bieger, T. & Laesser, C. (2002). Market segmentation by motivation: The case of Switzerland. *Journal of Travel Research*, 41 (1), 68-76.

Card, J. A. & Kestel, C. (1988). Motivational factors and demographic characteristics of travelers to and from Germany. *Society and Leisure*, 11 (1), 49-58.

Cohen, E. (1972). Toward a Sociology of International Tourism. *Social Research: An International Quarterly*, 39 (1), 164-182.

Correia A.; Pimpão, A. & Crouch, G. (2008). Perceived risk and novelty-Seeking behavior: The case of tourists on low-Cost travel in Algarve (Portugal). In Arch G. Woodside (Ed.): *Advances in Culture, Tourism and Hospitality Research, Vol. 2.* Emerald Group Publishing Limited. 1-26.

Crompton, J. L. (1979). Motivations for pleasure vacation. *Annals of Tourism Research*, 6(4), 408-424.

Dann, G. M. S. (1977). Anomie, ego-enhancement and tourism. *Annals of Tourism Research*, 4 (4), 184-194.

Dann, G. (1981). Tourist motivation: An appraisal. *Annals of Tourism Research*, 8 (2), 187-219.

Fortuna, C. (1995). Turismo, autenticidade e cultura urbana. *Revista Crítica de Ciências Sociais*, 43. Faculdade de Economia da Universidade de Coimbra.

Gnoth, J. (1997). Tourism Motivation and Expectation Formation. *Annals of Tourism Research*, 24 (2), 283-304.

Gunn, C. A. (1988). *Tourism Planning.* 2nd Ed. Taylor &Francis. New York.

Hair, J.F.; Anderson, R.E. & Tatham, R.L. (1998). *Multivariate data analysis.* Prentice Hall. England.

Hanqin, Z. Q. & Lam, T. (1999). An analysis of Mainland Chinese visitors' motivations visit Hong Kong. *Tourism Management.* 20 (5), 587-594.

Iso-Ahola, S. E. (1980). *The Social Psychology of Leisure and Recreation.* William C. Brown Co. Publishers. Dubuque.

Iso-Ahola, S. E. (1982). Toward a social psychological theory of tourism motivation: A rejoinder. *Annals of Tourism Research*, 9 (2), 256-262.

Iso-Ahola, S. E. (1989). Motivation for Leisure. In E.L. Jackson and T.L. Burton (Eds.): *Understanding Leisure and Recreation: Mapping the Past, Charting the Future*. Venture Publishing. USA. 247-279.

Janssens, W.; Wijnen, K.; Pelsmacker, P. & Kenhove, P. (2008). *Marketing Research with SPSS*. Prentice Hall – Finantial Times. England.

Kozak, M. (2002). Comparative analysis of tourist motivations by nationality and destinations. *Tourism Management*, 23 (3), 221-232.

Krippendorf, J. (1986). The new tourist – turning point for leisure and travel. *Tourism Management*, 7 (2), 131-135.

Law, R.; Rong, J.; Vu H. Q.; Gang, L. & Lee, H. A. (2011). Identifying changes and trends in Hong Kong outbound tourism. *Tourism Management*, 32 (5), 1106-1114.

MacCannell, D. (1976). *The tourist: a new theory of leisure class*. Macmillan. London.

McKercher, B. & Cross, H. (2003). Testing a cultural tourism typology. *International Journal of Tourism Research*, 5 (1), 45–58.

Mill, R.C. & Morrison, A.M. (1985). *The tourism system: An introductory text*. Prentice Hall International Editions. Englewood Cliffs, NJ.

Maslow, A. (1943). A theory of human motivation. *Psychological Review*, 50 (4), 370-396.

Maslow, A. (1954). *Motivations and Personality*. Harper & Low. New York.

Mayo, E. & Jarvis, L. (1981). *Travel Travelers - Psychological aspects*. CBI Pub. Co. Boston.

Pearce, P. L. (1988). *The Ulysses Factor: Evaluating Visitors in Tourist Settings*. Springer. NY.

Pearce, P. L. (1993). Fundamentals of Tourist Motivations. In D. Pearce & R. Butler (Eds.): *Tourism Research: Critiques and Challenges*. Routledge and Kegan Paul. London. 85-105.

Pearce, P.L. & Lee U. (2005). Developing the Travel Career Approach to Tourism Motivation. *Journal of Travel Research*, 43 (3), 226-237.

Pine, B. J. & Gilmore, J. H. (1999). *The experience economy*. Harvard University Press. Boston.

Pizam, A & Sussmann, S. (1995). Does nationality affect tourist behavior? *Annals of Tourism Research*, 22 (4), 901-917.

Plog, S. C. (1974). Why Destination Areas Rise and Fall in Popularity. *Cornell Hotel and Restaurant Administration Quarterly*, 14 (4), 55-58.

Prebensen, N. K. (2006). *A grammar of motives for understanding individual tourist behavior*. PhD thesis submitted for the Department of Strategy and Management at the Norwegian School of Economics and Business Administration.

Rapoport, R. & Rapoport, R. N. (1975). *Leisure and the Family Life Cycle*. Routledge. London.

Reis, E. (2001). *Estatística Multivariada Aplicada*. 2.ª Ed. Sílabo. Lisboa.

Richards, G. (2002). Tourism Attraction Systems. Exploring Cultural Behavior. *Annals of Tourism Research*, 29 (4), 1048-1064.

Rojek, C. (1995). *Decentring Leisure: Rethinking Leisure Theory*. SAGE. London.

Ross, E. & Iso-Ahola, S. (1991). Sightseeing tourists' motivation and satisfaction. *Annals of Tourism Research*, 18 (2), 226-237.

Ryan, C. & Glendon, I. (1998). Application of Leisure Motivation Scale to Tourism. *Annals of Tourism Research*, 25 (1), 169-84.

Ryan, R. M. & Deci, E. L. (2000). Self-determination theory and the facilitation of intrinsic motivation, social development, and well-being. *American Psychologist*, *55*(1), 68-78.

Uysal, M. & Hagan, L. R. (1993). Motivation of pleasure to travel and tourism. In M. D. O. M. A. Khan, T. Var (Eds.): *VNR'S Encyclopedia of Hospitality and Tourism*. Van Nostrand Reinhold. New York. 798–810.

Wang, N. (2000). *Tourism and Modernity: A sociological analysis*. Pergamum. Amsterdam.

Witt, C. & Wright, P. (1992). Tourist Motivation: Life after Maslow. In P. Johnson & B. Thomas (Eds.): *Choice and Demand in Tourism*. Mansell. London. 33-55.

Yavuz, N., Baloglu, S. & Uysal, M. (1998). Market Segmentation of European and Turkish Travelers to North Cyprus. *Anatolia*, 9 (1), 4-18.

In: Methods and Analysis on Tourism and Environment   ISBN: 978-1-62417-824-5
Editors: J.M.Jiménez, M.V.Vargas, F.J.O.Rosell et al. © 2013 Nova Science Publishers, Inc.

Chapter 8

ANALYSIS OF THE SPATIAL STANDARDS AND PERCEPTUAL COMPONENTS OF THE RECREATIONAL CARRYING CAPACITY APPLIED TO ARCHAEOLOGICAL SITES: CASE STUDY OF CASTELLET DE BERNABÉ (LLÍRIA, SPAIN)

María José Viñals, Pau Alonso-Monasterio and Mieria Alonso-Monasterio
Universitat Politècnica de València, Valencia, Spain

ABSTRACT

Planning and managing tourism in archaeological sites demands setting up specific instruments and tools to guarantee both the site conservation and the visitors' satisfaction. This chapter focuses on the analysis of spatial standards and perceptual components affecting the visitors' satisfaction in the framework of the Recreational Carrying Capacity Assessment. These standards have been obtained from scientific literature, proxemic studies and field studies.

The standards have been applied to the case study of the archaeological site of the Iberian village Castellet de Bernabé located in Llíria (Valencia, Spain). Methodologically, the analysis of this site is based on the study of the space where the activity is held, the natural, cultural and scenic resources involved, the recreational activities and the visitors' profile and behaviour.

1. INTRODUCTION

Heritage protection and preservation in areas of unique scientific, natural, cultural, artistic and/or historical value and the impacts of tourism have been traditionally important issues in the framework of heritage planning and management. Among the different tools applied to tourism planning and management, the Recreational Carrying Capacity Assessment (ReCCA) is one of the most recognized methods to guarantee the sustainability. ReCCA sets the limits of the established and desired site conditions according to the proposed recreational use level and the conservation goals. In general terms, the concept of Recreational Carrying Capacity addresses the question of how many people can be permitted into an area without risk of degrading the site and the visitors' experience on it (Pedersen, 2002). Traditionally, this tool has been a long-standing issue in outdoor recreation, guiding the decision making processes and becoming increasingly important since the 1960s, when the first rigorous applications of carrying capacity to outdoor recreation occurred. In this sense, Mathieson and Wall (1986), Kuss et al., (1990), O'Reilly (1991), Cifuentes (1992), McNeely et al., (1992), Butler (1996), Buchinger (1996), Liddle (1997), Chamberlain (1997), Clark (1997), and Middleton and Hawkins (1998), among others, have mainly worked with a perspective orientated to biophysical components and impacts prevention based on the study of thresholds or tolerance level beyond which further exploitation or use may impose strains on the site. Other authors have incorporated some social aspects of the visitors' experience. In fact, psychological and sociological components focused on visitors' perceptions have been studied by Shelby and Heberlein (1986), Harroun and Boo (1995), Tarrant and English (1996), Lindberg and McCool (1998) and Viñals et al., (2003), among others. During the evaluation seems to be necessary to consider some visitors' personality traits or cultural features such as behaviour and habits, beliefs, etc., being these components difficult to quantify and evaluate (Morant, 2007). Anyway, it is important to take into account, as Mann (2003) suggests, that recreation impacts differ with the type, timing, distribution of use, environmental setting, management actions, and people's expectations and norms. In this line, McCool (1996) suggested that more than the number of users, the problem of recreational use is related with the visitors' behaviour, because a large number of people can be accommodated in an area if there is enough education and access management.

Although ReCCA seems to be a simplistic and easy-to-implement tool, it is quite complex and works based on a systemic approach, examining area issues from different perspectives, studying specific site conditions and limiting factors (physical-ecological, socio-demographic and political-economic), and it must be considered within the framework of a huge planning process for tourism development.

In this sense, Severiades (2000) highlights that ReCCA is not just a scientific concept or formula to obtain a number beyond which development should cease, but a process where the limits must be considered as guidance in a dynamic temporal and spatial framework. Vera and Baños (2004) agree arguing that the reduction to a simple number is an abusive simplification.

In any case, ReCCA represents an important conceptual framework within which to view recreation management because it provides the basis for examining the interactions between recreational supply and demand considerations, between concerns about resource conditions and perceived recreational quality, and between the quantity of recreational opportunities supplied and the quality of experiences derived from them (Stankey and Manning, 1986).

2. OBJECTIVE AND METHODS

The inspiring principles to develop ReCCA for archaeological sites are on the basis that this tool fits well in these settlements because the space is perfectly delimited (López-Bonilla and López-Bonilla, 2007); and secondly, because developing simple and flexible management plans and tools like the ReCCA for this kind of sites, where responsible local authorities cannot afford great financial investments in tourism management, works better than any other more complex methodologies. The technical procedure for the analysis of ReCCA has been based on the analysis of its key components: a) space where the activity is held (size and features of the area); b) natural, cultural and scenic resources involved; c) recreational activities planned; and d) visitors' profile and behaviour.

The natural, cultural and scenic resources of the territory have been analysed following both, descriptive and evaluative process in the framework of the development of an Inventory and an Intrinsic and Recreational Assessment of the existing resources. In order to assess the intrinsic and recreational values, several criteria as significance, representativeness, and singularity have been considered in the intrinsic value analysis. Recreational criteria have taken into account attractiveness, accessibility, fragility/vulnerability, feasibility, availability, educational values and increasing awareness values. The information has been recorded onto base maps to allow the comparison of existing conditions and those defined as acceptable for the site. Therefore, physical and ecological standards of conservation were established and also the related-indicators. These standards indicate the minimal acceptable conditions and are often expressed as probabilities in relative terms (%) because absolute standards are unrealistic.

In relation with visitors, it is important to highlight that one of the goals when implementing the ReCCA pursued the visitors' satisfaction through a quality experience. In this sense, social conditions have been studied as part of the standards of quality. It is important to highlight that, to achieve this goal, a demographic visitor study is not enough but a visitor behaviour analysis is needed, to know the different types of visitors and their motivations or inner drives that cause people to take action to satisfy their needs. In any case, one of the biggest problems in this concern is that everyone has different needs, expectations and behavioural patterns. In the same way, as Southall (2009) wrote, it must be noted that experiences are inherently personal, existing only in the mind of an individual who has been engaged on an emotional, physical, intellectual, or even spiritual level. For these reasons, understanding the needs and expectations of the visitors' and designing activities to meet these is a relatively straightforward concept, but it is also vital to consider, rather than personal factors (age, gender, etc.), the cultural background (beliefs, rituals, values, ways of thinking, etc.) and social influences (references groups, lifestyle, etc.).

In this case study, the visitors' analysis was made through the study of compared cases in Spanish Iberian archaeological settlements. That is because this settlement was not regularly visited before the enhancement project conducted by this team. Nevertheless, it must be said that the existing studies analysing the visitors only included just a demographic approach, not enough for our purposes. In addition, several focus group meetings with stakeholders, interviews with interested people, and direct observation of visitors' perceptions and behaviour pattern in the pilot visits to the settlement were done in order to obtain an approach to this kind of information.

The process of setting up all the aforementioned components and data was drawn following the classical three consecutive level approach proposed by Cifuentes (1992) and Ceballos-Lascuraín (1996): Physical Carrying Capacity (PCC), Real Carrying Capacity RCC), and Effective Carrying Capacity (ECC). The standard of individual space requirements are directly linked with the Visitors' Psychological Comfort. Proxemic studies developed by Hall (1966) state that needs for interpersonal space in a social context is 120 cm. When developing dynamic activities, the World Tourism Organization (2005) talks about 4.00 m^2 which is also the standard space in recreational outdoor activities deduced by Morant (2007) and Morant and Viñals (2009) from several empirical works in protected areas. Then, it can be said that the area where one person feels comfortable sharing the space with a non-familiar person changes depending on the setting where they are.

The second level of the process is to evaluate the Real Carrying Capacity. This stage of the process deals basically with the study of the limiting factors, reducing the amount of visitors obtained from PCC calculation. This study includes the analysis of the site conditions, and the physical, ecological and social factors. It can be said that this stage is the most complex to address because the several variables influencing the analysis. It is necessary to take into consideration that this study can vary according to different settings, activities, resources or visitors' profile considered. Then, the limiting factors are not necessarily the same for each site. The process starts with the analysis of the physical conditions of the site (natural, cultural and historical settings and landscapes) and space availability (space limiting factors), considering the existence of restricted point zones (because archaeological resources are unique and fragile). Ecological constrains (ecological limiting factors) are related with the conservation and protection of the fauna, flora, soils, and geomorphic and hydrological elements in and around the site. Social limiting factors deal with some elements of the Visitors' Psychological Comfort. In order to establish physical, ecological and social standards, it was necessary to identify the desirable site conditions. This issue was considered within the context of conservation and protection goals, management objectives, and the implementation of preventive strategies. The Resources Inventory recorded the current status quo of the natural and cultural heritage, taking that as the minimal acceptable conditions for conserving the place but expecting to improve the site as much as possible. Furthermore, a direct and indirect, short-term and long-term impacts study was addressed in order to state the different levels of archaeological and natural resources degradation or even destruction and the preventive measures must be considered to enable the site to be presented to the public. Regarding the type of impacts, beyond the natural damage caused by weather, impacts due to visitors can be multiple. The most relevant detected in relation to the archaeological sites, were mechanical and occasionally voluntary degradations that exist under various forms. There is evidence that the wear and tear through abrasion provoked by the rubbing of shoes on the floors, and the destruction of the archaeological setting (fall of blocks and fabric degradation) are closely related with the action of stepping on the settlement structures. Littering is another action that usually is registered. Therefore, a detailed study evaluating the potential damage that the public access may provoke was carried out. Results of this study allowed to determine the appropriate areas for recreation (i. e. where materials and fabrics were inherently more resistant), establishing the fragile zones, and setting the visitors' touring pattern inside the site.

Limiting social factors are related to the needs, wants and expectations of people in determining appropriate uses of resources. In this kind of study, several variables conditioning the social standards must be taken into account: the scenery where the activity is developed (indoor, outdoor with/without physical barriers, grades, topography, floor conditions, length of the itinerary, etc.); the thermo-hygrometric features conditioning the human climatic comfort (weather limiting factors); the visitors' motivations and behaviour; the visitors' expectations, the existing facilities (facilities limiting factor); the safety conditions (safety limiting factor). Other social standards are usually considered, especially in sites highly frequented, as the visitors' perception of crowding and the number of encounters with others groups along the trail or in the site itself. Field observations show that most visitors like visiting these unique places in the context of a quite atmosphere, and the acceptable solitude level, which should be no longer than three groups along short trails per day. When McCool (1983) compared satisfaction ratings for wilderness visitors who reported that meeting more than 10 groups was "too many."

Figure 1. Settings where the recreational activities are hold. Left up: Trail. Left down: Picnic area. Right: Archaeological settlement of the Castellet de Bernabé (Llíria, Valencia).

The third analytical level is the Effective Carrying Capacity (ECC), dealing with the managing capacity. ECC is defined as the sum of conditions that the site administration requires in order to carry out its functions and objectives (Tran Nghi et al., 2007), and it is a crucial concern in implementing recreational carrying capacity. Measuring managing capacity is not an easy task, since many variables (several of which are quite subjective) are involved, such as policy measures (preventive and protection measures, flow management policies, etc.), legislation (mandatory permits, regulations, etc.), infrastructure, facilities and equipment, staff (number and qualifications) or funding. In this sense, planning tools, such as zoning, and management techniques as visitor flow management, can mitigate the recreation impacts. According to Manning (1979), other available techniques are to reduce the amount of use through restrictions; accommodate more use by supplying additional opportunities; modify the character of use to reduce its impact, or harden the resource base to increase its resiliency. Moreover, alternative fields of actions must be evaluated, and strategy for tourist development formulated. Additionally, the use of adequate information, interpretation, education, and the involvement of the visitors in the preservation process can help to achieve the conservation goals. Then, raising visitors' awareness and their integration in the protection process do not only help site preservation but also provide a better quality experience. On the other hand, an effective legal framework could help to reduce/mitigate the negative impacts from recreation in order to preserve valuable resources.

Regarding the staff members it must be highlighted that firstly it is necessary to count on a sufficient number of people for addressing managerial, conservation monitoring and recreational tasks. Moreover, staff members must receive appropriate qualifications through regular training programs. In this sense, financial support is always necessary to maintain heritage conservation, at least in the first stages of the enhancement process. Later on, some funds can be retrieved with ticketing policies, fees, etc. and also from donors. Anyway, it must be noticed that funding is an important limiting factor in the framework of the effectiveness of the managing plan.

3. CASE STUDY OF THE ARCHAEOLOGICAL SITE OF THE CASTELLET DE BERNABE (LLIRIA, VALENCIA, SPAIN)

Currently, most Spanish accessible archaeological sites are related to the Greco-roman civilization, such as the World Heritage site (WHs) of Mérida (Badajoz) or Las Médulas (León). There are also internationally renowned prehistoric archaeological WHs such as the Altamira Palaeolithic Rock Art Cave (Santander) or the important human fossils settlement of Atapuerca (Burgos). All of them constitute significant attractions of a successful tourism offer. Although there are no sites of the Iberian period in the World Heritage List, some of them have been restored in order to enhance their resources for tourism purposes.

The Castellet de Bernabé has been the archaeological site where this methodology has been applied in the framework of a recreational enhancement process in order to identify the type and use level that this space and its visitors can support. According to the excavation works of Ballester (1945) and Guérin (1984), the Castellet de Bernabé is a 1,000 m^2 fortified typical Iberian village located on the top of a hill, inhabited between the 4th and the 3rd centuries BC, located in the Mediterranean mountains of Llíria (Valencia, Spain). The Iberians were one of the most important western Mediterranean civilizations. They were a diverse group with common cultural characteristics and, like other Mediterranean peoples of the time (Greeks, Phoenicians, Etruscans, Carthaginian), they possessed a developed and complex civilization with urban and trade networks. From the urban planning point of view, it presents a central main street with houses, larders, workshops, mills, furnaces, cistern, forges and stables on both sides, enclosed by a stone wall. The village held fifty people in, and the houses were built with stone bases with rows of mud bricks or adobe facing on top; having flat roofs made of beams with branches, which were then covered with thick layers of mud mixed with rosmarine straws. Some of the buildings had one or two floors and the entrances had wood doors.

The RCCA of the archaeological site of the Castellet de Bernabé has been applied to three different spaces: the archaeological settlement itself, its nearby picnic area, and a lineal interpretive trail connecting the settlement with the nearest town Bodegas de Campo. Visitors can access by walking, cycling or horse riding (Figure 1).

Once the settlement was zoned, only one area was identified to develop recreational activities due to safety reasons and the fragility of the rest of the rooms and archaeological structures. Then the available space for the visit was 224.04 m^2 (central street of the village).

If the needed space for each visitor developing a group activity in outdoor spaces with physical barriers is 4 m^2, a simple calculation brings up a maximum of 56 people (PCC) visiting the site at the same time.

Related to the Real Carrying Capacity (RCC), it must be said that ecological limiting factors are not relevant in the settlement, but landscape ones are because the village is located on the top of a hill and panoramic views are available in any direction, being the landscape vulnerability too high, even considering the historical landscape as a central argument of the interpretation programme. It is considered that the largest side of the settlement has 34.00 m, so to guarantee the appreciation of sights (considering 1.20 m as interpersonal distance), the groups should be of 28.3 people.

In relation to safety, grades higher than 5%, irregular topography and holes inside the settlement have been observed as difficulties to take into consideration, especially for kids and elder visitors. In this way, entering and getting out of the settlement was through a narrow ramp of 1.30 m width (only one way flow) and 11.20 m length. Thus, the visitors could access the site were the result of dividing the ramp length per 1.20 m (interpersonal distance), and this is 10 people (9.3 people).

Other visitors' comfort issues, as the perception of crowding and the number of encounters with others groups, have influenced the analysis. In this case, the suggested number of encounters, knowing the needs of this interpretative audience, is zero. It means that only one group can visit the settlement at the same time. Regarding the adequate group size, several educational research and museums as the American Educational Research Association (2003), the National Gallery Management[1] authorities (UK) or the Alhambra managers[2] (Spain) recommend groups of less than 30 people. The final RCC for the archaeological settlement is 10 people, which is the most restrictive number obtained from the different calculations.

The limiting factors considered for determining Effective Carrying Capacity (ECC) dealt with preventive and protective measures, the touring pattern, the facilities, the regulations, the staff, and the funding capacity. It must be highlighted that the staff and policy makers motivation for heritage conservation was always worthy to mention although the financial support was weak because of budgetary reasons. Nevertheless, an adequate number of informative and interpretative institutional and private qualified services and dissemination materials have been provided; as well as some managing techniques and tools that contributed to mitigate the recreation impacts. On the other hand, visiting the site without guide is not allowed. Probably, the existent staff could manage a larger number of visitors but due to the fragility of the site and the insufficient budget to maintain site conditions, this option was not suitable. It was established therefore for the ECC the mentioned peak number of 10 people per day.

In relation to the picnic area, the analysis shows that RCC numbers practically fits in the PCC. This area measures 445.17 m^2 and it holds 3 picnic tables (8 persons per table) and 6 benches (4 persons per bench). This means a total of 48 people. Then, it can be said that in this area, the limiting factors are the existent facilities. In any case, it would be good to recall that this area is located beside the settlement that has a more restrictive carrying capacity. Then, not all the people enjoying the picnic area could visit the archaeological site.

---

[1] http://www.nationalgallery.org.uk/visiting/organise-a-group-visit/, (accessed 3 September 2011).
[2] http://www.alhambra.org/esp/index.asp?secc=/alhambra/visitas (accessed 3 September 2011).

The path connecting the Castellet de Bernabé to Bodegas de Campo is a 3,900 m one-way multi-use trail, having an average of 2.00 m width. It is an easy hiking trail with low level of difficulty because grades are less than 5% (according to the ranges proposed by the U.S. Army Corps of Engineers (2008). The different users of this trail cause impacts on the resources at different levels, being horse riding and bicycling more impacting activities than hiking. They cause ecological impacts to the vegetation (loss and degradation) and soil erosion, and also disturbances to the fauna. The PCC analysis applied to this trail considering the standard of 4.00 m^2 for pedestrians developing outdoor activities in a space without barriers bring us the number of 1,950 hikers. In these multi-use trails with horse riders and cyclists, the standard of space requirements are 10 linear metres per user and 1.50 m safety distance in parallel in order to guarantee a safety space among the group practitioners to prevent accidents or collisions[3]. These spatial needs for horses have been monitored by means of some surveys campaigns addressed to horse-riders groups and following the proposals from the U. S. National Parks[4] and the Australian National Parks Authorities[5]. Therefore, the PCC calculated was 390 riders or cyclers.

After that, RCC was established by applying the limiting factors. Then, for the conservation of the physical and ecological site conditions, and taking into account the short length and narrowness of the trail, and according to empirical previous experiences, it is recommended a standard of trail linear occupancy of 10% in order to minimize impacts, facilitate flows mobility and provide psychological comfort. Therefore, calculations must consider only 390 m.

The social limiting factors regarding the Psychological Comfort of users (included horses) considered the group size, the number of encounters with other groups and the length and the distance between the different groups. Other standard was the minimum distance between groups to avoid visual contact and the persecution sensation. This standard was established in 50 m following Cifuentes (1992). In the establishment of the group size, behavioural patterns of horses (animals' affinity, hierarchy, etc.) and riders (experience, ethics, behaviour, etc.) in walks for pleasure, recommend 10 horses. This number is also justified by safety reasons for riders, for preventing impacts. Other studies admit bigger group size than this, but due to the special conditions of Mediterranean ecosystems it has been proposed a more reduced figure. Between 4 and 6 horses would be the perfect number to guarantee harmony among the animals; and between 8 and 10 as the maximum suggested. Nevertheless, it has been highlighted that is important to restrict this activity during the wet season to avoid soil erosion. Then, RCC of the trail comes from the consideration of the 390 linear meters occupied by groups of 10 horses or cyclists spreading each along 100 m. If we add 50 m more in order to avoid visual contact, it means 150 m for each group. On the other hand, as the trail is 2.00 m width, and safety distance is 1.5 m, users only can go in one direction within the same path. Then, RCC for horses and cycles results from dividing 390 by 150 giving us a number of 2.6 groups of 10 users on the trail at the same time, following the same direction and keeping, at least, a distance of 50 m between them. The touring pattern followed according to the interpretation programme designed for the trail, recommended to stagger, as possible, the groups to avoid crowding in the different interpretation stations.

---

[3] Reglamento de circulación (España), sección 3°, art. 85).
[4] http://www.nps.gov/cany/planyourvisit/horseshoecanyon.htm (accessed 5 September 2011).
[5] http://www.australianalps.environment.gov.au/caring/horse-riding.html (accessed 6 September 2011).

The RCC calculation for pedestrians follows the same steps. Then, having a distance of 390 m and taking an average group size of 3-4 people (not guided groups) that is the usual number according to Fix and Loomis (1997), Gimblett et al., (2001), Hall (2001), Hesselnatt et al., (2003), and if 1.20 m is needed by each hiker, then the group needs 4.80 m. Adding 50 m to avoid visual contact between groups, it results in 55 m needed for each hiking group. Then, in 390 m, the number of groups that fit at the same time in the trail is 7 groups of 4 hikers.

Summarising, the RCC for the trail considering all the users, it results in 7 groups of hikers and 2.6 groups of riders and cyclists, this is only one way, as they can't come encounter each other because of the trail width. This data represents the peak carrying capacity in a given moment, taking into account only the spatial standards.

Finally, the managing limiting factors associated to the trail analysis of the Effective Carrying Capacity (ECC) are related with the lack of staff and funds to manage visitors' flows.

CONCLUSION

As concluding remarks of this work it could be pointed out that the Recreational Carrying Capacity Assessment seems work adequately in determining the adequate number of visitors in archaeological sites, considering the spatial and social requirements needed to enjoy a quality experience. In this line, determining Recreational Carrying Capacity for archaeological sites should be always subjected to the heritage conservation and protection goals. In this sense, the spatial standards and perceptual components only address adequately the peak use level of the site in a given moment. This analysis would not be enough to guarantee the site conservation because impacts from recreation are cumulative and it is necessary to consider the frequency use level.

Limiting factors are multiple and change on each case study. In archaeological sites, the available space is one of the most restrictive. Regarding the consecutive level of analysis (PCC, RCC and ECC), it is recommended to implement the most restrictive results. The analysis pattern is usually as follows: Physical Carrying Capacity shows the broadest approach; then the Real Carrying Capacity decreases when applying the limiting factors, and finally the Effective Carrying Capacity (related to visitors' management) is normally the most restrictive approach (although it would not always be applicable when dealing with archaeological sites). When a recreational activity needs for different settings (i.e. settlement, trail, picnic area, etc.) to be developed, each area should be analysed independently, in order to compare the results to establish the final Carrying Capacity according to the most restrictive.

When animals are involved in the activity (horses in this case), a Psychological Comfort analysis should be carried out especially for them, due to their behavioural patterns and its strong influence over the visitors' quality experience.

Regarding the results from the Recreational Carrying Capacity Assessment applied to the Castellet de Bernabé, it could be concluded that the settlement should be visited in groups of 10 people to provide a satisfactory experience. Some physical elements linked to safety measures (i.e. bottleneck effect in some crucial points) of the site strongly condition this number. Secondly, a multi-use trail access to the archaeological site presents some complexities due to its one-way sense of circulation, its reduced width in some sections and its multi-users condition. Therefore, 7 groups of 4 hikers and 2.6 groups of 10 cyclists or riders were established, sharing the trail simultaneously following the same direction. The picnic area, with 48 people, presents the largest Recreational Carrying Capacity because it is a facility of intensive use. Finally, managing visitors in archaeological sites highlights the undeniable need for involving local staff in order to guarantee the preservation of such fragile and irreplaceable heritage.

REFERENCES

American Educational Research Association (2003). Class size: counting students can count. *Essential Information for Education Policy*, 1 (2), 1-4.

Ballester, E. (1945). Las Actividades del S. I. P. *Archivo de Prehistoria Levantina II*. Valencia.

Buchinger, M. (1996). *Turismo, recreación y medio ambiente. Problemas y soluciones*. Ed. Universo, Buenos Aires.

Butler, R. W. (1996). The concept of Carrying Capacity for Tourism Destinations: dead or merely buried? *Progress in Tourism and Hospitality Research*, 2, 283-293.

Ceballos-Lascurain, H. (1996). *Tourism, Ecotourism and Protected Areas*. IUCN Gland.

Chamberlain, K. (1997). Carrying capacity. *UNEP Tourism Newsletter*, 8, 1–8.

Cifuentes, M. (1992). *Determinación de la Capacidad de Carga Turística en áreas protegidas*. Ed. Turrialbe (Costa Rica), WWF-Catie, 34.

Clark J. (1997). *Coastal Zone Management Handbook*. Lewis Publishers, Florida.

Fix, P. & Loomis, J. (1997). The economic benefits of mountain biking at one of its meccas: an application of the travel cost method to mountain biking in Moab, Utah. *Journal of Leisure Research*, 29 (3), 342-352.

Gimblett, H. R.; Richards M. T. & Itami R. M. (2001). RBSim: Geographic Simulation of Wilderness Recreation Behavior. *Journal of Forestry*, 99, 4(1), 36-42.

Guérin, P. (1995). El poblado de Castellet de Bernabé (Llíria) y el horizonte ibérico pleno edetano. Tesis de Doctorado. Universitat de València, València.

Hall, T. (1966). *The Hidden Dimension*. Anchor Books, New York.

Hall, T. (2001). Hikers' Perspectives on Solitude and Wilderness. *International Journal of Wilderness*, 7, 2, 20-24.

Harroun, L. A. & Boo, E. A. (1995). *The search for visitor carrying capacity*. Draft paper, World Wildlife Fund, Washington, DC.

Hesselna, H; Loomis, J.; González-Cabánc, A. & Alexander, S. (2003). Wildfire effects on hiking and biking demand in New Mexico: a travel cost study. *Journal of Environmental Management*, 69, 4, 359-368.

Kuss, F., Graefe, A. & Vaske, J. (1990). *Visitor Impact Management*. National Parks and Conservation Association, Washington.

Liddle, M. (1997). *Recreation Ecology. The ecological impact of outdoor recreation and ecotourism*. Ed. Chapman & Hall.

López Bonilla, J. M. & López Bonilla, L. M. (2007). *La capacidad de carga psicológica del turista como indicador del turismo sostenible, Boletín de ICE*, 2911, 25-35.

Mann, C. (2003). *Concepts for Recreation Management: Carrying Capacity & Limits of Acceptable Change*. Institute of Forest Policy, PowerPoint presentation.

Manning, R. E. (1979). Impacts of recreation on riparian soils and vegetation. *Water Resources Bulletin*,15, 30-43.

McCool, S. F. (1983). The National Parks in Post-Industrial America. *Western Wildlands, 9* (2), 14-19.

McCool, S. F. (1996). *Limits of Acceptable Change: A Framework for Managing National Protected Areas: Experiences from the United States*. Unpublished paper. Missoula, MT: School of Forestry, University of Montana.

Mathieson, A. & Wall, G. (1986). *Turismo: Repercusiones económicas, físicas y sociales*. Ed. Trillas, México.

Mcneely, J. A., Thorsell, J. W. & Ceballos-Lascuráin, H. (1992). *Guidelines: Development of national Parks and protected areas for tourism*. OMT/UNEP-IE/PAC, Technical report, 13, 53 pp.

Middleton, V. & Hawkins, R. (1998). *Sustainable tourism: a marketing perspective*. Ed. Butterworth-Heinemann, Oxford.

Morant, M. (2007). *Desarrollo de un modelo para la determinación de la capacidad de carga recreativa y su aplicación espacios naturales protegidos de laComunidad Valenciana*. Tesis Doctoral inédita. Univ. Politècnica de València.

Morant, M. & Viñals, M.J. (2009). Modelo para evaluar la capacidad de carga recreativa en áreas de uso intensivo de espacios protegidos. Casos de estudio de la Comunidad Valenciana (España). In: López Olivares (ed.): *Turismo y gestión de espacios protegidos*, Ed. Tirant lo Blanch, Valencia. 618-636.

O'Reilly, A. M. (1991).Tourism carrying capacity. In Medlik (ed.): *Managing Tourism*. Ed. Butterworth-Heinemann, Oxford. 301-306.

Pedersen, A. (2002). *Managing Tourism at World Heritage Sites: a Practical Manual for World Heritage Sites Managers*. UNESCO World Heritage Centre, Paris.

Severiades, A. (2000). Establishing the social tourism carrying capacity for the tourist resorts of the east coast of the Republic of Cyprus. *Tourism Management*, 21, 147-156.

Southall, C. (2009). The value of cultural awareness. *Tourism insights*, August 2009.

Stankey, G.H. & Manning, R.E. (1986). *Carrying capacity of recreational settings: a literature review*. INT 4901 Publication 166. Washington, DC.

Stankey, G.H. & McCool, S.F. (1984). Carrying Capacity in recreational settings: Evolution, appraisal and application. *Leisure Sciences*, 6 (4), 453-473.

Tarrant, M.A. & English, D.B.K. (1996). A Crowding-Based Model of Social Carrying Capacity: Applications for Whitewater Boating Use. *Journal of Leisure Research, 28* (3), 155-168.

Tran Nghi; Nguyen Thanh Lan; Nguyen Dinh Thai; Dang Mai & Dinh Xuan Thanh. (2007). Tourism carrying capacity assessment for Phong Nha-Ke Bang and Dong Hoi, Quang Binh Province. *VNU Jour. Science, Earth Sciences*, 23, 80-87.

Vera, F. V. & Baños, C.J. (2004). Turismo, territorio y medio ambiente. *Papeles de Economía Española*, 102, 271-286.

Viñals, M. J.; Morant, M.; El Ayadi, M.; Teruel, L.; Herrera, S.; Flores, S. & Iroldi, O. (2003). A Methodology for determining the recreational carrying capacity of wetlands. In: Garrod and Wilson (eds.): *Marine Ecotourism. Issues and experiences*. Ed. Channel View Pub., Clevedon, England, 79-99.

World Tourism Organization. (2005). *Indicators of sustainable development for tourism destinations. Guidebook*. WTO, Madrid.

In: Methods and Analysis on Tourism and Environment   ISBN: 978-1-62417-824-5
Editors: J.M.Jiménez, M.V.Vargas, F.J.O.Rosell et al. © 2013 Nova Science Publishers, Inc.

Chapter 9

IMAGE OF EXTREMADURA AS A TOURISTIC DESTINATION: FIDELITY FACTOR IN COUNTRYMAN TOURISM[1]

Marcelo Sánchez-Oro Sánchez
and Aurelio Moreno Fernández-Durán
University of Extremadura,
Research Group Sustainable Local Development (DELSOS), Spain

ABSTRACT

It has been noted that the relationship between the returnees and their descendants with Extremadura, in terms of their visits and their attachment to it, is very high. This, beyond any considerations, presents the interest in knowing the characteristics of this influx and the social, cultural economic and touristic impact on the towns of this region, which is mostly rural.

This article seeks to address the study of perceptive and symbolic elements which constitute the image of Extremadura in this segment of the population. Thus, for instance, we analyze the perception of the region harbored by these tourists in comparison with that of the rest of the country. We also address the satisfaction with the touristic experience, and the assessment of the services carried out in these towns. Finally, the opinions on the region in relation with some of its symbolic aspects like backwardness, old age or unemployment.

Our hypothesis is that a good perception of these central elements of the region contribute substantially to reinforce the visits by this part of this segment of the population with a subsequent fidelity of these tourists towards the destination of Extremadura.

---

[1] This article is a product of the data obtained from PRI08A045/ returns and «Countryman» tourism in neorurality. Motivations, orientations and their contribution to the rural development of extremadura. grupo desarrollo local de la uex (delsos).

1. INTRODUCTION

This article has, as its main aim to unveil the perception of Extremadura by the segment known as "countryman tourism[2], people who are native to the region who once had to go to other parts of the nation, looking for improvements in their quality of life. Today, they return to Extremadura during holiday periods adopting behavioral patterns of eminent touristic character.

For the present case, the selected sample represents people who, in most cases, were born in Extremadura, and have been living outside for an average period of 35 years. Eight out of every ten returnees acknowledge to visit Extremadura every year (once or twice).

The surveys have been done in the regions where they habitually live, that is to say, outside Extremadura, although they have been asked about Extremadura. The origin of this contact has been the regional houses in the respective autonomous regions.

The sample is constituted by 480 informants[3], who live in Catalonia (29.17%), Andalusia (12.50%), Community of Madrid (46.88%) and Euskadi (the Basque Country) (11.46%).

For us, this group constitutes a unique source for assessing the image of Extremadura with regard to aspects like: the touristic roles of the Extremadura returnees, opinion on the general situation of the towns and rural areas of Extremadura, opinion on the general situation of the towns and rural areas of Extremadura by the returnees in comparison with other regions, opinion of the returnees on what they identify the rural world of Extremadura with y, assessments on the quality levels of the different services of the region.

2. THE TOURISTIC ROLE OF THE RETURNED EXTREMADURANS

The preoccupation for the delimitations of the touristic role of the travelers as a referent of Cohen`s work[4] (1972), which establishes a typology based on the degree of authenticity sought by the tourists in their trips. The other axis of delimitation of this role is the degree of alienation which the tourists have in their everyday life (the higher or lower degree/motivation for the search of places for relaxation, tranquility and finding nature), therefore, it is possible to establish types of travelers who embody, in higher or lower degree, the role of the tourist. Pearce (1982) insists on these taxonomies by establishing 14 categories of travelers, among which we can find the so called "tourists". Pearce's classification (1982:155) is based on the behavior of these travelers, which led to describe 22 different types of conducts, which he denominated roles; therefore delimitating what applies to be considered to be tourism and what does not.

As a consequence, we base our work on the hypothesis that only parts of this type of visitors, emigrants who return to Extremadura, play a fairly authentic touristic role. The basic

---

[2] For a better comprehension of this segment of countryman tourists, we reccommend to consult Pérez Rubio and García García.

[3] The distribution of the simple matchs the proportionality criteria with respect to the Extremaduran emigrants who live in the different regions of Spain. The following sample values have been assigned for the random selection of this sample: being the level of trustworthiness of 95% and the maximum permissible error of ± 4.5%.

[4] In Castaño (2005: 92 and 79) there is a synthetic summary by different authors who elaborate typologies of tourists based on their motivations and expectations of the trip.

differentiation, in our opinion, lies in the motivation, as admitted by them, to go to Extremadura. Motivation is accepted as a central concept in understanding the behavior of these tourists, as well as the process of choosing destination and the formation of touristic images. This is because this represents the engine which decides the human actions, including touristic behavior (Castaño 2005:116).

As noted previously, motivations play a determinant role to clarify the touristic role. We consider that those motivations which deal with relax, tranquility and nature, are typical of the touristic role, rather than other motivations like meeting relatives and friends. We proceeded to group the motivational scale into three categories: firstly, those returnees who consider their main motivation to be aspects which deal with leisure and recreation (23.4%) make up the group that we consider the most touristic role, and therefore they are the so called countrymen tourists. Other returnees affirm that the motivation for their trip is their attachment to their family and friends (66.2%), and therefore touristic interest becomes secondary. Finally, a 10.3% express other types of reasons to travel, different from the previously mentioned ones, and therefore they don't have a touristic motivation.

Henceforth, we will use the previous three categories as critical variables of our analysis.

Table 2 relates the motivations included in the three previously mentioned categories to the origin of the returnees. As we can see, leisure and recreation are the main motivations for people from Madrid (36%), followed by the people who live in Andalusia (22%).

Table 1. Motivations to visit Extremadura

Motivation:	Percentage
Relaxation and tranquility	20.5
Meeting their relatives	61.0
Meeting their friends	5.3
Contact with nature	2.1
Devotion to religious patrons	1.1
Cheaper holidays	0.8
Following traditions	4.6
Other motivations	4.6
Total	100.0

Source: Own Elaboration.

Table 2. Autonomous Region[*]. Established motivations (Percentages)

Region	Motivations		
	Leisure and recreation	Meetings, attachment	Other motivations
Catalonia	12.9	78.6	8.6
Andalusia	22.0	74.6	3.4
Madrid	36	48.2	15.8
Euskadi	0.0	100	0.0
Sample total	23.4	66.2	10.3

Source: Own Elaboration.

Table 3. Motivations for the visit[*]. Declared Expenses (Percentages)

How much money do you spend when you go to Extremadura?					
	Between 100 and 500	Between 501 and 1.000	Between 1.500 and 2.000	More than 2.001	Total
"Countryman"tourist role (leisure and recreation)	44.9%	31.8%	14.0%	9.3%	100%
"Returned emigrant" role (meetings and attachment)	29.5%	35.3%	24.7%	10.5%	100%
Other motivations	46,5%	20,9%	16,3%	16,3%	100%
Sample totals	34,8%	33,0%	21,3%	10,8%	100%

Source: Own Elaboration.

Table 4. Motivations for the visit[*]. Length of stay (percentages)

How long do you usually stay in your Extremaduran town?					
	One week	Two weeks	Three weeks	More tan three weeks	Stay length indicator
"Countryman tourist" role (leisure and recreation)	36.8%	25.5%	7.5%	30.2%	0.43
"Returned Emigrant" role (Meetings and attachment)	33.8%	19.9%	10.5%	35.8%	0.48
Other motivations	35.6%	20.0%	8.9%	35.6%	0.48
Sample total	34.7%	21.3%	9.6%	34.5%	

Source: Own Elaboration.

If we consider the returnees whose main motivations to go back to the region are leisure and recreation as the most purely touristic role, we can minimally establish this group. With respect to their economical expenses (table 3), those who go to Extremadura for recreation purposes are the ones who keep the lowest expense rate, as 45% of them spend between 100 and 500€, as opposed to those with different motivations. We conclude that the purely touristic role is associated to lower expenses than those of the returnee who doesn't associate the visit to touristic purposes.

The length of their stay in the region (table 6) is also inferior among those whose motivation is leisure and recreation, so a 62.3% of them tend to stay between one and two weeks in the region; whereas those whose reasons to travel are meetings with relatives and friends present major levels of dispersion, a 46.3% can be said to spend more than 3 weeks in Extremadura.

In terms of the synthetic indicator of permanence we can establish that, in a range of 0 to 1, the level of those who seek leisure is 0.43, whereas those who travel for social reasons show a level of 0.48.

The place chosen for fun and leisure by the three groups of tourists is, in most cases the town of stay, but in the case of those who travel mainly for leisure and recreation purposes, a 3.6% of them chooses the city instead, as opposed to the lower 1.3% of the tourists who travel in order to meet people.

Table 5. Motivations for the visit[*]. Where they usually spend their leisure time (percentages)

Where do you spend your leisure time in Extremadura?				
	Town of stay	Neighboring towns	In the city	Total
"Countryman tourist" role (leisure and recreation)	95.5%	0.9%	3.6%	100.0%
"Returned emigrant" role (meetings and attachment)	96.4%	2.3%	1.3%	100.0%
Other motivations	91.3%	2.2%	6.5%	100.0%
Sample totals	95.7%	1.9%	2.4%	100.0%

Source: Own Elaboration.

Table 6. Motivations for the visit[*]. Consumption in restaurants

Activity carried out in Extremadura: Restaurants				
	Daily	From time to time	Never	Total
"Countryman tourist" role (leisure and recreation)	5.9%	84.2%	9.9%	100%
"Returned emigrant" role (meetings and attachment)	8.1%	71.0%	20.9%	100%
Other motivations	8.5%	55.3%	36.2%	100%
Total	34	322	89	445
Sample total	7.6%	72.4%	20.0%	100%

Source: Own Elaboration.

Table 7. Motivations for the visit[*]. Satisfaction with their visits to Extremadura. Satisfaction indicator

Satisfaction levels with their visits to Extremadura					
	Very much	Fairly satisfied	Scarcely satisfied	Little satisfied	Unsatisfied	Indicator
"Countryman tourist" role (leisure and recreation)	56.8%	40.5%	2.7%	0.0%	0.0%	0.89
"Returned emigrant" role (meetings and attachment)	51.8%	43.4%	4.5%	0.3%	0.0%	0.87
Other motivations	60.4%	29.2%	8.3%	0.0%	2.1%	0.86
Sample total	53.8%	41.3%	4.5%	0.2%	0.2%	0.87

Source: Own Elaboration.

An indicator of this segment's consumption is restaurants, as those whose motivations are purely touristic are the ones who use these services more often. If we look at the data of those who affirm that they never go to a restaurant, in the case of the touristic role, it is only a 9.9%, whereas in the case of the returnee who looks to meet people, it reaches 21%.

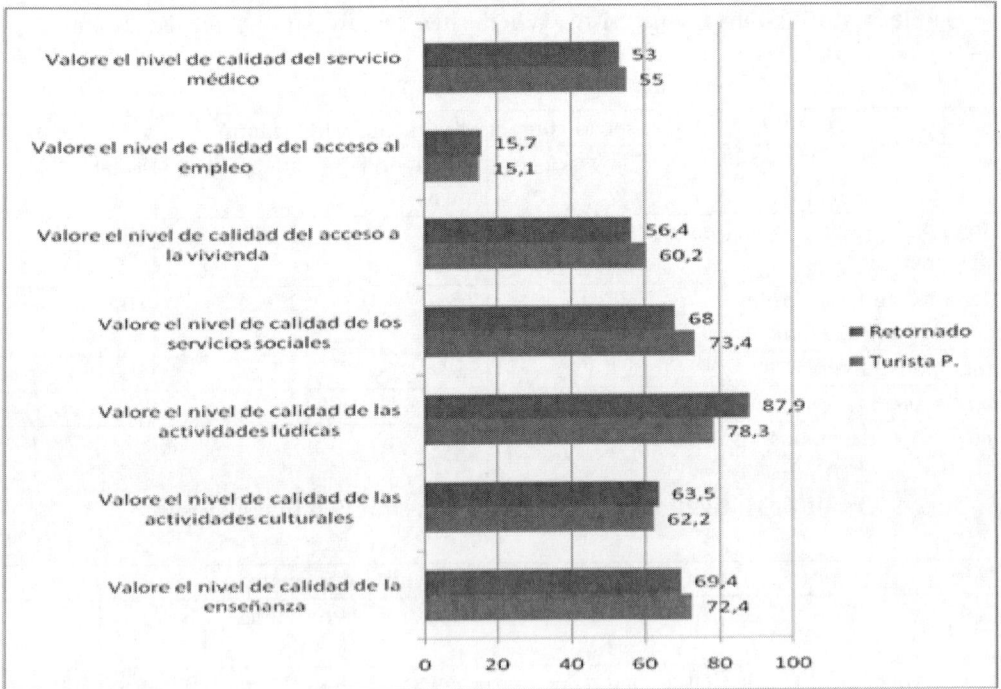

Source: Own Elaboration.

Figure 1. Assessment of the different aspects of Extremadura as touristic destination.

We must also stand out that, despite not appearing in the tables, the place chosen for accommodation does not represent significant differences between the different types of visitors, so a 94.5% of the countrymen tourists stay in their own houses or their relatives, and only a 3.6% of them stay in a rural hotel, pension, or hostel.

3. THE IMAGE OF EXTREMADURA AS TOURISTIC DESTINATION

The first observation is that the degree of satisfaction with the visit to Extremaura is very high. If we look at the satisfaction indicator on table 9, it shows that the average satisfaction level is 0.87, being that of the countrymen tourists the most elevated (0.89). This constitutes valuable data for establishing this type of tourism.

The assessment of the different aspects of Extremadura as touristic destination done by the countrymen tourists, is in general "Very good + Good" as shown in all the selected aspects of this evaluation, except for the case of Access to employment, which is the worst valued aspect. Graph 2 shows this information with the percentage values of "Very good + Good".

The quality of the recreation activities offered in the towns of the region is the service which both subgroups, tourists and returnees, rate better, as "very good or good". In any case, the highest rating of these types of services is the one held by countrymen tourists, of whom an 88% have a very high regard. Among the rest of the services, the average level of regard is above 50%, and those who appreciate it the most are the returnees, as opposed to tourists:

medical services, social services, education, etc. In general, we can affirm that the returnees value the public benefits of the region more positively.

A detailed breakdown of these assessments lets us go deeper into their keys. We must consider the positive evaluation of these services as an important source for motivation for returning to the region, both as a tourist or as a returned emigrant. It is well known that in traditional areas of sun and beach tourism of Spain, these additional services become an extra support to reinforce the touristic influx and for this reason Extremadura must plan the expansion and the maintenance of these benefits having these potential users in mind, that is to say, not only thinking about the native neighbors of rural towns and regions. It seems clear that many of the recreational activities in these towns have the purpose of reinforcing this touristic attraction, but what we can deduce from this data is that this strategy must contemplate the rest of the services.

In the following tables, we add a synthetic indicator to the percentage distribution which lets us concentrate the distribution in a single digit.

With regard to this, although it must be understood with a broader view, we must approach cultural activities which constitute a significant touristic attraction for many regions and towns of Extremadura. The rating does not reach the 0.7 indicator, although it is very close to this point. It is interesting to stand out that among the countrymen tourists a 37.8% of them rate it as "mediocre" or "bad", a value which makes us reflect on possible ways for improvement and adaptation to the countrymen tourists' needs.

The holiday and recreational activities are considerably important for this sector, not only the quantity of them but also the quality, which is what the following question in this questionnaire is aimed at. For countrymen tourists, the quality of them is above the rest of services evaluated in this article, a very positive factor for tourism. Only 21.7% of the tourists rate it as mediocre or bad. We are therefore facing an aspect which significantly reinforces the influx of tourists in the rural areas of this region.

Table 8. Motivations for the visit[*]. Assess the quality level of the cultural activities. Evaluation indicator (0 very bad; 1 very good)

Assess the quality level of cultural activities						
	Very Good	Good	Mediocre	Bad	Very Bad	Indicator
"Countryman tourist" role (leisure and recreation)	11.2%	51.0%	33.7%	4.1%	0.0%	0.67
"Returned emigrant" role (meetings and attachment)	9.9%	53.6%	30.0%	5.5%	1.0%	0.66

Source: Own Elaboration.

Social services (benefits for the elderly, infants, youths, etc;) are also highly rated by this section of countrymen tourists, with a rating indicator over 0.7. This type of services must be cautiously looked at, as a significant part of countrymen tourists look for these essential aspects of improvement of life quality with respect to the regions where they usually live.

They constitute a primary attraction factor which seeks not only to revitalize our rural spaces but also to make the investments performed in this field profitable.

The medical services, closely linked to social services, obtain a very good rating by the countrymen tourists. Nonetheless, it seems clear that there are still aspects to improve, as almost 13% of this segment estimates that the situation is in "very bad" or "bad" conditions. The importance of these services has already been suggested since a particular sector of countrymen tourists seeks these particular complementary services in their touristic destinations, sometimes becoming the determinant factor for their final decision. Besides, the image of the region can be damaged by denial of these services. It must be taken into account that these evaluations are done by comparing these services to those of the autonomous regions where the interviewees live.

Graph 2 includes in a synthesized way the ratings of the evaluation indicator which countrymen tourists give to the different services in Extremadura. The first bar represents the average evaluation (0.65), quite high. This rating is even higher if we dismiss the lowest rated factor which is employment access, which in our opinion is the least relevant factor to establish the motivations of countryman tourism in the rural regions of Extremadura, so that if we eliminate the employment factor, the evaluation of theses services goes up to 0.69.

Table 9. Motivations for the visit[*]. Evaluate the quality level of the recreational activities. Evaluation indicators (0, very bad; 1 very good)

Assess the quality level of recreational activities					
	Very Good	Good	Mediocre	Bad	Very Bad	Indicator
"Countryman tourist" role (leisure and recreation)	30.9%	47.4%	19.6%	2.1%	0.0%	0.77
"Returned emigrant" role (meetings and attachment)	28.2%	59.7%	11.1%	0.7%	0.3%	0.79

Source: Own Elaboration.

Table 10. Motivations for the visit[*]. Rate the quality level of the medical services. Evaluation indicators (0, very bad; 1 very good)

Rate the quality level of the medical services					
	Very Good	Good	Mediocre	Bad	Very Bad	Indicator
"Countryman tourist" role (leisure and recreation)	8,8%	46,1%	32,4%	8,8%	3,9%	0.62
"Returned emigrant" role (meetings and attachment)	6,7%	46,2%	33,1%	10,4%	3,7%	0.61

Source: Own Elaboration.

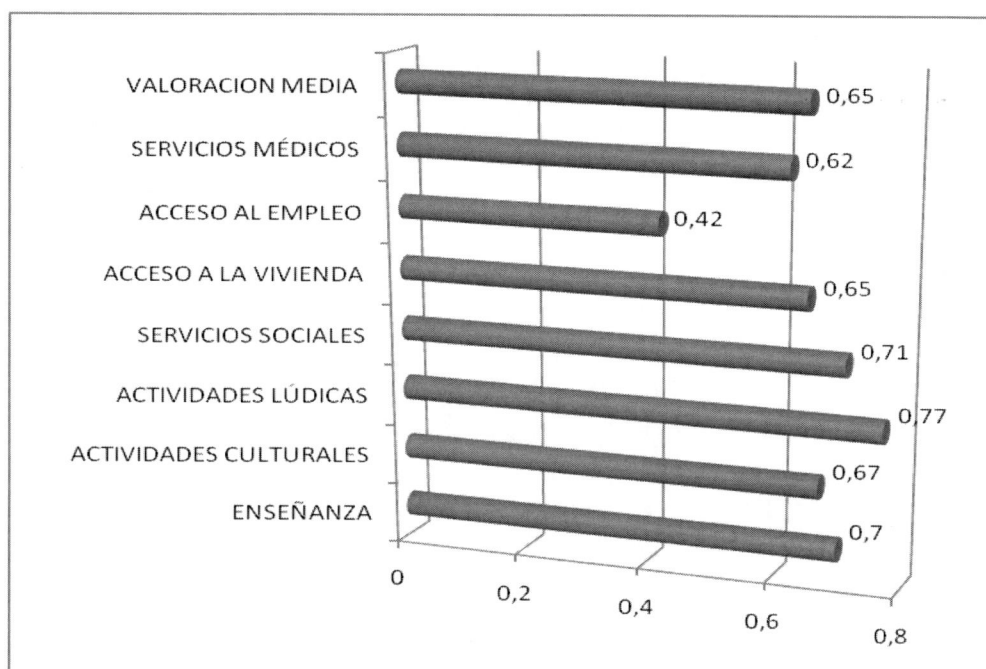

Source: Own Elaboration.

Figure 2. Evaluation indicators of the quality of the services in Extremadura by countrymen tourists. Evaluation indicators (0, very bad; 1 very bad).

4. VALUES WITH WHICH THE EXTREMADURAN RURAL WORLD IS IDENTIFIED WITH

The people who visit the region, having strong roots in it and despite not living in it, express very positive judgments about the Extremaduran rural space. In table 16 we can see that when asked about their opinions on the general situation of the villages and towns of Extremadura, more than half of them affirm that it is good or very good. This positive assessment of the rural space in which they enjoy their holidays is slightly minor for the countrymen tourists. If we analyze the indicator for this type of tourists we see a 0.67.

The evaluation of the Extremaduran rural space when compared to what they know of the rest of the autonomous regions is less positive, as comparatively our rural space would be in an inferior situation according to the informants being the compared evaluation indicator of around 0.5. It is particularly revealing that a 9.2% of the interviewed countrymen tourists and a 12.1% of other returnees consider the situation of the Extremaduran rural space to be bad or very bad when compared to the rest of the country.

It seems evident that a positive evaluation of the services that people give and receive in this region can substantially contribute to maintain the region's capacity to attract countryman tourism. Nonetheless, another relevant aspect is the values associated to the region, understood as symbolic elements, strong ideas that are linked to the parts or even the whole territory. In this association, the marketing campaigns done in Extremadura by private agents acquire special relevance. In this respect, it is necessary to remember the important effort made by the regional administration in order to change and improve the image of Extremadura both inside and outside its territory by means of the "Marca Extremadura" (brand of Extremadura).

Table 11. Motivation for the visit[*]. Opinion on the general situation of the towns and rural areas. Evaluation indicator of the situation of the villages and towns

Opinion on the situation of the towns and rural areas of Extremadura						
	Very Good	Good	Mediocre	Bad	Very Bad	Indicator
"Countryman tourist" role (leisure and recreation)	19.3%	50.5%	27.5%	1.8%	0.9%	0.67
"Returned emigrant" role (meetings and attachment)	16.8%	58.4%	22.9%	1.9%	0.0%	0.70
Other motivations	14.6%	50.0%	33.3%	2.1%	0.0%	0.62
Sample total	17.1%	55.7%	25.1%	1.9%	0.2%	0.68

Source: Own Elaboration.

The promoters of the "Marca Extremadura" hold that the brand is one the most important variable strategies for this autonomous region. It is not only a mere name and logo, it is the identity hallmark of Extremadura and its image does not only comprise the riches of its towns and peoples, but also the intangible and emotional aspects which are the essence of the region (…)[5].

Table 12. Motivation for the visit[*]. Opinion on the general situation of the Extremaduran towns in comparison with those of other autonomous regions. Compared evaluation indicator

Opinion on the general situation of the Extremaduran towns in comparison with those of other autonomous regions						
	Very Good	Good	Mdiocre	Bad	Very bad	Indicator
"Countryman tourist" role (leisure and recreation)	12.0%	46.3%	32.4%	8.3%	0.9%	0.56
"Returned emigrant" role (meetings and attachment)	10.1%	45.8%	32.0%	10.8%	1.3%	0.54
Other motivations	15.6%	46.7%	22.2%	13.3%	2.2%	0.60
Sample total	11.1%	46.0%	31.2%	10.5%	1.3%	0.55

Source: Own Elaboration.

As held by professor Castaño (2005:116) the process of formation of a particular touristic destination has been described by different authors from who we mention Reynolds (1965), who defined such process as "a mental construct based upon a few impressions chosen from a flood of information on a particular destination and upon a lot of information about such

---

[5] www.marcaextremadura.es.

destination". The sources of information would basically be promotional literature (travel brochures, specific publicity, posters, etc.), the opinion of others (family/friends, travel agents), and the general media (magazines, newspapers, books, the internet, television, etc.).

**Table 13. Motivations for the visit[*]. Assess the quality levels of the social services.
Evaluation indicator (very bad; 1 very good)**

Assess the quality levels of social services						
	Very Good	Good	Mediocre	Bad	Very Bad	Indicator
"Countryman tourist" role (leisure and recreation)	13.8%	59.6%	22.3%	4.3%	0.0%	0.71
"Returned emigrant" role (meetings and attachment)	14.3%	53.7%	24.4%	5.6%	2.1%	0.68

Source: Own Elaboration.

In the case of countrymen tourists who visit the region, in most cases every year, the image of Extremadura is associated to a series of believes which we synthesize in the following graph. In it we can stand out the idea of healthy environmental surroundings, followed by the idea of an advantaged region, with traditional ideas. The last symbolic value is that of freedom, with a 49% versus the idea of "social control" which has less support. Therefore, the main value to identify the region with for this group is the one referred to the environment.

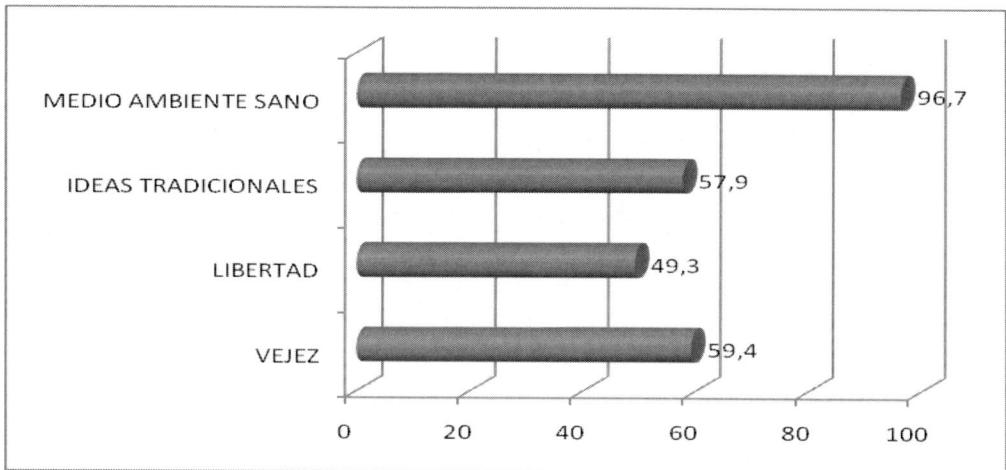

Source: Own Elaboration.

Figure 3. Values with which the image of Extremadura is associated with by countryman tourism. Percentages.

With regard to the first value, the "old age vs young age" dilemma, 6 out of every 10 countrymen tourists identify the regional rural space with old age, and only 2 of them identify it with young age. This might be true but in view of the incentive of touristic aspects in the region, this image must be changed. This is the primary effort of the "Marca Extremadura" campaign, which tries to associate the region to successful singers, basketball players or young and renowned journalists. It seems clear, however, that this identification is not associated with the rural space, but rather with the notion of a few cities which are advantaged if compared to the rest of Extremadura.

A small group of countrymen tourists identify the region's rural space with the idea of freedom (5 out of every 10). It seems clear that traditionally rural areas are associated with social control and group identity vs. individuality. The relevant data is that 3 out of every 10 countrymen tourists associate the Extremaduran rural world with social control, a higher percentage than that of the returned emigrants (25.9%).

A 58% of the interviewed countrymen tourists also identify Extremadura with traditional ideas, which is a higher percentage than that of the returnees. There are still a few (2 out of every 10) who identify our rural space with a "new mentality".

Finally, there is a wide unanimity in linking the region with a healthy environment (96.7%).

CONCLUSION

The relationship between the returnees and their offspring with Extremadura, in terms of their visits, is very close. This had us study their characteristics, as well as the impact produced on the rural towns in which they spend their holidays.

The group of returnees is large, which makes it necessary to establish a typology in order to discern which ones present a behavior closer to the touristic role. Motivations are a determinant factor to clarify this role. Let us consider, in this piece of work, that those motivations related to relax and the search for tranquility, or a natural environment, are more closely related to the touristic role than other motivations like meeting old friends and relatives. We have proceeded to group the returnees' motivations in three different categories: the returnees who express that their main reasons for the visit are aspects related to leisure and recreation (23.4%). We identify the purely touristic role with this group, being therefore the countrymen tourists. Other returnees manifest that their reason to travel is their attachment to their old friends and relatives, so the touristic interest becomes something secondary.

One of the most significant findings of this article is this group's elevated degree of satisfaction with their visits to Extremadura: being the average indicator a 0.87, being that of the countrymen tourists the highest with 0.89, which is a fundamental value for the strategies of establishing this type of tourism.

Another aspect to be taken into account is the quality of services in the rural areas. For instance, the recreational activities of the rural towns are very highly regarded by both groups, tourists and returnees, especially the countrymen tourists with a 88%. We must bear in mind that the positive evaluation of these services (recreational, cultural medical, social services, etc.) is an important source of motivation for returning to the region, both as a tourist or as a returned emigrant.

The evaluation of the Extremaduran rural space in comparison with what they know from other autonomous regions is less positive though. Comparatively, the Extremaduran rural space is in worse conditions, according to the informants, around 0.5 in the case of the compared evaluation. It is however revealing that a 9.2% of the countrymen tourists and

121% of the returned emigrants thinks that the situation of the Extremaduran rural space compared to that of the rest of Spain is "bad or very bad".

The values which are associated to the Extremaduran rural space are also a source for studying the image of the region. With respect to the "old age vs. young age" dilemma, 6 out of every 10 countrymen tourists identify the rural space of this region with old age, whereas only 2 out of 10 identify it with young age. This evaluation may be right, but in view of improving tourism in the region it's an image that must be changed. A small group of countrymen tourists identifies the region with the idea of freedom (5 out of 10), and yet 3 out of 10 countrymen tourists associate it to social control. Countrymen tourists, in higher percentages than the returned emigrants, also identify Extremadura with traditional ideas (58% of the interviewees). Only 2 out of 10 people identifies the region with a "new mentality", that is to say, with the idea of modernity.

REFERENCES

Castaño, J. M. (2005). *Psicología social de los viajes y del turismo*, Ed. Thomson. Madrid.

Cohen, E. (1984). The sociology of tourism: Approaches, Issues and Findings. *Annual Review of Sociology*, 10, 373-392.

Gobernando Arribas, R. (2008). La estratificación social. En Iglesias de Ussel y Trinidad: *Leer la sociedad*. Tecnos. Madrid.

Gutiérrez Brito (2007). *La investigación social del turismo*. Ed. Thomson. Madrid.

Pearce, L. Philip. (1982). *The Social Psychology of Tourist Behaviour*. Oxford. Pergamon Press.

Pérez Rubio, J. A. & García García, Y. (2005). *Turismo rural en Extremadura*. El caso del "turismo paisano". Estudios Agrosociales y Pesqueros, 206.

Reynolds, W. H. (1965). El Papel de la imagen construida por los clientes. *California Management Review*. 7 (10), 69-76.

In: Methods and Analysis on Tourism and Environment   ISBN: 978-1-62417-824-5
Editors: J.M.Jiménez, M.V.Vargas, F.J.O.Rosell et al. © 2013 Nova Science Publishers, Inc.

Chapter 10

THE "COUNTRYMAN TOURISM" IN RURAL AREAS: THE CASE OF EXTEMADURA (SPAIN)

Y. García García, R. Blanco Gregory and J. A. Pérez Rubio
University of Extremadura, Caceres, Spain

ABSTRACT

"Countryman Tourism" is a category scarcely considered by experts, scholars and policy makers when it comes to developing rural areas. However, in the search for new segments of a profitable and stable rural tourism, it is necessary to identify and specify the functions that they play.

This tourism seeks the imagined habitat from personal experience where family life is essential to repeat the visit. Staying in rural areas from which they originally come is characterized by a practice of consumption, which on the one hand, helps to maintain the rural economy; and on the other hand, has different nuances with regard to generic rural tourism. The subject of this paper is to describe and analyze this type of rural tourist communities in which we present the findings and partial results of the research project: "Returned and countryman tourists" in the neo-rural. Motivations, orientations and their contribution to rural development in Extremadura".

1. INTRODUCTION

The countryman tourist is a category which has been considered less significant by scholars and the people responsible for the rural development policies. Nonetheless, throughout the process of identification of actors in the new scenario of rural spaces, their identification and the specification of the functions they carry out become necessary. Both the residential experience of the returnees and the visit of the countrymen tourists have to do more with the "logic of feelings" and the "call of the land". Both of them seek the imagined habitat from the personal experience, in which life with the family is essential for repeating the visit and the continuity of the residence in the rural space. Also, their visits to the rural regions where they come from are characterized by a practice of goods consuming which, on the one hand, helps the rural economy; and on the other hand, presents different nuances in terms of behavioral patterns, with respect to other types of tourism.

The returnees and the "countrymen" tourists are particularly important in rural areas, especially in regions like Extremadura where the agrarian tradition and the processes of emigration have had a great historical weight. What seems obvious is the positive effect that these visits have for the development of rural spaces, both from a socioeconomic perspective (alternative to agricultural production as a way of contributing as a new source of income and employment) and from a socio-cultural perspective (maintaining population in rural areas and contributing to the conservation and protection of natural resources and the rural space).

Nevertheless, the research in this area is scarce and the absence of data creates one more difficulty for its chapter. The tourism of countrymen is a category overlooked by researchers of tourism as well as by scholars and people responsible for policies of development in rural areas. For this reason, in the search for new profitable and stable segments in rural tourism, it is necessary to identify and specify the roles played. We understand this as a category to be considered for it plays a role in the revitalization of rural life, especially in areas far from the urban centers.

Taking as a base the partial results obtained from the research project *Returnees and "countrymen tourists", motivations, orientations and their contribution to the rural development of Extremadura*, in this chapter we attempt to quantify and evaluate a set of issues that have so far been ignored. All this in order to obtain an approximation of these returnees as "countrymen tourist", rural visitors motivated primarily both by family and community ties. Thus, the main aim of this chapter is to describe the role of this typology of tourist in rural communities, to identify and define their motivations, expectations and idiosyncrasies.

2. RETURNEES AND RURAL TOURISM: THE CASE OF THE "COUNTRYMAN" TOURIST

Rural tourism in Extremadura has experienced a significant expansion in the last few years. According to the data provided by the survey of occupancy of rural tourism accommodation of the National Institute of Statistics, the number of travelers has increased over the last decade uninterruptedly, moving from 30,192 tourists in rural lodgings in 2001, to 107,526 as to 2010. The increase has been significant, followed by a rapid development of tourism activity in rural spaces. This data suggests that, as in other regions of the inland country, there has developed a tendency towards the intensification of this sort of tourism in Extremadura (from 2007, this sector is also suffering the effects of the recent economic recession). However, despite the fact that the tendency in rural accommodation is growing, there is an ignored contingency in these statistics that are part of the overall numbers. We refer to family tourism and more specifically to countrymen tourists. This phenomenon has been controversial in its evaluation because, in spite of being overlooked by the researchers and the people responsible for tourism policies and rural development, it has been "vindicated" by the responsible for local policies and development agents, as a basic element of promotion and as a source of employment for the small towns with little chances of touristic promotion.

There is no generally accepted conceptual framework to define or even denominate this type of tourism and there is little research dealing with it. It has been even referred to it as a "hidden" phenomenon given that, as manifested by Volo and Giambalvo (2005), it is hidden for it refers to an activity of touristic consumption of economic relevance, not voluntarily reported and ignored by the standard system of tourism statistics. With respect to this typology, Yagüe (2002) uses a denomination of "traditional" rural tourist as well as *return* tourist, the tourists who, having a life and a job in the city, go back to the town of origin, where they probably still have family and friends, in order to spend their holidays. Pérez Rubio and García García (2005; 95), when referring to rural tourism, used the denomination of "countryman tourist", to define the tourist who visits the autonomous region, local region or area of origin where he or his ancestors come from; but does not reside there. García González, et al., (2008) speaks about *tourism of return* as a typology not contemplated neither in the prevailing conception of tourism nor in official statistics. Other authors like Reyes Morales, et al., (2009; 71) analyze the *nostalgic tourism* as the kind of tourism conformed by the migrants who return periodically from their places of residence to their community of origin for short periods of time. Dominguez Arcos (2011) considers that the better possibilities of mobility and contact enjoyed by the contemporary migrants explain, to a large extent, the development of a new form of tourism known as *tourism of roots* or *nostalgic tourism*, which refers to emigrants, especially economic, who return to the area of origin at certain times to visit their loved ones.

With respect to the general concept of tourism, it refers to the activity of visitors and, in that sense, the World Tourism Organization (2008) regards as visitor any traveler with touristic aims; and it defines a touristic travel as "that realized by a traveler to a destination outside their usual environment for a period of less than twelve months, with any primary purpose (leisure, business, or other personal reasons) other than being employed by an entity resident in the country or place visited". Logically, all visitors, whose main purpose is entertainment or other personal reasons in rural areas can be abstractly considered as tourists, but it is also the main reason of the trip that helps determine if this can be considered a touristic trip. In this sense, the International Recommendations for Tourism Statistics (2008) classifies the tours depending on the main subject referring to nine categories; and among them is that of the main reason for trips *Visits to relatives and friends*. Therefore, we are obliged to believe that the returned visitor which we come to describe as "countryman" goes on a holiday and as such, it must be said that the presence of visitors in these rural towns during holiday dates must be understood as a segment of rural tourism.

Certainly, there exist flows of this type of tourists in Extremadura who stay there particularly during significant holidays such as summer holidays or Easter. The volume of these "tourists" is difficult to quantify due to its mobility and to the type of accommodation (mainly the family house or their own), but it is a demonstrable fact that the increase of rural populations in times of vacation or social and religious celebrations. In certain occasions, the stereotyped image of the rural Extremaduran space is not fully in line with reality. It is clear that not all the rural areas fit into an attractive touristic scenario and many of them are virtually far from this vision, particularly at certain times of the year in which such factors like the weather conditions and lack of resources disarticulate bucolic images of rural areas. Nonetheless, we note that in Extremaduran villages with little chance of promoting tourism, that is to say, with few or no resources to promote rural tourism-related activities, the periodic visits of emigrants and their descendants suppose the generation of additional revenue primarily to the service industry (small businesses, hotels, transport, etc); and to construction (in the adaptation, rehabilitation and construction of houses).

The origin of these processes of return in Extremadura must be found in the flows of emigrants who abandoned the region and settled in industrial centers during the 60's and 70's. The proportion of emigrants who left Extremadura was in relative terms higher than that of other autonomous regions with similar socioeconomic structures. The bulk of the migratory contingent of Extremadura during these years was composed primarily of the young working population from the rural areas. However, following the thesis by Pérez Rubio and García García (2005), our research suggests that the flow of countrymen tourists are not only formed by the Extremadurans who emigrated in the 60's and 70's, and we can approach the different social segments that conform this contingent of visitors harbored in the rural space of Extremadura. We can distinguish three types of visitors within countrymen tourism:

- The visitors who belong to the first generation of emigrants had as main motivation the improvement of their purchasing power. Nowadays, this sort of visitors have accelerated the tendency towards buying homes, with the purpose of avoiding certain obligations by their relatives and also with the hope of returning eventually in a definite way after retirement.
- A second contingent is the conformed by the descendants of the first generation of emigrants. This segment has a less homogeneous profile than the previously mentioned visitor, and they have a very different behavior with regard to the culture of mobility, as well as less commitment to the rural community where they belong. Even though the length of their stays and the number of visits may be more reduced than their predecessors, according to the data exposed by Pérez Rubio and García García (2003) they recur more frequently to catering services, they assist to more cultural events, they visit places different from their places of origins, etc.
- Another contingent is the constituted by those who, having a good academic formation, found better job opportunities in urban centers outside the region. With a higher purchasing power and a major mobility capacity, their behavior coincides in part with the previously mentioned, although their patterns of leisure and free time tend to be more diversified in space and time, that is to say, visits tend to be more itinerant and they use to be surrounded by friends and acquaintances.

According to the last data at our disposal provided by the Spanish Statistic Institute, Census of January 1st, 2010, there are 1,558,656 people in Spain who were born in Extremadura. More than half of them (950,729 people) continue to live in this region, whereas the rest (607,927) are living in municipalities of other parts of the Spanish territories. If we temporally analyze the series of individuals who were born in Extremadura but moved to other autonomous regions, we appreciate how the percentage of Extremaduran emigrants has decreased in the four most populated regions throughout the last ten years, presenting the highest rates of decrease in the country. The rest of autonomous regions mostly present an increase of population born in Extremadura. This can be due, among other reasons, to the phenomenon of returnees, that is to say, the emigrants who return to Extremadura. The profile of these Extremadurans who return would predominantly be that of the "retired", who departed to the most industrialized cities during the 60's and 70's and go back to where they were born in order to enjoy a more relaxed life.

Madrid and Catalonia continue to be the autonomous regions which absorb the largest volume of Extremaduran emigrants. In the Community of Madrid there are more than 219,644 people born in Extremadura, whereas Catalonia has 136,461 people registered in its four provinces. Following these, the most common destinations are Andalusia (with 61,309 Extremadurans) and the Basque Country (58,344), each of the rest of autonomous regions harbor less than a 5% of the total of emigrants from Extremadura.

3. METHODOLOGY

Based on the observed data, the goal of this chapter is to obtain an approximation of the "countrymen" tourists as Extremadurans who return to rural spaces where they come from. In order to approach this segment of the market in rural tourism by means of empiric evidence, it was considered appropriate to carry out a research by conducting a survey on the Extremaduran population of these four communities, which, as we have stated previously, absorb the vast majority of the migrant population of this region. Also, the informants are especially qualified to give knowledge of the characteristics of this touristic typology which can influence the developed future of our peoples.

According to international recommendations for tourism statistics WTO (2008) the surveys, based on a stratified sample which uses spatial, demographic and socioeconomic criteria, can be efficient and adequate tools to measure the internal touristic activity. For this reason, in order to conduct our research and analyze a representative sample, given the difficulties to have a certain knowledge of the number, the distribution and other basic demographic characteristics of the people who, being from Extremadura, reside outside the region, we opted for conducting our research through the application of a survey aimed at the Extremaduran population that resides in the four regions which absorb the vast majority of emigrants from Extremadura (Andalusia, Catalonia, Madrid and the Basque Country). The informants are especially qualified to give knowledge of the characteristics of these two segments of the population which can influence the developed future of our peoples.

After the introduction of the data in the system for their computational analysis, and after the reduction of information by means of the laborious task of coding all variables of each question, we used the computer program SPSS v.15 for the treatment of the information and its statistic analysis.

The survey is aimed at the population who lives outside Extremadura. The information about this universe, in order to obtain the minimal necessary number of interviews to carry out, was obtained from the data offered by the National Institute of Statistics about the number of Extremaduran inhabitants outside the region and their spatial distribution. For the design of the samples we used the information of the municipal Census correspondent to 2010, reaching the level of disaggregation by regions of residence.

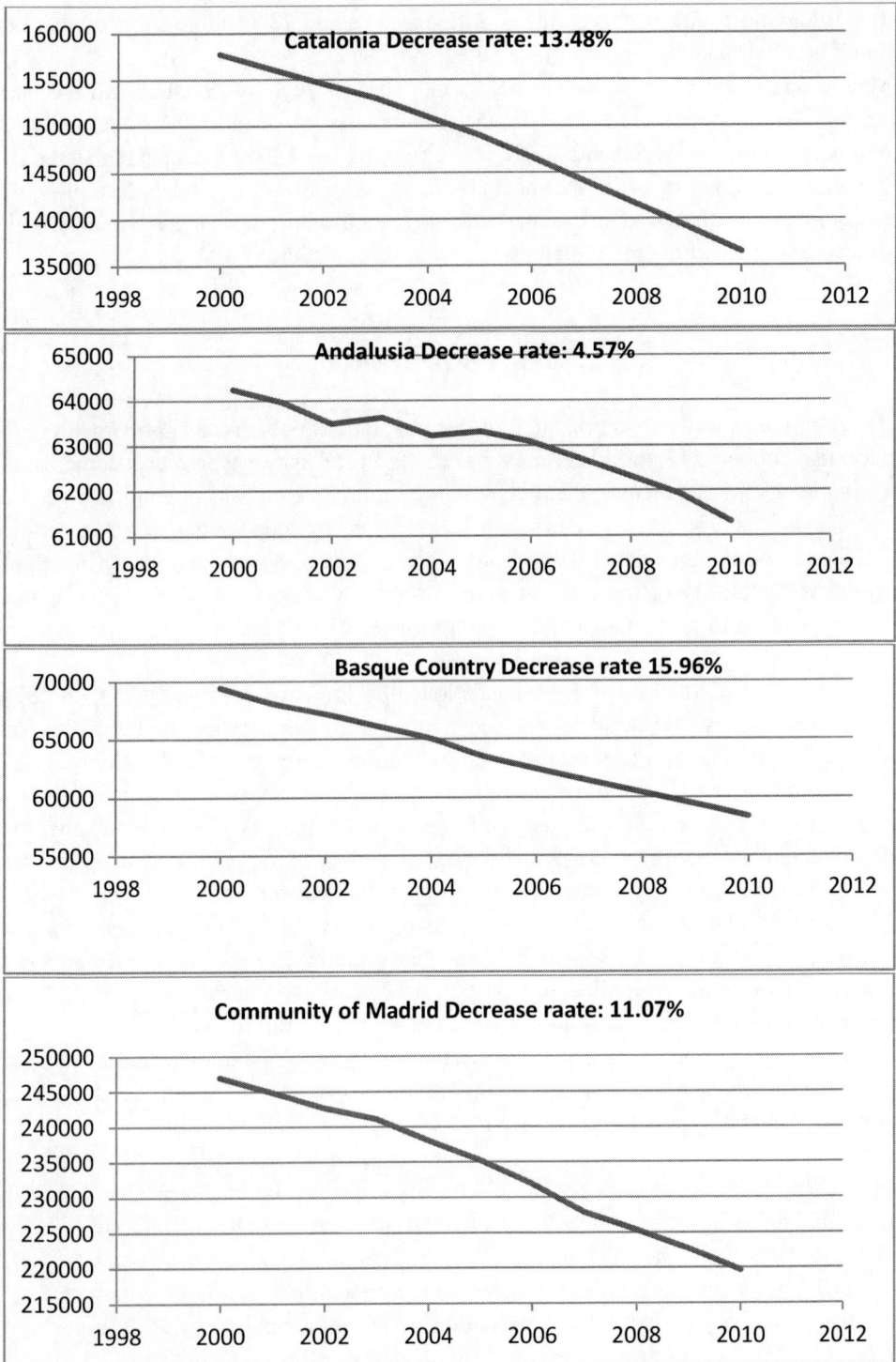

Source: Compiled from data of the National Statistics Institute.

Figure 1. People born in Extremadura who live in other regions (2000-20102010).

The sampling was performed with a selection of the different sampling units in a random way proportional to the number of Extemaduran inhabitants who reside in each of the regions under research. The application of the sampling methodology and proportional allocation was made at a level of reliability of 95%, and the maximum permissible error considered is ±4.5%. The bulk of the designed sample was 474 surveys, although eventually 480 were done. The distribution was determined based on the population percentage by autonomous regions: Andalusía (12.5%), Catalonia (29.17%), Madrid (46.88%) and Basque Country (11.46%). The questionnaires were completed by means of personal interviews between February and June 2010.

4. APPROACH TO THE "COUNTRYMAN" TOURIST PROFILE

In this section we present the most significant results obtained in this field. We will attempt to highlight the main aspects that refer to the returnees, who, responding to the reflections and ideas shown in the previous sections, we have denominated as "countrymen tourists".

The analysis of the obtained results in the developed field research, was carried out based on the three social segments that conform what we know as "countrymen tourism": the group formed by the emigrants of first generation, the group of the generational shift (those who call themselves emigrants and are older than 50 years old), and the group formed by those who emigrated in more recent times (those who consider themselves emigrants and are no older than 50 years old. With respect to the decade in which they abandoned the region, it can be seen that the bulk of interviews was done with those who left Extremadura before the 70's, especially those who departed to Catalonia and the Basque Country. This contingent belongs to the first generation of emigrants, whose main motivation was the improvement of their purchasing power.

Nowadays, this sort of visitors (those who emigrated in prior decades to the 70's) have accelerated the tendency towards acquiring homes, with the object of avoiding family obligations, but also with the hope of returning in a definite way sometime after retirement, something affirmed by a 40% of the emigrants who reside now in Catalonia and the Basque Country, a 34% of those who emigrated to Madrid, and almost a 29% of the Andalusians.

The profile of the countryman tourist is mostly characterized by being older than 55 years old (more than 66.7% of them). It is Madrid that contains the highest percentage of individuals under 35 years old. We assume that this group is mostly formed by the countrymen visitors who have a good academic formation and found better job opportunities in the urban centers in which they studied. In fact, a 75% of these visitors, younger than 35 years old who reside in Andalusia have a college degree, same as a 31% of the Catalonians and a 20% of the Madrilenians. Generally this portion has a higher purchasing power and a better mobility capacity, being their leisure strategies more diversified in space and time, that is to say, their visits are more itinerant and they tend to tend to be surrounded by friends and acquaintances.

One of the most revealing aspects to be mentioned in countrymen tourism is the well defined characterization among these three groups analyzed both with regard to the returnees' level of education as well as their socio-professional activities. Given the lack of research in this respect, we turned to the results provided by our interviews in order to identify the visitors who come from the articulated segments and generated from this process of return.

The visitors who belong to the first generation of emigrants, whose main motivation was the improvement of purchasing power, are mostly pensioners and housewives. Almost a 75% of the countrymen tourists either do not have a formal education or it is very basic.

However, the "countrymen" tourism formed by the descendants of the first generation of emigrant, have a less homogeneous profile with respect to socio-professional activities, predominating skilled workers, service industry workers and middle technicians and employees. We must highlight the large percentage of individuals of this group who studied vocational training (23.6 %) whereas a 20% of them have complete college formation. These characteristics will help understand, as we will see later, the fact that this type of visitors has clearly distinct behavioral patterns during their stay in Extremadura if compared to their ancestors.

The third analyzed group is the one constituted by those who abandoned Extremadura mainly with the object of obtaining a high academic formation and found better job opportunities in urban centers outside the region. They are the interviewed who consider themselves emigrants and abandoned the region after the 70's. This segment of rural tourism shows the percentage of individuals with the highest degree of completed college education, a 34 % of the interviewed. We can consequently see the importance of this group of countrymen tourists, service industry and white collar workers of other industrial sectors. We can affirm that almost a 50% of the visitors have these types of professions. Approximately, a 30% of them work as qualified skilled workers, whereas a 27% and a 13.5% work in administrative positions and the service industry respectively.

This indicates that the "countrymen tourists" have their recruiting base in professional activities linked to the service sector and qualified or semi-qualified positions. The preponderance of these occupations in "countrymen" tourism can be influenced by the better formation of both the emigrants' descendants and the emigrants with higher academic education. The data indicates that nowadays there isn't a relation between the professions linked to those workers who ended up in the industrial sector mainly as unskilled workers, as it happened with the emigrants of the 60's and 70's. This variable has been pointed out in the surveys, that is to say, the existence of a type of tourism formed by the offspring of those emigrants who have different levels of formation as well as different and superior jobs compared to those of their parents.

At this point, we try to describe and analyze this typology of tourists based on aspects which deal with the frequency of the visits to Extremadura and their reasons, the type of accommodation used, the consumption habits (use of catering and cafeteria services), the places chosen for shopping and leisure, their expenses, the days of stay, the degree of satisfaction and finally the evaluative aspects and opinions on the region's rural areas.

With respect to the assiduity with which our informants travel to Extremadura, the data shows that the vast majority of the interviewed people visit the region every year, being just a few who have returned from one to three times. The results confirm that the vast majority of emigrants return to their birth towns and villages every year, and so do the visitors that who make up the generational change who emigrated in the decades of the 60's and 70's. Furthermore, data shows that the distance that separates them from Extremadura does not represent a problem when it comes to travelling to this region. The residents of the most remote regions like the Basque Country and Catalonia declare travelling there every year in a

76 % and 72 % respectively. It is therefore noted that in the Extremaduran towns, even those with little chances of touristic promotion, that is to say, with little or no resources to promote tourism-related activities, there are still frequent and periodic visits by these emigrants and their descendants; who constitute the bulk of what we here denominate "countryman" tourism. With regard to the time of the year most frequently chosen to visit Extremadura, it can be seen that there are diverse patterns of behavior in the analyzed groups. The returnees who form the first group of emigrants and their descendants take advantage of the Easter break, as well as the summer holidays to visit the towns of villages where they grew up. However, the most recent emigrants tend to choose other touristic destinations for their summer holidays.

Moreover, when these emigrants choose to travel to their birthplaces, very few of them do it on their own. The group of emigrants who left in the 60's and 70's choose to travel with their couple or partner. The group that corresponds with those who abandoned the region in more recent times tends to do so with other relatives, friends and acquaintances. Finally, the last group of emigrants who make up the generational shift, show completely different patterns of behavior, as they tend to travel with a group of friends or with the family (more than 3 people).

In general terms, all those who return to their birthplaces do so with the main aim of seeing their relatives and friends. The third goal of their visit is the search for relaxation and tranquility. While meeting their relatives is the most compelling reason for all the emigrants from Extremadura, it is exclusively different in the case of those who live in Madrid, who also point out as their main motivation, "relax and tranquility". In the case of the residents of Madrid and Andalusia, apart from "relax and tranquility" we also consider their will to get into contact with nature, and therefore we come to understand the natural resources of Extremadura as a powerful attraction for a large percentage of these Extremaduran emigrants. On the contrary, the "relatives" factor is the main and almost only reason for the emigrants who reside in the Basque Country.

If we analyze the reasons why these emigrants go on visits depending on the social segments that they belong to, we can see that the patterns of behavior are similar in the three groups under study. As first motivation, we can see the family as the most powerful attraction, followed by their friends. This motivation nourishes the classification which we constantly refer to, the "countryman" tourist whose profile is characterized by the three groups already analyzed. The tourists' profile therefore inclines secondly towards visiting friends and enjoying some relax and tranquility.

With respect to the type of accommodation used when they visit Extremadura, we observe that the patterns of behavior are different in the three groups analyzed. Most of the emigrants of first generation have their own house in this region, whereas their descendants and those who emigrated after the 70's tend to choose the house of their relatives more frequently. The descendants of the first generation of emigrants have a different conduct with regard to the culture of mobility and less commitment with the rural community where they belong, although the length of their stay and the number of visits can be more reduced than those of their ancestors, although, according to the exposed results, it is more frequent for them to use public accommodation.

According to the last published data referred to the year 2010, the average stay in Extremadura in rural touristic accommodation was of 2.34 days. It seems clear that "countryman" tourism generally offers an average length of stay way above any sort of tourism developed in rural areas. 6 out of every 10 "countrymen" tourists affirm that they stay in the region for at least two weeks.

With regard to the frequency with which they visit bars and cafés during their stay in Extremadura, the three analyzed groups show an homogeneous behavior and, therefore, we can affirm that the frequency with which they use these catering services during their stay is high, given that practically half the interviewed people affirm that they use this type of services from time to time, and the other half confirm that they visit bars and cafés daily. The decision of using restaurant services during their visits to their birthplaces or their ancestors' birthplaces show diverse behaviors. Also, we can observe that the "countryman" tourist has a high consumption capacity in the visited place. It is those who emigrated more recently, as well as the visitors who make up the generational shift, that use restaurant services with more assiduity; something logical considering that this group of people stay in their friends' houses and public accommodations. Restaurants, bars and cafés are resources which are used habitually by countrymen tourists, unlike other types of tourists.

Nonetheless, it is clear that the stay in the rural areas where they or their ancestors come from is characterized by a practice of consumption which, on the one hand, helps maintaining the rural economy, and on the other hand, presents different nuances in terms of consumption patterns with respect to other types of tourism, for "countrymen" tourists spend most of their money (accommodation, shopping, catering, leisure) in the towns and areas where they reside during vacation.

"Countryman" tourism undoubtedly shows consumption patterns which differentiate it from any other type of tourism that takes place in rural areas, as an 82 % of the visitors do their shopping in the town or village where they stay. The consumption practiced by these countrymen tourists is one of proximity: purchases are done in "their town", pointing out with this that they shop in the centers where they live or spend their stay (therefore different from the city as they do shopping there with less frequency). This confirms the economic impact that these visits have on the regions' municipalities; focusing on: important expenses on second homes, hotels, catering services, purchases of food and products of daily consumption, etc; and all this in the rural town where they stay. If we add that approximately a 34.5% of "countrymen" tourists of first generation spend an average of 500-1,000 € every time they visit the region, and that a 40% spends more than 1,000 €, we can figure out the economic impact that these visits represent for their places of origin, which are, in most cases, rural centers.

Similarly, "countrymen" tourists tend to stay most of the time in the town or village of visit for leisure. This elevated percentage who declare to stay in the town for fun, is key to detect sources of income different from the traditional in the rural space of Extremadura, which in this case it is its returnees and the expenses they make during their visits. In fact, many of the celebrations of towns which traditionally were celebrated during different time of the year have been moved to traditional holiday time so that the returnees guarantee their success, both because of the influx of more people in town, and the increasing revenue which their visits entail.

It seems clear that "countryman" tourism developed both by the generational shift and those who abandoned the Extremaduran rural spaces more recently, have a different conduct with respect to the mobility culture, given that these two groups manifest that during their stay they use to visit historic places or attend cultural events more frequently than those who belong to the first generation of emigrants, even though the behavioral patterns of the latter are also high in this respect.

The level of satisfaction shown by the "countryman" tourists is elevated. Nonetheless, with the objective of attempting to amplify the information, it seems interesting to recur to the elaboration of an indicator that can synthesize, in a single numeric value, the degree of satisfaction of this segment of rural tourism in their visits. The resulting satisfaction indicator (Si) [1] for the visits conformed by the emigrants of first generation is equal to 0.86 and 0.88 for recent emigrants. The descendants of the first wave of emigrants show a very homogeneous satisfaction indicator with respect to the previous groups with an indicator value of satisfaction of 0.87. We can therefore say that, in general, "countryman" tourists feel very satisfied with their visits to Extremadura, with a 95% of the people manifesting a high level of satisfaction.

"Countrymen" tourists hold a very good opinion of the towns and rural areas of Extremadura. More than a 72% manifests a good or very good opinion of the Extremaduran villages, towns and rural zones. A 40% of the countrymen tourists who emigrated in the 60's and 70's and their descendants have manifested that they wouldn't install again in Extremadura. However, more than a 52% of those who emigrated recently declare that they would actually do so. In all the analyzed groups there are plenty of affirmations that they would install again in Extremadura in case of retirement, although the possibility of finding a job position in this region seems to acquire importance.

The level of their descendants' attachment to the region is considerably high as more than a 72% of them feel a strong attachment to the region. Moreover, the indicator that synthesizes in a single numeric value the degree of attachment by this segment of rural tourism to their ancestors' region (Ai) [2] shows a similar value (0.7165). In addition, the feeling of being Extremaduran reaches percentages above 75% in the analyzed groups of "countrymen" tourists.

CONCLUSION

It results evident that the study of "countryman" tourism is aimed at the visits of those Extremadurans who reside outside the region and return periodically throughout the year. From this group we distinguish those who live outside the region in the 60's and 70's, and those who emigrated in later times. Within the typology of "countryman" tourism, we analyzed a third group constituted by the generational shift of the first emigrants. This group is also part of the visitors whom we also come to denominate "countrymen" tourists.

In conclusion, as a way to finish this piece of work, it must be noted that "countryman" tourism rebels as an important segment to be taken into account and that can certainly contribute to the economic development of rural spaces. We consider this to be a category

---

[1] The construction of the indicator is the following: $Si = [(\%Very\ much \times 4) + (\%Quite \times 3) + (\%Some \times 2) + (\%A\ little \times 1) + (\%None \times 0)]/400$. The indicator varies from 0 to 1, so that the closer to 1, the closer to total satisfaction, and the closer to 0, the closer to total dissatisfaction.

[2] The construction of the indicator is the following: $Ai = \dfrac{\%Very\ much \times 4 + \%Quite \times 3 + \%Some \times 2 + \%A\ little \times 1 + \%None \times 0}{400}$. The indicator varies from 0 to 1, so that the closer to 1, the closer to total satisfaction; and the closer to 0, the closer to total dissatisfaction.

which plays a significant role in the revitalization of rural life, especially in the areas that are far from urban centers. This is because countrymen tourists, in their visits, show consumption practices which, on the one hand, help maintain the rural economy, and on the other hand, present varied patterns in terms of consumption behavior with respect to other kinds of tourism. "Countrymen" tourists stay for an average period which is way higher than any other type of conventional tourist in rural zones. They make most of their expenses (accommodation, shopping, restaurant and entertainment) in the municipality where they spend their vacation, and they are a satisfied sort of tourism, with a great appreciation for the places that they visit and their locals.

REFERENCES

Dominguez Arcos, F. (2011). Los viajeros del siglo XXI: la repercusión del público inmigrante en la industria turística española. *Revista de investigación en turismo y desarrollo loca,*. Vol 4, N° 9.

García González, J.; Cebrián Abellán, F. & Panadero Moya, M. (2008). El turismo de segunda residencia en el interior peninsular. *Scripta Nova. Revista Electrónica de Geografía y Ciencias Sociales.* Vol. XII, núm. 270 (94).

Pérez Rubio, J. & García García, Y. (2005). Turismo Rural en Extremadura. El caso del turismo "paisano" en *Revista Española de Estudios Agrosociales y Pesqueros.* 206, 87-111.

Reyes Morales, R.; Mata Sánchez, N. D.; Gijón-Cruz, A. S.; Cruz Contreras, A. C. & López Platas, S. (2009a). Impacto del turismo nostálgico y las remesas familiares en el desarrollo de la comunidad rural oaxaqueña, *Migración y Desarrollo*, 12, 69-88.

Reyes Morales, R.; Mata Sánchez, N. D.; Gijón-Cruz, A. S.; Cruz Contreras, A. C. & López Platas, S. (2009b). Impactos del turismo nostálgico en una economía con flujos migratorios a los EE.UU., *Migración y Desarrollo*, 12, 1-23.

Volo, S. & Giambalvo, O. (2008). Tourism statistics: methodological imperatives and difficulties. The case of residential tourism in Island communities. *Current Issues in Method and Practice.* 11, 369-380.

World Tourism Organization (WTO) (2008). *International recommendations on tourism statistics.* Department of Social and economic Affairs. Statistics Division. Estudios de métodos Serie M No. 83/Rev.1. Madrid/Nueva York.

Yagüe Perales, R.M. (2002). Rural tourism in Spain, *Annals of Tourism Research*, 29 (4), 1101-1110.

In: Methods and Analysis on Tourism and Environment   ISBN: 978-1-62417-824-5
Editors: J.M.Jiménez, M.V.Vargas, F.J.O.Rosell et al. © 2013 Nova Science Publishers, Inc.

Chapter 11

INTERNATIONAL REGULATION OF THE RIGHT OF ACCESS TO INFORMATION IN ENVIRONMENTAL MATTERS

Alma Patricia Domínguez Alonso
University of Castilla-La Mancha, Spain

ABSTRACT

The right of access to environmental information involves both the right to seek and obtain information held by public authorities, and the right to receive environmentally significant information from those authorities, who should collect it and disseminate it with no need for a prior request. The Aarhus Convention is the chief international instrument in the field, and this paper analyzes its main contents and its application in the European Union.

1. INTRODUCTION. IMPORTANCE AND INTERNATIONAL RECOGNITION OF THE RIGHT OF ACCESS TO ENVIRONMENTAL INFORMATION

A guaranteed and effective public right of access to environmental information and the dissemination of such information contributes vitally to a greater awareness of environmental matters, to more effective public participation in environmental decisions and, in short, to improvement of the environment.

Indeed, access to environmental information plays a key role in involving the public and educating society in environmental matters, constituting a vital instrument for any informed involvement in public affairs (see Various Authors, coord. Magariños, 2009), *Derecho al conocimiento y acceso a la información en las políticas de medio ambiente*. National Institute of Public Administration, Madrid). It has two aspects: the right to seek and obtain information held by public authorities, and the right to receive environmentally significant information from those authorities, who should collect it and disseminate it with no need for a prior request.

Public participation in environmental decision-making, for its part, involves three spheres of public action: the authorization of certain activities, the approval of plans and programs, and the preparation of generally applicable legal or regulatory provisions.

Closely related to the above is the right of access to justice, with the object of ensuring citizens' right of access to the courts in order to obtain a review of decisions that may have impaired their democratic environmental rights.

Citizens' right to seek and obtain environmental information held by public authorities, developed internationally as a general principle in early treaties and summits, especially following major nuclear accidents, was established in the European sphere with the publication of Directive 90/313/EEC of 7 June 1990 (Directive 90/313 was transposed into Spanish law by Law 38/1995, December 12th, on the right of access to information in environmental matters).

Principle 10 of the 1992 Rio Declaration on Environment and Development links the achievement of sustainable development to public participation, access to information and access to justice:

> "Environmental issues are best handled with participation of all concerned citizens, at the relevant level. At the national level, each individual shall have appropriate access to information concerning the environment that is held by public authorities, including information on hazardous materials and activities in their communities, and the opportunity to participate in decision-making processes. States shall facilitate and encourage public awareness and participation by making information widely available. Effective access to judicial and administrative proceedings, including redress and remedy, shall be provided."

It is also worth noting the Sofia Guidelines, endorsed at the Third Ministerial Conference "Environment for Europe" in 1995, on access to environmental information and public participation in environmental decision-making.

After this came the adoption at international level of the United Nations Economic Commission for Europe Convention on Access to Information, Public Participation in Decision-making and Access to Justice in Environmental Matters, in Aarhus on 25 June 1998. The Aarhus Convention recognizes the rights of access to relevant environmental information, of participation in environmental decision-making processes, and of access to justice where such rights are denied.

2. ANALYSIS OF THE AARHUS CONVENTION ON ACCESS TO INFORMATION AND PUBLIC PARTICIPATION IN ENVIRONMENTAL DECISION-MAKING

The Aarhus Convention of 25 June 1998 sets out from the recognition in its Preamble that every person has the right to live in an environment adequate to his or her health and well-being, and the duty, both individually and in association with others, to protect and improve it for the benefit of present and future generations. It links the exercise of this right/duty with the recognition and regulation of three instrumental rights: the right of access to environmental information, the right to take part in decision-making on or affecting the environment, and the right of access to justice.

Thus it states that the public should have access to effective judicial mechanisms so that its legitimate interests are protected, and provisions protecting the environment may be respected. With the recognition and regulation of these three rights it develops the principles and basis of "participatory environmental democracy".

The purpose of the Aarhus Convention, which has, to date, been ratified by 40 countries (see the site http://www.unece.org/env/pp/ratification.htm, checked on 25 October 2011) and by the European Union (Council Decision 2005/370/EC), is to establish a harmonized framework in Europe so that the three rights may be effectively exercised.

Unlike most international environmental conventions, which regulate relations between the signatory countries, the Aarhus Convention recognizes the rights of individuals, and provides a procedural regulation of relations between States and individuals.

Pursuant to the Convention's article 3(5), its provisions will not affect "the right of a Party to maintain or introduce measures providing for broader access to information, more extensive public participation in decision-making and wider access to justice in environmental matters than required by this Convention."

The Convention defines "environmental information" as any information in written, visual, aural, electronic or any other material form concerning:

a) The state of elements of the environment, such as air and atmosphere, water, soil, land, landscape and natural sites, biological diversity and its components, including genetically modified organisms, and the interaction among these elements;

b) Factors, such as substances, energy, noise and radiation, and activities or measures, including administrative measures, environmental agreements, policies, legislation, plans and programs, affecting or likely to affect the elements of the environment, and cost-benefit and other economic analyses and assumptions used in environmental decision-making;

c) The state of human health and safety, conditions of human life, cultural sites and built structures, inasmuch as they are or may be affected by the state of the elements of the environment.

"The public" is defined, also in article 2, providing definitions, as one or more natural or legal persons, and, in accordance with national legislation or practice, their associations, organizations or groups.

"The public concerned" is in turn defined as the public affected or likely to be affected by, or having an interest in, the environmental decision-making. For the purposes of this definition, non-governmental organizations promoting environmental protection and meeting any requirements under national law will be deemed to have an interest.

Regarding access to environmental information, the Convention requires the signatory countries to ensure that their public authorities, in response to a request for environmental information, make such information available to the public, within the framework of national legislation, including, where requested, copies of the actual documentation containing or comprising such information, regardless of whether such documents also include other information:

a) Without an interest having to be stated by the public;
b) In the form requested unless:
    i.   It is reasonable for the public authority to make it available in another form, in which case reasons shall be given for making it available in that form; or
    ii. The information is already publicly available in another form.

Environmental information will be made available as soon as possible and at the latest within one month after a request has been submitted, unless the volume and the complexity of the information justify an extension of this period up to two months after the request. The applicant will be informed of any extension and of the reasons justifying it.

A request for environmental information may be refused if the public authority to which the request is addressed does not hold the environmental information requested; if the request is manifestly unreasonable or formulated in too general a manner; or if it concerns material in the course of completion or internal communications of public authorities where such an exemption is provided for in national law or customary practice, taking into account the public interest served by disclosure.

A request for environmental information may also be refused if the disclosure would adversely affect the confidentiality of proceedings of public authorities, where such confidentiality is provided for under national law; international relations, national defense or public security; the course of justice, the ability of a person to receive a fair trial or the ability of a public authority to conduct an enquiry of a criminal or disciplinary nature; the confidentiality of commercial and industrial information, where such confidentiality is protected by law in order to protect a legitimate economic interest; intellectual property rights; the confidentiality of personal data and/or files relating to a natural person where that person has not consented to the disclosure of the information to the public, where such confidentiality is provided for in national law; the interests of a third party which has supplied the information requested without that party being under or capable of being put under a legal obligation to do so, and where that party does not consent to the release of the material; or the environment to which the information relates, such as the breeding sites of rare species.

However, the aforementioned grounds for refusal are to be interpreted in a restrictive way, taking into account the public interest served by disclosure, and whether the information requested relates to emissions into the environment.

As regards public participation in decisions relating to specific activities, the Convention's article 6 provides that when an environmental decision-making process begins, the public concerned will be informed, either by public notice or individually as appropriate, early in an environmental decision-making procedure, and in an adequate, timely and effective manner,

The information will relate in particular to the proposed activity, including the application on which a decision will be taken; the nature of possible decisions or the draft decision; the public authority responsible for making the decision; the envisaged procedure, including, as and when this information can be provided: the commencement of the procedure; the opportunities for the public to participate; the time and venue of any envisaged public hearing; the public authority from which relevant information can be obtained, and where the relevant information has been deposited for examination by the public; the relevant public authority or any other official body to which comments or questions can be submitted and the time schedule for transmittal of comments or questions; and an indication of what environmental information relevant to the proposed activity is available; and the fact that the activity is subject to a national or transboundary environmental impact assessment procedure.

Public participation procedures will include reasonable time-frames for the different phases, allowing sufficient time for informing the public and for the public to prepare and participate effectively during the environmental decision-making.

It is of the utmost importance that States take measures to provide for early public participation, i.e. when all options and solutions are open and the public may have a real influence.

The signatory countries must require the competent public authorities to give the public concerned access for examination, upon request where so required under national law, free of charge and as soon as it becomes available, to all information relevant to the decision-making that is available at the time of the public participation procedure.

The relevant information will include at least:

a) Description of the site and the physical and technical characteristics of the proposed activity, including an estimate of the expected residues and emissions;
b) Description of the significant effects of the proposed activity on the environment;
c) Description of the measures envisaged to prevent and/or reduce the effects, including emissions;
d) Non-technical summary of the above;
e) Outline of the main alternatives studied by the applicant; and
f) Accordance with national legislation, the main reports and advice issued to the public authority at the time when the public concerned is to be informed.

Procedures for public participation will allow the public to submit, in writing or, as appropriate, at a public hearing or inquiry with the applicant, any comments, information, analyses or opinions that it considers relevant to the proposed activity.

Regarding public participation during the preparation of executive regulations or generally applicable legally binding normative instruments, the Convention requires that States should fix time-frames sufficient for effective participation; publish draft rules or otherwise make them publicly available; and give the public the opportunity to comment, directly or through representative consultative bodies.

3. THE AARHUS CONVENTION'S RATIFICATION AND ENTRY INTO FORCE IN THE EUROPEAN UNION

European Council Decision 2005/370/EC ratified the Aarhus Convention for the European Union, requiring from that moment that EU legislation be made consistent with the Convention's provisions, which are applicable both to Member States and to EU institutions.

Thus to guarantee its application to EU institutions, Regulation 1367/2006 of 6 September was adopted, on the application of the provisions of the Aarhus Convention on Access to Information, Public Participation in Decision-making and Access to Justice in Environmental Matters to Community institutions and bodies. This Regulation amends certain provisions of Regulation 1049/2001 of 30 May regarding public access to European Parliament, Council and Commission documents.

In this same field the European Union adopted its Directive 2003/4/EC of the European Parliament and of the Council of 28 January 2003 on public access to environmental information and repealing Council Directive 90/313/EEC and Directive 2003/35/EC of the European Parliament and of the Council of 26 May 2003 providing for public participation in respect of the drawing up of certain plans and programs relating to the environment and amending, with regard to public participation and access to justice, Directives 85/337/EEC and 96/61/EC.

As precedents to these provisions it is worth noting the Fourth and Fifth Environment Action Programs, incorporating into EU environmental policy the contents of the Rio Declaration's Principle 10.

This was developed, before and after the signing of the Aarhus Convention, by various directives regulating the right of access to information and to participate in certain decisions concerning the environment. These include Directive 85/337/EEC of 27 June on the assessment of the effects of certain public and private projects on the environment, Directive 90/313/EEC of 7 June on the freedom of access to information on the environment, Directive 96/61/EC of 24 September concerning integrated pollution prevention and control, Directive 96/62/EC of 27 September on ambient air quality assessment and management, Directive 2000/60/EC of 23 October establishing a framework for Community action in the field of water policy, and Directive 2001/42/EC of 27 June 2001 on the assessment of the effects of certain plans and programs on the environment.

4. LEGISLATION ON THE RIGHT TO INFORMATION IN MEXICO

Mexico is notable internationally for its advanced legal framework for access by citizens to government information. The Federal Law on Transparency and Access to Governmental Public Information, published in the Federal Official Journal on 11 June 2002, provides quick and simple channels allowing the right of access to information to be exercised freely by any citizen, from wherever he/she may be – over the internet, by post or in person at Liaison Units – and for whatever purpose may be sought.

Article 6 of the Political Constitution of the United Mexican States, amended in 2007, provides that for the exercise of the right of access to information, the Federation, States and Federal District will, in the sphere of their various responsibilities, be governed by the following principles and guidelines:

I.   All information held by any federal, state or municipal authority, entity, body or agency is public and may be withheld temporarily only on grounds of public interest as specified by law. In the interpretation of this right the principle of maximum publicity should prevail.

II.   Information relating to private life and personal data will be protected on the terms and with the exceptions provided by law.

III. Everyone will have free access to public information with no need to demonstrate an interest or to explain what it is to be used for, as well as to his/her personal data or to a rectification of such data.

IV. Timely mechanisms for access to information and review procedures will be established. These procedures will be conducted before specialist and impartial bodies or agencies, autonomous in their operation, management and decisions.

V. Those subject to these requirements should keep their documents in up-to-date administrative archives and will disclose full and up-to-date information in the available electronic media on their management indicators and use of public resources.

VI. Those subject hereto should make public the information regarding public resources to be handed over to natural or legal persons in the way determined by law.

VII. Any infringement of provisions in the field of access to public information will be punishable as provided by law.

The purpose of the Transparency Law, as stated in its article 1, is to provide what is required "to guarantee access for everyone to information held by the various branches of government, autonomous constitutional bodies or bodies with legal autonomy, and any other federal agencies."

All the governmental information to which the Law refers is public, and private individuals will have access to it on the terms provided in the legislation.

The Transparency Law created the Federal Institute for Access to Public Information and Data Protection (IFAI, with the website www.ifai.org.mx/, checked on 7 November 2011) as an independent body with the necessary autonomy and authority to oversee compliance with the law, to review cases in which the authorities deny access to information and to determine if the information requested by individuals is public, reserved or confidential.

According to article 37 of the Transparency Law, the IFAI's functions are interpreting the Law in the administrative sphere; hearing and resolving upon appeals for review filed by applicants and establishing and reviewing criteria for the classification, declassification and custody of reserved and confidential information; assisting the General National Archive in the preparation and application of criteria for cataloguing and preserving documents, and organizing the files of official agencies and bodies; supervising and, in case of infringement, making recommendations to official agencies and bodies so that the provisions of article 7 may be complied with; guiding and advising individuals regarding requests for access to information; providing technical support to official agencies and bodies in the preparation and implementation of their information programs provided for in article 29(VI); drawing up forms for requests for access to information, and for accessing and rectifying personal data; and providing general guidelines and policies for the handling, maintenance, security and protection of personal data held by official agencies and bodies.

With regard to the environment, back in 1996 the General Law on Ecological Balance and Environmental Protection (LGEEPA) was amended so as to provide for the right of everyone to environmental information.

But since the adoption of the Federal Transparency Law, this latter law is the legal text of reference for access to environmental information.

The portal of the Ministry of the Environment and Natural Resources (SEMARNAT) includes a special section on "Transparency", setting out the applicable legislation in the field. It also has a section on public participation and mechanisms in the environmental field allowing citizens to exercise their right to participation in conditions of equality. These notably include the various civic participation bodies operating in the sector in which civil society is represented, along with public consultations, petitions and class actions. Moreover the comprehensive public information offered by the SEMARNAT site includes annual reports on the state of the environment in Mexico (see http://www.semarnat. gob.mx/informacionambiental/Documents/sniarn/index_informes.html, checked on 6 November 2011).

CONCLUSION

The Aarhus Convention is the chief international instrument about the right of access to environmental information that involves both the right to seek and obtain information held by public authorities, and the right to receive environmentally significant information from those authorities, which should collect it and disseminate it with no need for a prior request.

European Council Decision 2005/370/EC ratified the Aarhus Convention for the European Union, requiring from that moment that EU legislation be made consistent with the Convention's provisions, which are applicable both to Member States and to EU institutions.

Thus to guarantee its application to EU institutions, Regulation 1367/2006 of 6 September was adopted, on the application of the provisions of the Aarhus Convention on Access to Information, Public Participation in Decision-making and Access to Justice in Environmental Matters to Community institutions and bodies.

REFERENCES

Garrido, N. (2008). La participación de los ciudadanos y usuarios en los órganos colegiados del agua, in: *Ciudadanos y usuarios en la gestión del agua*, Pamplona: Thomson-Civitas.

Delgado, F. (2004). *La trasposición de la Directiva Marco de Aguas en España*, *RAP*, 165.

Fanlo, A. (2003). La adaptación de la Administración pública española a la Directiva marco comunitaria del agua, in: *Aplicación en España de la Directiva Europea Marco de Aguas*, Ecoiuris.

Magariños, A. (2009). *Derecho al conocimiento y acceso a la información en las políticas de medio ambiente*. Madrid: National Institute of Public Administration (INAP).

Villanueva, E. (2009). *El ejercicio del acceso a la información pública en México. Una investigación empírica*, Mexico: UNAM Legal Research Institute.

In: Methods and Analysis on Tourism and Environment   ISBN: 978-1-62417-824-5
Editors: J.M.Jiménez, M.V.Vargas, F.J.O.Rosell et al. © 2013 Nova Science Publishers, Inc.

Chapter 12

ENERGY EFFICIENCY OF THE EUROPEAN LISTED HOTELS AND STOCK MARKET VALUE

Esteban Pérez-Calderón, Patricia Milanés-Montero and Javier Ortega Rossell

University of Extremadura, Caceres, Spain

ABSTRACT

For the listed hotels to work with an optimal level of energy efficiency is a double source of value creation. Firstly, the improvement of expenditure increases the operating result and thus the financial benefit; secondly, they achieve social benefit from the environmentally responsible behavior and thus their stakeholder social satisfaction (which ultimately becomes a financial gain on the revaluation of the shares and / or market share).

The present chapter examines whether the shareholders of the European listed hotels during 2003-2007 reward those who obtain higher levels of energy efficiency. The results found no evidence of a positive relationship between share appreciation and higher levels of energy efficiency. Likewise, the shareholders also revalued more to those companies that have chosen a policy of disclosure of information on their performance in energy efficiency as part of its environmental responsibility strategy.

1. INTRODUCTION

Climate change has already been a reality for some years now, being responsible for additional deaths all over the world due to the disasters caused. It also represents a threat in terms of a greater risk of disease, hunger, floods and droughts due to the changes in the different eco-systems that are being provoked. One of the main causes of global warming are CO_2 emissions due to the use of fossil fuels to obtain energy. Thus, one of the topics of the greatest interest that is gaining ground today is that of energy efficiency. There are clear references to the increasingly greater importance placed on efficiently consuming energy on the agendas of international work institutions such as the United Nations, Greenpeace or the

World Trade Organization. In this way, we can manage to reduce CO_2 emissions and actively combat the global warming of our planet (Greenpeace & EREC, 2008; UNWTO, 2008; EEA, 2008).

Large hotel chains are a focus of attention because the services that they provide and the quality standards that they offer require greater consumption of energy, water or different types of fuel. Sustainable tourism is a reality with great influence and it is estimated that there will be increased growth in coming years. It follows that there is an increasing importance in energy efficiency for the tourist sector in general and the hotel sector in particular (UNWTO, 2008).

In this scenario, a listed hotel business has a twofold reason for acting. On one hand, producing a high level of energy efficiency will mean savings in the use of resources, which will have a direct effect on the profit and loss account, and the profit of the financial year. On the other hand, in addition to the positive effect of this higher profit on the willingness of investors when it comes to financing the company, we would have added motivation involved for all of the stakeholders (including investors) related to a group of companies respectful of the environment by managing to provide its services consuming the optimum energy level. This demonstrates its concern about the environmental impact involved in its business in this way.

This chapter analyses the degree of energy efficiency achieved by large listed European hotel corporations, which have greatest interest in these measures. We intend to quantify the percentage of large hotel groups that are working efficiently so as to see to what extent the leading representatives of this sector have in adapting their strategies on matters of energy efficiency to current demands (staff training policies, remodeling of buildings and installations, investments in equipment, production processes, etc.).

Another observation is to ascertain the relationship between the generation of value achieved by the extra valuation realized by the shareholders, which in part is due to the concern that the company has, on one hand, in improving the profit and loss account by controlling costs that involve proper management of energy consumption and, on the other hand, by demonstrating responsible environmental behavior. In this latter case we have found studies that relate the distribution of information about the environment to the share price, but none where it establishes a relationship between the energy saving factor and the valuation that the capital market of the company makes.

We can highlight the following contributions from our chapter. The first one is to study the large listed hotel groups in Europe. Thus, while we can cite an extensive set of literature in which efficiency in hotels located in different regions or any country specifically was analyzed, none has been undertaken dealing with large listed European hotel corporations in an organized securities market. The most recent studies that we can cite that are similar to ours are (Önüt & Soner, 2005; Deng & Burnet, 2000; Deng, 2003; Khemiri & Hassairi, 2005). As can be seen, the preliminary studies do not cover a supra-national zone like Europe or listed companies. The second contribution is that we are focusing on the analysis of the efficiency of energy consumption and not on that obtained in the use of a set of general data inputs such as staff, material, food and drink provisions, financial costs and other costs. The third is that no work has been found that relates the recognition of the capital market to responsible energy consumption.

2. PRODUCTIVE EFFICIENCY
IN THE HOSPITALITY SECTOR AND ITS EFFECTS

There are quite a few studies on productive efficiency in large hotels in the review of the most recent literature. In one of the most cited works, Barros (2004), starting from the point of the estimated costs limit, obtained a very low level of efficiency of 21.6% in a sample of 42 Portuguese guesthouses in the years 1999-2001. In successive works (Barros and Alves, 2004) in a sample of 42 hotels between the years 1999-2001, a study is made of the relationship between efficiency and public or private ownership of the establishments. It concludes that the change in technical efficiency experienced is assessed on the basis of the total efficiency and efficiency of scale. Perrigot et al., (2009) worked with 15 large European hotel chains. The objective of their paper is to analyze efficiency in large French hotel holding companies with regard to their type of ownership: franchise vs. private owners. It turns out that the hotel chains composed of franchises and privately-owned hotels are the ones with greatest technical efficiency.

In the international sphere, above all in the Asian pacific, we have very recent studies such as Wang et al., (2007) that analyze a sample of 66 international hotels in Taiwan for the years 1992-2002. They apply a Stochastic Frontier (SFA)-malmquist Analysis. As data inputs, they used employees cost, restaurant area, number of rooms and other operating costs. As data outputs, they take the number of rooms occupied, income from the restaurant and other operating income. The conclusions that they reach are that local policy acts as a factor that places conditions on the level of efficiency achieved by these companies due to the effect on other operating costs.

Neves & Lourenço (2009) determine the efficient frontier using a sample of 83 hotels throughout the world for the years 2000 to 2002. The data inputs they use for resources used are current assets, net fixed assets, net assets, the costs of goods and services and output data such as total income and EBITDA. The main conclusions that they reach would be: first, efficiency of scale has a greater effect than technical efficiency, and management must pay greater attention to improving the productivity of their businesses. Most of the companies deal with decreases in scale in the period analyzed, perhaps due to their underused capacity since they have certain lower take-up rates.

Hu et al., (2010) worked with a panel of data from 66 international hotel companies in Taiwan between the years 1997-2006. Results highlight the fact that the Taiwanese hotels can improve their consumption by 8.85%. Cost efficiency is seen to be influenced by the environmental factors analyzed, with the most efficient ones being the hotels that form part of a chain as compared to the independents; the number of tourist guides and proximity to international airports.

In reviewing the literature we also find some studies that associate related voluntary patterns of behaviors with environmental measures and profits obtained by these companies (Vidovic and Khanna, 2007; Lyon and Maxwell, 2008; Portney, 2008). More specifically, we have studies that have demonstrated evidence of positive relationships between responsible environmental behavior and the reaction of capital markets (Clarkson et al., 2004; Derwall et al., 2005).

3. ASSUMPTIONS, METHODOLOGY AND DATA

In this chapter, we would like to determine the relationship that is established between the efficient consumption of the different supplies, the dissemination of information in this respect and the recognition made by the shareholders. As a work hypothesis we have:

H1: "Large European hotels with higher indices of dissemination of information regarding energy efficiency are also the ones that attain the highest levels of efficiency."

In principle, it is to be expected that we will find ourselves with a positive relationship between greater transparency and information that is issued publicly and the companies with highest levels of efficiency.

H2: "Shareholders of large European hotels reward the companies with higher levels of energy efficiency."

In this case, we also expect a positive relationship between the valuation of the capital markets and the level of information distributed about measures and commitment to energy efficiency.

To do this we use three types of statistical techniques, the Stochastic Frontier (SFA) Analysis, cluster analysis and lineal regression.

One of the most commonly used models in much of the literature on hotel efficiency is the SFA. This is a parametric and stochastic method, which makes it possible to distinguish the influence of noise and the inefficiency borne by each company analyzed. There have been many investigations since the pioneering work of Farrel (1957) that have used the optimum efficiency frontier. Their proposal is to distinguish between production units with regard to their improved use of technique, technology, administration, geographical location, size, and type of ownership; amongst other factors we have to be able to observe these uses in the review of the literature carried out. The first pieces of work are those from Aigner et al., (1977) and Meeusen and Van den Broeck (1977). We apply SFA in this chapter, with these pieces of work being based on a short cross-sectional sample where all of the variables are quantities. The starting model is represented in the following expression:

$$\boxed{Y_i = f(X_iB) + e_i} \quad i = 1, 2, \ldots n; \tag{1}$$

$$\boxed{\log y_i = \beta_0 + \beta \log x_i + e_i} \quad ; \tag{2}$$

$$\boxed{\log y_i = \beta_i + \beta \log x_i + v_i} \quad ; \tag{3}$$

The subscript i refers to the ith production unit. The variables used in the model relate to what is described below:

- y_i: output obtained;
- x_i: inputs vector consumed;

- β: parameters vector to be estimate;
- β_0: optimal efficiency frontier parameter to be estimate;
- β_i: parameter to i hotel, being $\beta_i = \beta_0 - u_i$;
- e_i: term error, $e_i = v_i - u_i$. This is a random disturbance with a twofold component. The first of these, v_i, sets out the effect of random factors that cannot be controlled by the production units. It is assumed that this is independent with respect to the explanatory variables (x_i) and technical inefficiency (u_i), as well as being symmetrically distributed with zero average and a σ_v^2 constant variance, that is to say $N(0, \sigma_v^2)$.

With respect to the second component, u_i, represents the inefficiency for each production unit in particular. In this case, this likewise involves a random disturbance that takes non-negative values ($u_i \geq 0$) which are symmetrically distributed with zero average and a σ_v^2 constant variance, that is to say $N(0, \sigma_u^2)$. In this case we are also going to assume that u_i is distributed independently and in an identical way with respect to the term v_i.

The production efficient frontier identifies the maximum quantity of product that a particular production unit can obtain or the profits that it has been possible to generate (output) based on a set of consumed resources (input). In this first analysis, we obtain the relative position of each one of the hotel groups with respect to the efficient frontier according to their energy consumption, for every year and for the whole of the study period.

In order to classify the hotels of our sample into homogenous groups according to their characteristics, we use the groups or cluster analysis. In our case, to group the companies together we use the K-measurements non-hierarchical (quick cluster) method. This technique is a useful method for making a division of individuals into k-groups, where this k number must be set on an a priori basis (Ferrán-Arranz, 2001). We aim to check whether the level of information dissemination (nie -variable-) concerning actions of the hotels analyzed on energy management in these periods is associated with those with a higher revaluation of their shares and/or with higher energy efficiency levels, in addition to other factors such as profitability or size.

Lastly, if our first hypothesis is agreed, i.e., the disclosure level of information is related with the efficiency level attained, then we will use a lineal regression model. Therefore, the independent variable is the market revaluation companies and we have some financial variables and the efficiency level as dependent variables. We can ascertain to what extent the energy efficiency obtained by the hotels studied places conditions on the behavior of their shareholders.

This methodology would be framed within what is known as a fundamental analysis that consists of inferring the market value of book securities of the companies, without taking into account the listed prices of its stocks in the capital markets (Bauman, 1996). The Ohlson model (1995) is the model of reference to carry out this type of analysis and, therefore, we apply it in this chapter.

$$\boxed{VM_{it} = f(H_{it-1}) + e_{it}};$$
$$(4)$$

$$\boxed{vm_{it} = \gamma_0 + \gamma\,(vc_{it-1}, o_{it-1}) + e_{it}};$$
$$(5)$$

The subscript i refer to the i-th firm and t to the year. The model variables relate to what is described below:

- vm_{it}: market value;
- γ: parameter vector to be estimated;
- vc_{it-1}: book values vector; o_{it-1}: other information that may be conditioning the value reached by vm_{it-1} (both accounting variables and other information are delayed a year as the market value of a period is updated according to the information provided in the previous period);
- e_{it}: error term.

To realize the study the following functions are defined:

- Production function:

$$\log I_i = \beta_0 + \beta_1 \log(x) + e_i, \tag{6}$$

where: $\log(I_i)$, logarithm of annual revenue (€); $\log(x)$: logarithm of energy consumption (€); e_i: error term with two components, u_i and v_i, as explained in the analysis of the methodology previously.   .

- Linear regression:

$$vmit = \beta 0 + \beta 2 vcit\text{-}1 + \beta 1 rit\text{-}1 + \beta 3 efit\text{-}1 + eit, \tag{7}$$

where: vm_{it}, market to book ratio, equal to the ratio between market value and book value; vc_{it}: book value represented by the shareholders funds, this variable is delayed a year; r_{it}: net income, this variable is delayed a year; ef_{it}: energy efficiency for each hotel (SFA, frontier v.4.1c output), this variable is delayed a year; e_{it}: error term. Except vm and ef, all variables have been deflated using the value of total assets.

The data used in the analysis are provided by the AMADEUS database. The work sample was composed of all hotel companies with the same sector code[1]. The years of study are 2003 through 2007. The resulting data panel comprises 22 large hotel groups throughout Europe with a resulting total of 110 observations.

As regards the variable used, in addition to those detailed above, it would be necessary to consider two indices for dissemination of information. One of these refers to energy efficiency (nie); the other refers to level of dissemination of environmental information (nim). We use both indices in the cluster analysis in order to distinguish companies that publicly demonstrate the commitment to energy and environmental savings, based upon the volume of information issued with respect to these sections. In addition, in order to do the SFA, it would be necessary to consider the entry for other operating costs as a proxy of energy consumption, as we do not have specific details about this piece of data. Under the heading of other

---

[1] The code used in AMADEUS to limit the search is Primary Nace Rev 2 Code = 5510, Hotels and similar accommodation.

operating costs, energy consumption is accounted along with taxes, insurance and other supplies, even though the cost of the different energy sources is very important in these types of companies.

Frontier Tool v.4.0 and the statistical package Stata v.9.0 software was used for data processing and application of different statistical techniques are needed.

4. EMPIRICAL RESULTS

In the cluster analysis, we can clearly check how two groups of companies are obtained. The companies of a larger size, profitability, energy efficiency and the level of dissemination with respect to energy efficiency, are grouped together in the mid-term in one of these. The other group displays opposing characteristics, of a lesser size, profitability, energy efficiency and the level of dissemination with respect to energy efficiency. The valuation made by the market in the medium term for these groupings is very similar, being slightly higher in the second case, as we can see in Table 1. That is to say, in the medium term, the market is clearly not rewarding the companies that are demonstrating greater energy savings and it is concerned with disseminating information about the measures and commitments referring to energy efficiency.

ANOVA shows us how the environmental information level (nim), the energy efficiency information level (nie), the estimated efficiency level (ef) and the total assets (at) are significant. That is to say, that they have been factors that have had an influence on the formation of the groupings, which supports the homogeneity of the characteristics of the hotels in the classification made.

Table 1. K-means Clusters and Anova

	Clusters		ANOVA	
	1	2	F	Sig.
vm	2.23	2.09	.056	.816
nim	.22	1.75	39.568	.000
nie	.08	1.18	59.526	.000
ef ^{2}	.2783	.7270	10.741	.004
at	113417.32	3167267.39	2756.802	.000
roe	.0380	.0992	.428	.520
roi	.0690	.0961	.226	.640

Likewise, having obtained the coefficient of the factors analyzed in the lineal regression concerning the initial data panel, the sole positive and significant variable is the profit of the period, as was expected because this is established in this way by the theoretical model. This relationship is increased if we do the same regression for only the more developed countries that have more consolidated, regulated and internationalized capital markets. We have not obtained significant influence in any of the two previous regressions; between the market value and a higher level of efficiency of the hotels analyzed for the years of study (see Table

---

[2] Estimated technical efficiency from 2003 to 2007. Frontier v.4.1c output.

2). This shows us a lack of evidence about whether the market is taking account of the fact that the company makes an effort to obtain a greater saving in its energy consumption.

It is seen from the efficiency analysis for the years 2003 through 2007, that a very low level of 24.04% efficiency is obtained in the medium term, but we do not find any of the companies analyzed in the optimum energy consumption frontier. In addition, great differences are obtained between the efficiency levels attained by some companies and others, with the hotels of the countries being the ones that obtain greater levels of efficiency.

Table 2. Linear Regressions. Coefficients and Significance of Variables

	Reg. I		Reg. II	
	Coefic.	**P>t**	**Coefic.**	**P>t**
const	-9.048586	0.212	7.389959	0.269
vc	-.2599367	0.822	-1.417863	0.302
r	5.767687	0.058	9.351432	0.006
e	12.15013	0.132	-5.832992	0.417
R^2	.66423602		.80258766	

CONCLUSION

Regarding the results obtained, for the sample of hotels and years analyzed, shareholders do not seem to be rewarding, in an additional manner, those listed European hotels that technically demonstrate a greater degree of efficiency. In addition, neither is there any observation that these shareholders have a clear willingness for the hotels to demonstrate greater attention to disseminating information about indicators, the design of strategies, business lines and commitments concerning energy efficiency. In our opinion, this behavior is causing the following:

- This is a very recent pattern of behavior. From the analysis made we have seen how only some visionary companies, leaders in their sector at the European and international levels, have been concerned for some years with energy efficiency from a twofold perspective of a technical viewpoint and one that meets the satisfaction of stakeholders (not just shareholders).
- Except in very specific cases, the information about energy efficiency is issued without sufficient detail; it is prepared in a subjective way and it is not audited-verified by independent bodies or experts in the interests of these hotels. This would be the main reason for the lack of confidence in capital markets regarding this type of information.
- One big limitation of this chapter may be the variable taken as an approximation about energy consumption, with this detracting from the results, with outstanding work to be done in the future, in doing this same study but with precise or approximate measurements in energy consumption.

We cannot clearly relate the revaluation of the company in the capital markets to its energy efficiency or dissemination of information about its measures and commitments related to the same. What is indeed clear is that those companies with a higher level of efficiency are obtaining a smaller impact on these costs as regards its profit and loss account and, hence, greater profits and levels of profitability. On the other hand, whilst shareholders do not reward these forms of behavior, the stakeholders may do so. Here we are referring to the clients, workers, suppliers, local institutions or society in general, with this assuming a bonus in terms of reputation, image, sales and productivity.

With this chapter, we orientate the companies in such a way that they can redirect their energy consumption policies by investing in new technologies, the adaptation of their installations, work routines or the training of their personnel. From the stock market perspective, the chapter does not provide results that show evidence of an increase in the revaluation of the shares as the best indices of efficiency or with these forms of behavior. It is foreseeable that in the very near future this stakeholder (shareholder), to a large extent, will be more sensitive to these forms of behavior and reward them.

Our chapter can also be used for European institutions and bodies to control to what extent the large European countries, leaders in the sector and a reference point for the rest, use the designed agenda. Therefore, they can control how the proposals made are having an effect, and in what way it will be necessary to redesign or modify the strategic plan for energy efficiency in hotels.

REFERENCES

Aigner, D. J.; Lovell, C. A. K & Schmidt (1977): Formulation and estimation of stochastic frontier production function models. *Journal of Econometrics*, 6, 21-37.

Barros, C. P. (2004). A stochastic cost frontier in the Portuguese hotel industry. *Tourism Economics* 10, 99-120.

Barros, C. P. & Alves, P. (2004). Productivity in tourism industry. *International Advances in Economic Research* 10, 215-225.

Bauman, M. P. (1996). A review of fundamental analysis research in accounting. *Journal of Accounting Literature*, 15, 1-33.

Clarkson, P. M.; Li,Y. & Richardson, G. D. (2004). The market valuation of environmental capital expenditures by pulp and paper companies. *The Accounting Review*, 79, 329-353.

Deng, S. (2003). Energy and water uses and their performance explanatory indicators in hotels in Hong Kong. *Energy and Buildings,* 35, 775-784.

Deng, S. & Burnett, J (2000). A study of energy performance of hotel buildings in Hong Kong. *Energy and Buildings,* 31, 7-12.

Derwall, J.; Guenster, N.; Bauer, R. & Koedjijk, K. (2005). The eco-efficiency premium puzzle, *Financial Analysts Journal*, 61(2), 51–63.

European Energy Agency (EEA) (2008). *Energy and environment report 2008.* EEA report nº6/2008. Available from: http://www.eea.europa.eu, accessed 11-11-2009.

Farrel, M. J. (1957). The measurement of productive efficiency. *Journal of the Royal Statistical Society* 120, 253-290.

Ferrán-Arranz, M. (2001). *SPSS para Windows. Análisis estadístico.* McGraw-Hill, Madrid.

Greenpeace & European Renewal Energy Council, EREC (2008). Energy Revolution. A *sustainable global energy outlook*. Available from: http://www.greenpeace.es, accessed 11-11-2009.

Hu, J-L.; Chiu, C-N.; Shieh, H-S & Huang, C-H. (2010). A stochastic cost efficiency analysis of international tourist hotels in Taiwan. *International Journal of Hospitality Management* 29, 99-107.

Khemiri, A. & Hassairi, M. (2005). Development of energy efficiency improvement in the Tunisian hotel sector: a case study. *Renewable Energy, 30*, 903-911.

Lyon, T. & Maxwell, J. (2008). Corporate social responsibility and the environment: a theoretical perspective. *Rev. Environ. Econ. Policy, 2*, 240-260.

Meeusenm, W. & Van den Broeck, J. (1977). Efficiency estimation from Cobb-Douglas production functions with composed error, *International Economic Review*, 18, 435-444.

Neves, J. C. & Lourenço, S. (2009). Using data envelopment analysis to select strategies that improve the performance of hotel companies. *International Journal of Contemporary Hospitality Management 21 (6), 698-712.*

Ohlson, J. A. (1995). Earning, book value and dividends in equity valuation. *Contemporary Accounting Research*, 11, 661-687.

Önüt, S. & Soner, S. (2005). Energy efficiency assessment for the Antalya Region hotels in Turkey. *Energy and Buildings, 38*, 964-971.

Perrigot, R., Cliquet, G, & Piot-Lepetit, I. (2009). Plural from chain and efficiency: insights from the French hotel chains and the DEA methodology. *European Management Journal* 27, 268-280.

Portney, P. R. (2008). The (not so) new corporate social responsibility: an empirical perspective. *Rev. Environ. Econ. Policy, 2*, 261-275.

United Nations of World Tourism Organization, UNWTO (2008*). Climate Change and Tourism: Responding to the Global Challenges*. Available from: http://www.unwto.org, accessed 21.01.2010.

Vidovic, M. & Khanna, N. (2007). Can voluntary pollution prevention programs fulfill their promises. Further evidence from EPA's 33/50 Program. *J. Environ. Econ. Manage*, 53, 180-195.

Wang, Y. H.; Lee, W. F. & Wong, C. C. (2007). Productivity and efficiency analysis of international tourist hotels in Taiwan: an application of the stochastic frontier approach. *Taiwan Economic Review 35, 87-114.*

In: Methods and Analysis on Tourism and Environment   ISBN: 978-1-62417-824-5
Editors: J.M.Jiménez, M.V.Vargas, F.J.O.Rosell et al. © 2013 Nova Science Publishers, Inc.

Chapter 13

CATEGORIES OF EUROPEAN EXCHANGE-LISTED HOTELS ACCORDING TO THEIR LEVEL OF ENVIRONMENTAL INFORMATION DISCLOSURE

Patricia Milanés-Montero, Esteban Pérez-Calderón and María Luisa Pajuelo-Moreno

University of Extremadura, Badajoz, Spain

ABSTRACT

There is not a specific accounting regulation that allows recognizing, measuring and disclosing comparable information in the Annual Accounts about the commitment they have made, in spite of accounting this information could be an important means of evaluating the environmental behavior of the hotel chains. In addition to it, though the disclosure of environmental information by companies has been the subject of many studies (Zeghal & Ahmed, 1990, Deegan & Gordon, 1996, Hackston & Milne, 1996; Archel & Lizarraga, 2001, etc.), most of these have confined themselves to analyzing annual reports in a single country. Only a few studies have made comparisons between companies across various European countries (Aranguren & Ochoa, 2008). Due to this situation, this chapter provides empirical evidence on environmental information disclosure by the main European exchange-listed hotel chains in the European Union countries and it finds Exchange-listed hotels.

1. INTRODUCTION

Most of the published studies in relation with the disclosure of environmental information by companies have confined themselves to analyzing annual reports in a single country. Only a few of them have made comparisons between companies across various European countries (Aranguren & Ochoa, 2008). Castelo & Delgado (2009) analyzed research in southern Europe, noting that the volume of research published is equally distributed between empirical and theoretical studies. The empirical research shows a slight qualitative bias and most empirical studies relate to the researchers' country of origin. Accordingly there is a need to contribute to research on social and environmental accounting in the countries of southern Europe and to widen its geographic scope.

Table 1. Cluster analysis and tables of frequencies (variable: country);
ANOVA (Cluster Analysis)

VARIABLES	F	Sig.
	Media cuadrática	gl
A1_ISO 14000	.	.
A2_EMAS	.	.
B1_INFORMA WEB	15.942	.000
C1_NO DOCUM	74.379	.000
C2_CCAA	.	.
C3_MEMORIA	.	.
C4_INF SEPAR	483.280	.000
D1_INF CUALIT	.	.
D2_INF CUANT	.	.
D3_INF POSIT	.	.
D4_INF NEGAT	.	.
E1_RECURSOS	141.913	.000
E2_EMISIONES	174.207	.000
E3_ENERGIA	141.913	.000
E4_PRODUCTOS	248.657	.000
E5_GS E INVERS	483.280	.000
E6_OTRA INF	483.280	.000
F1_N° PAGS	96209.388	.000

Moreover the existing literature on environmental accounting in the hotel trade is very limited (Chung & Parker, 2009), so there is a significant gap in research to be filled on the combined fields of social and environmental accounting and management, financial control and hotel management, in line with the Global Reporting Initiative (GRI) proposal, based on the economic, social and environmental "triple bottom line" approach.

Given this need and the utility of having specific accounting standards for disclosure by companies of environmentally responsible actions, this chapter provides empirical evidence on environmental information disclosure by the main European exchange-listed hotel chains in EU countries. Our analysis focuses on the population of exchange-listed hotels owned within the EU registered in the Amadeus database in 2007, to avoid any effects of the economic crisis on these firms' net worth and results or even on their environmental behavior (See Table 1).

2. PREVIOUS STUDIES IN RELATION WITH THE DISCLOSURE OF ENVIRONMENTAL INFORMATION

Most of the literature on social and environmental accounting has focused on companies' social and environmental reporting (Russell & Thomson, 2009), given the lack of consideration of social costs and benefits in their financial statements. This result is a not wholly accurate representation of companies' economic reality, and the main problem in accounting for environmental measures affecting that economic reality is their monetary *valuation*, i.e. monetizing social costs and environment-related benefits for which there is no market benchmark.

Final cluster centers

VARIABLES	Conglomerado				
	1	2	3	4	5
A1_ISO 14000	2	1	2	1	2
A2_EMAS	2	1	2	2	2
B1_INFORMA WEB	1	1	1	1	2
C1_NO DOCUM	2	2	2	2	0
C2_CCAA	2	2	2	2	0
C3_MEMORIA	1	1	1	1	0
C4_INF SEPAR	1	1	2	1	0
D1_INF CUALIT	1	1	1	1	0
D2_INF CUANT	1	1	2	1	0
D3_INF POSIT	1	1	1	1	0
D4_INF NEGAT	1	1	2	1	0
E1_RECURSOS	1	1	2	1	0
E2_EMISIONES	1	1	2	1	0
E3_ENERGIA	1	1	2	1	0
E4_PRODUCTOS	1	1	2	1	0
E5_GS E INVERS	1	1	2	1	0
E6_OTRA INF	1	1	2	1	0
F1_N° PAGS	38	176	1	134	0

Frequencies: Aa_PAIS (Cluster C1)

		Frequency	Percentage	Valid Percentage	Accumul. Percentage
Country	Spain	2	66.7	66.7	66.7
	UK	1	33.3	33.3	100.0
	Total	3	100.0	100.0	

Frequencies: Aa_PAIS (Cluster C2)

		Frequency	Percentage	Valid Percentage	Accumul. Percentage
Country	France	2	25.0	25.0	25.0
	Romania	1	12.5	12.5	37.5
	UK	5	62.5	62.5	100.0
	Total	8	100.0	100.0	

Little research work has involved comparative studies between countries, and what work there has been, focuses on comparisons between European countries (Aranguren & Ochoa, 2008), especially Germany and the UK (Roberts, 1991; Adams & Frost, 2006, Hibbitt, 2003). These studies demonstrate the existence of significant differences in the degree and nature of information supplied on social responsibility across companies in the various countries, even among those belonging to the same sector.

In particular, Aranguren & Ochoa (2008) analyze environmental information disclosure practices, among other aspects, of Spanish firms listed on the Ibex35 and of German ones listed on the Dax30. Using a disclosure index constructed on the basis of the content of annual reports and other annual reporting used by companies to publicize their socially responsible behavior, the authors conclude that German companies have a higher disclosure index than Spanish ones.

There are two approaches in research on environmental accounting (Ball, 2004):

- The *conventional* approach, which explores its potential as a meeting point between the organization and society, allowing the former to show or justify the transparency of its processes in response to *external* pressure (Gray, 2002, Neu et al., 1998). Indeed, a tendency is appreciable in research on the disclosure of environmental information to demonstrate that the voluntary nature of such disclosures is a strategy intended to legitimate corporate activities in the eyes of the community (Lehman, G., 2004; Hopwood, 2009). Accordingly it might be argued that management regards annual reports as a publicity device to counter the adverse perception that some sectors of society have of modern-day business (Neu et al., 1998). This may be seen in the study by Husillos (2007), who, after applying content analysis methodology to analyze the environmental information disclosed on financial statements by companies listed between 1997 and 1999 for continuous trading on the Madrid stock exchange, concludes that those companies released environmental information to influence society's perception of them, and that the information was sharply biased to suit the companies' interests. According to Hopwood (2009), some forms of reporting may be skillfully used to show little information on the company, despite the reports' apparent openness. Hence the urgent need to research the field.
- The *current* stance, backed by just a few studies, regards environmental accounting from an internal organizational perspective, i.e. as a tool for capturing aspects of *internal* policy processes as a reaction by the organization to external demands (Larrinaga & Bebbington, 2001).

Moreover a widespread trend is observable (Llull, 2004) towards firms putting environmental contents in an *ad hoc* report in which, rather than providing quantitative data, the narrative part is used to give a view of the company justifying its actions (KPMG, 1993; Giner, 1992; Moneva & Llena, 1996; Peyró, 1997; Ripoll & Crespo, 1998; Archel & Lizarraga, 2000; Harte & Owen, 1991; Roberts, 1991; Niskala & Pretes, 1995; Deegan & Rankin, 1996; De Beelde & Willequet, 2000), which makes comparisons difficult. Negative aspects are rarely mentioned. The author attributes this state of affairs to the lack of compulsory accounting standards relating to environmental information, validated by independent experts. Moreover, though companies that do not supply environmental information remain in the majority, their number has gradually fallen in recent years. Those that do report, do so not in their annual accounts but in their directors' report and the annual report in which they provide general data on the company's business.

In this same regard, Russell & Thomson (2009) argue that most of the literature on social and environmental accounting focuses on companies' external social and environmental reports (Thomson, 2007) on a basis of on political economics theory (Putxi, 1991) and stakeholder theory (Owen & Swift, 2001). Deniz (2007) attributes this fact to the plethora of information required to give an overview of a company's environmental performance that is not contained in the annual accounts and which may directly or indirectly affect its net worth (emission and discharge figures, energy, water and materials consumption, strategic resources, certain biological and biochemical indicators, general principles and programs). The Global Reporting Initiative proposal is the chief and best-known one in relation to these alternative forms of reporting of environmental information, such as environmental reports and sustainability reports.

Moneva & Hernández (2007) analyze the degree to which corporate social responsibility (CSR) practices are incorporated in the management of small and medium-sized firms through an analysis of sustainability information in reports made in accordance with the Global Reporting Initiative (GRI) principles. They also determine their forms of accountability to stakeholders. Their findings show that information is insufficiently developed, and geared more to environmental practices than to economic and social issues.

Llena (1999) defines an indicator of accounting function relevance as the sum, for each firm surveyed, of values corresponding to a series of variables including calculation of environmental costs and margins, accounting records for environmental items, disclosure of environmental information, publication of economic/financial environmental information, and separate reporting of environmental financial items, *inter alia*.

Despite the scarcity of literature relating to environmental accounting in the hotel trade (Chung & Parker, 2009), there are a few studies on the issue, such as that by Llull (2004), who analyzes the annual accounts and reports of tourist accommodation providers in the Balearic Islands, and in particular their annual accounts, directors' report, chairman's report or letter to shareholders and general information on the company, and finds that they do not include significant information in their annual accounts and that those which do disclose some information do so in their annual reports and in very small quantities. More specifically: a) in the annual accounts and directors' reports deposited at the register of companies there is not one reference to environmental aspects by any of the firms analyzed; b) the only references to the environment found appear in the chairman's letter to shareholders, or in other sections of the annual report; c) in no case is quantitative information offered, and what is generally highlighted are the awards and distinctions received.

3. DESIGN OF THE VARIABLES TO MEASURE THE LEVEL OF DISCLOSURE OF ENVIRONMENTAL INFORMATION

In conceiving the variables to measure the level of disclosure of environmental accounting information by our population of European exchange-listed hotels we took account of the classification scheme devised by Aranguren & Ochoa (2008) on the basis of classic social and environmental disclosure studies, the disclosure index devised by Archel &

Lizarraga (2001), the initiatives of various international bodies (the European Union, OECD, Global Compact and, in particular, the GRI), and the classification scheme of the social responsibility rating agency Sustainable Investment Research International Company (SiRi), an international organization that analyzes the social and environmental activities of firms on the world's main financial markets.

The variables in our analysis are devoted to aspects of the disclosure of environmental accounting information; variables relating to the following are included:

A. The firm's undertaking of a certified environmental commitment:

Variables	Values	Conding
A1. Procurement of ISO 14000 certificates. Prizes and awards	Yes/No	1/2
A2. EMAS certification. Preparation of environmental reports. Verification	Yes/No	1/2

B. (General) economic/financial information disclosed on the Internet:

Variables	Values	Conding
B1. Reporting on corporate website	Yes/No	1/2

C   The document used to disclose environmental information:

Variables	Values	Conding
C1. No reporting in any document	Yes/No	1/2
C2. Reporting in annual accounts (on environmental investments, spending and provisions	Yes/No	1/2
C3. Reporting in notes to the accounts, tables or other documents (chairman's letter to shareholders, etc.)	Yes/No	1/2
C4. Reporting in a separate report (sustainability report, corporate governance, etc.)	Yes/No	1/2

D. Characteristics of the environmental information disclosed:

Variables	Values	Conding
D1. Qualitative information	Yes/No	1/2
D2. Quantitative information	Yes/No	1/2
D3. Positive information (environmental achievements)	Yes/No	1/2
D4. Negative information (environmental impacts)	Yes/No	1/2

E. Content of the environmental information supplied (Aranguren & Ochoa, 2008):

Variables	Values	Conding
E1. Resource consumption and conservation (commodities, water, recycled water)	Yes/No	1/2
E2. Emissions, discharges, waste and impact on ecosystems	Yes/No	1/2
E3. Energy	Yes/No	1/2
E4. Products	Yes/No	1/2
E5. Environmental spending and investment	Yes/No	1/2
E6. Other information	Yes/No	1/2

F.   The volume of environmental information disclosed (quantity):

Variables	Values	Conding
F1. Number of pages	0	0
	1	1
	2	2
	3	3
	38	38
	134	134
	176	176

All these variables are expressed in dichotomous terms (Y_i will be = 1 where the aspect appears in the accounting information and = 2 where it does not appear).

The statistical techniques applied to the data, using the statistics program SPSS version 15.0, after recoding of qualitative variables, separation of quantitative one (number of pages) on a quartile basis and analysis of the correlations between the study variables using Pearson's linear correlation coefficient, was cluster analysis (Ward's agglomerative hierarchical method and the non-hierarchical K-means (quick cluster method), so as to seek to identify various levels of environmental information disclosure across European exchange-listed hotels.

The analytical methodology used to obtain the values of these variables was content analysis, consisting of sorting the information disclosed in annual reports into various sets of aspects covering the environmental issues to be analyzed (Archel & Lizarraga, 2001; Husillos, 2007; Krippendorf, 1990). In particular we analyzed the content of all the information supplied on the corporate websites (Adam & Frost, 2006) of the hotels in the population, i.e. their annual accounts, directors' report, annual report, chairman's letter (Archel & Lizarraga, 2001) and sustainability or corporate governance report, as applicable (Aranguren & Ochoa, 2008; Buhr & Freedman, 1996; Hibbitt, 2003).

Frequencies: Aa_PAIS (Cluster C3)

		Frequencies	Percentage	Valid Percentage	Accumul. Percentage
Area	Bulgaria	1	1.7	1.7	1.7
	Cyprus	5	8.6	8.6	10.3
	France	4	6.9	6.9	17.2
	Greece	4	6.9	6.9	24.1
	Hungary	1	1.7	1.7	25.9
	Poland	1	1.7	1.7	27.6
	Portugal	1	1.7	1.7	29.3
	Romania	38	65.5	65.5	94.8
	Ukraine	1	1.7	1.7	96.6
	United Kingdom	2	3.4	3.4	100.0
	Total	58	100.0	100.0	

Table 1. Categories of European exchange-listed hotels identified according to their level of environmental information disclosure

Categories of hotels	Hotels with a high disclosure level (C1)	Hotels with a medium disclosure level (C2)	Hotels with a zero disclosure level (C3)
Hotels included	Nh Hoteles Sol Melia Intercontinental HG Whitbread	Intercontinental HG Millenium&Copthorne Mwb Group Holdings THR Marea Neagra Les Hotels De Paris Lonrho Catering Int Services HydroHotel Eastbourne	Rest of the hotels in the population. most of them: 58 (See Table 1)
Document used to disclose environmental information	Notes or tables to their annual accounts and, in particular, in an EMAS-type sustainability report	Only in the notes or tables to their annual accounts	-
Characteristics of information disclosed	-The information supplied concerns the consumption and conservation of resources, emissions, discharges and impacts on ecosystems, energy and environmental spending, among other aspects -All these hotels report more qualitative than quantitative information, and more positive than negative information	They provide only generic qualitative data on their good intention	-
Volume of information disclosed	It is the cluster that discloses most information, measured by the number of pages	They report very briefly, in less than one page	-

4. CATEGORIES OF EUROPEAN EXCHANGE-LISTED HOTELS IDENTIFIED ACCORDING TO THEIR LEVEL OF ENVIRONMENTAL INFORMATION DISCLOSURE

The results of cluster analysis on the information supplied in the dendrogram show the existence of five clusters or different behaviors across the population of 69 European exchange-listed hotels forming the study population. The variables that proved to be significant, and, therefore, differentiating features of these five clusters (See Table 1) were B1 (Disclosure or otherwise of general economic/financial information on the internet), C4 (Disclosure of environmental information in a separate report: sustainability report, corporate governance, etc.), E1-E6 (Content of environmental information disclosed: resources, emissions, energy, products, spending and investment, other information) and F1 (Volume of information disclosed, measured in number of pages). Given the similarity between the values of the reporting variables in clusters 1, 2 and 4, each consisting of a single hotel, we opted to group these three clusters in a single one (C1: 1, 2, 4).

So we may conclude that among the European exchange-listed hotels registered in Amadeus, i.e. those forming our population, three categories or clusters may be distinguished according to their level of environmental information disclosure on the Internet: high (C1), medium (C2) and low (C3), made up of 3, 8 and 58 hotels respectively. If we focus on the variables that are significant in the sets, the main differences between the clusters are shown in Table 1:

CONCLUSION

To conclude, it is worth noting that the behavior of the population of European exchange-listed hotels analyzed as to the disclosure of information on their environmental commitment largely coincides with the microeconomic scenario outlined by Llull (2004). This author also distinguishes between:

a) Firms that present no environmental information, a practice most often due to the virtual non-existence of accounting standards in the field and to the fact that the environmental impact of their business activities is negative, among other aspects;

b) Firms which report information in their notes or annexes to their traditional annual accounts or in other separate documents on the environment (an option characteristic of firms with major impacts), either because they are sensitive to demand from society for this type of information, or because they want to take advantage of the environmental variable as an instrument of marketing policy to improve their company's public image, or because they believe that by supplying additional voluntary information they can anticipate standards and thereby influence them or pre-empt them.

As to the characteristics and volume of the information disclosed, our results coincide with those obtained by the Intergovernmental Working Group of Experts on International Standards of Accounting and Reporting (ISAR, United Nations). This institution, following a survey on more than 200 multinational firms belonging to various sectors, not including the tourism industry, found that the environmental information supplied by companies is in most cases qualitative rather than quantitative and refers to environmental achievements rather than to negative impacts on the environment.

The results obtained, though they have the primary limitation of having only statistical validity, corroborate the conclusions offered by the prior literature as to the absence in hotels' annual accounts of economic and financial information of an environmental nature, impeding a representation of those firms' economic reality.

REFERENCES

Adams, C. A. & Frost, G. R. (2006). Accessibility and functionality of the corporate web site: implications for sustainability reporting. *Business Strategy and the Environment*, 15(4), 275-287.

Aranguren, N. & Ochoa, E. (2008). Divulgación de información sobre empleados y medioambiente en España y Alemania: una nota de investigación. *Revista de Contabilidad*, 11(2), 123-142.

Archel, P. & Lizarraga, F. (2000). La divulgación de información medioambiental en España: evolución de la misma en el período 1995- 1998. *Comunicación presentada al IX Encuentro de Profesores Universitarios de Contabilidad*, 259-271. Las Palmas de Gran Canaria.

Archel, P. & Lizarraga, F. (2001). Algunos determinantes de la información medioambiental divulgada por las empresas españolas cotizadas. *Revista de Contabilidad-Spanish Accounting Review*, 44(7), 129-153.

Ball, A. (2004). A sustainability accounting project for the local government sector? Testing the social theory mapping process and locating a frame of reference. *Critical Perspectives on Accounting*, 15, 1009-1035.

Buhr, N. & Freedman, M. (1996). A comparison of mandated and voluntary environmental disclosures. *Critical perspectives on Accounting Conference*, New York.

Castelo, M. & Delgado, C. (2009). Research on social and environmental accounting in Southern European countries. *Revista Española de Financiación y Contabilidad*, 144, 663-675.

Chung, L. H. & Parker, L. D. (2009).: Managing social and environmental action and accountability in the hospitality industry: A Singapore perspective. *Accounting Forum*, doi: 10.1016/j.accfor.2009.10.003.

de Beelde, I. & Willequet, E. (2000). External environmental reports: comparing practices in european countries. *XXIII Annual Congress of European Accounting Association*. Munich.

Deegan, C. & Gordon, B. (1996). A study of the environmental disclosure practices of Australian corporations. *Accounting and Business Research*, 26(3), 187-199.

Deniz, J. J. (2007). La regulación de la información contable medioambiental en España. La Resolución del Instituto de Contabilidad y Auditoría de Cuentas de 25 de marzo de 2002. *Contaduría y Administración*, 221, 163-192.

Giner, B. (1992). La responsabilidad social de la empresa: la información medioambiental. *Técnica Contable*, 527, 681-692.

Gray, R. (2002). The social accounting project and Accounting, Organizations and Society: privileging engagement, imaginings, new accountings and pragmatism over critique. *Accounting, Organizations and Society*, 27(7), 687-708.

Hackston, D. & Milne, J. J. (1996). Some determinants of social and environmental disclosures in New Zealand companies. *Accounting, Auditing and Accountability Journal*, 9(1), 77-108.

Harte, G. & Owen, D. (1991). Environmental disclosure in the annual reports of British companies: a research note. *Accounting, Auditing and Accountability Journal*, vol. 4, n° 3.

Hibbitt, C. (2003). *External environmental disclosure and reporting by large European companies. An economic, social and political analysis of managerial behaviour*. Tesis Doctoral. Limperg Instituut.

Hopwood, A. G. (2009). Accounting and the environment. *Accounting, Organizations and Society*, 34, 433-439.

Husillos, F. J. (2007). An approach to the environmental disclosures of the listed Spanish firms form the legitimacy theory. *Revista Española de Financiación y Contabilidad*, 133, 97-121.

Kippendorf, K (1990). *Metodología de análisis de contenido: teoría y práctica*. Paidos. Barcelona.

KPMG (1993). *KPMG International Survey of Environmental Reporting*. KPMG Peat Marwick. Thorne.

Larrinaga, C. & Bebbington, J. (2001). Accounting change or institutional appropiation? A case study of the implementation of environmental accounting. *Critical Perspectives on Accounting*, 12, 269-92.

Lehman, G. (2004). Social and environmental accounting. Trends and thoughts for the future. *Accounting Forum*, 28, 1-5.

Llena, F. (1999). *La contabilidad en la interacción empresa-medio ambiente: su contribución a la gestión medioambiental*. Tesis Doctoral no publicada, Universidad de Zaragoza.

Llull, A. (2004). *Contabilidad medioambiental y desarrollo sostenible en el sector turístico. Tesis Doctoral*. Universitat de les Illes Balears. Illes Balears.

Moneva, J. M. & Llena, F. (1996). Análisis de la información sobre responsabilidad social en las empresas industriales que cotizan en bolsa. *Revista Española de Financiación y Contabilidad*, 87, 361-401.

Neu, D.; Warsame, H.; Pedwell, K. (1998). Managing public impressions: environmental disclosures in annual reports. *Accounting, Organizations and Society*, 23(3), 265-82.

Niskala, M. & Pretes, M. (1995). Environmental reporting in Finland: a note on use of annual reports. *Accounting, Organizations and Society*, 17, 595-612.

Owen, D.L. & T. A. Swift (2001). Social accounting, reporting and auditing: Beyond the rhetoric?, *Business Ethics: A European Review* 10(1), 4-8.

Peyró, E. (1997). *Información social y ambiental en España: Un estudio empírico*. IX Congreso de AECA, 681-703. Salamanca.

Ripoll, V. M. & Crespo, C. (1998). Costes derivados de la gestión medioambiental. *Técnica Contable*, 591, 169-180.

Roberts, C. B. (1991). Environmental disclosures: a note on reporting practices in mainland Europe. Accounting, *Auditing and Accountability Journal*, 3(4), 62-71.

Russell, S. & Thomson, I. (2009). Analysing the role of sustainable development indicators in accounting for and constructing a Sustainable Scotland. *Accounting Forum*, 33, 225-244.

Thomson, I. (2007). Accounting and Sustainability: Mapping the Terrain. *Sustainability Accounting and Accountability*. In Russell, S.; Thomson, I. (2009). Analysing the role of sustainable development indicators in accounting for and constructing a Sustainable Scotland. *Accounting Forum*, 33, 225-244.

Zeghal, D. & Ahmed, (1990). Comparison of social responsibility information disclosure media used by Canadian firms. *Accounting, Auditing and Accountability Journal*, 3(1), 38-53.

In: Methods and Analysis on Tourism and Environment   ISBN: 978-1-62417-824-5
Editors: J.M.Jiménez, M.V.Vargas, F.J.O.Rosell et al. © 2013 Nova Science Publishers, Inc.

Chapter 14

AN INITIAL APPROACH TO CALCULATION OF THE CARBON FOOTPRINT IN THE LODGING INDUSTRY

Adelaida Ciudad-Gomez

University of Extremadura, Caceres, Spain

ABSTRACT

Environmental indicators are a tool allowing companies to measure the effect their activity has on the environment in which they operate and its progress, as well as to allow both internal and external reporting of their environmental behaviour, and one of these indicators is the *carbon footprint*, a parameter expressed in *equivalent carbon dioxide* tons, and which has become widely publicized in recent years.

However, when it is used by companies, the problem is found that there is no universal consensus over its definition and calculation, preventing comparison between companies.

So until a general consensus is reached, the intention of this chapter is to be an initial proposal for homogenization of calculation of the carbon footprint for companies in the lodging sector, using methods based on suggestions by and contributions from international organizations.

INTRODUCTION

One of the most important environmental indicators, the *carbon footprint*, a parameter used to quantify the effect of the *greenhouse gases* (GHG), has become famous in recent years. According to *Carbon Trust* (2007 b, pp. 10) is defined as *"the total set of greenhouse gas emissions caused by an individual or organisation, event or product. It should be expressed in carbon dioxide equivalent (CO2e)"*.

The carbon footprint, based on the *ecological footprint* of REES and WACHERNAGEL (1996, pp. 160) applied to companies, is a single-index indicator which is an important tool in management of CO_2 emission reduction and the fight against climate change.

But there is no general consensus over its definition nor how it should be calculated, which hampers the comparison of information supplied by companies with regard to their GHG emissions and carbon footprint, even though, in 2007, the ISO, WRI and WBCSD signed a *Memorandum of Understanding* (ISO, 2008, pp. 2) in which they announced their cooperation to promote GHG accounting and reporting standards.

The existing differences are basically caused by two fundamental questions: which gases to include, and scope.

Some studies recommend including emissions of various greenhouse effect gases (Doménech, 2004; POST 2006; Carbon Trust, 2007; European Commission, 2007; ETAP, 2007; BSI, 2008; Perry et al., 2008; Wiedmann, 2009; ADEME, 2007), while others taking only CO_2 into account (BP, 2007; Global Footprint Network, 2007; Wiedmann y Minx, 2008). The former would provide a more complete view, while the other, as WIEDMANN and MINX (2008, pp. 5) point out, would facilitate calculation and is the clearer, more practical solution.

In terms of scope, this can cover direct emissions (Scope 1), indirect emissions from purchased electricity (scope 2), and even indirect emissions from other sources (scope 3), these last being highly ambiguous and discretional.

Therefore, taking into account the fact that the *carbon footprint* is becoming one of the main environmental indicators and that there is no general consensus with regard to its definition and calculation, the purpose of this chapter is to open a debate over the need to develop internationally *agreed* guidelines taking in the existing proposals, defining and delimiting the scope of its calculation and resolving the ambiguity and discretional nature of *scope 3*, presenting an initial approach to it, based on suggestions by and contributions from international organizations.

It adopts simple, easily used methods, so that it can be used by any kind of lodging establishment, regardless of its size or category.

MATERIALS AND METHODS

This chapter has been prepared using the ideas and suggestions of the most important methodological frameworks for carbon footprint calculation, one of which is the *Greenhouse Gas Protocol (GHG Protocol),* an initiative of the *World Resources Institute* (WRI) and *World Business Council for Sustainable Development* (WBCSD), which proposes standards and procedures for quantification and control of GHG emissions, grouped in three fields or spheres (WRI and WBCSD, 2004), as well as a new standard being developed, *"Corporate Value Chain (Scope 3) Accounting and Reporting Standard"*, that will provide a standardized method to inventory the emissions associated with individual products across their full life cycles and of corporate value chains, taking into account impacts both upstream and downstream of the company's operations (WRI and WBCSD, 2010).

The *International Organization for Standardization* is developing another methodological framework: ISO 14064: 2006 contains a set of criteria for GHG accounting and verification compatible with the GHG Protocol (WRI y el WBCSD, 2004); and it is developing another two standards, ISO 14067 *"Carbon footprint of products - Requirements and guidelines for quantification and communication"* and ISO 14069 *"GHG -*

Quantification and reporting of GHG emissions for organizations (Carbonfootprint of organization)".

As well as these standards, other notable regional contributions are the *Bilan Carbone* (ADEME-France, 2007) and the *Publicly Available Specification* 2050 (BSI/ DEFRA/ CarbonTrust-UK, 2008), with specifications on the GFG emissions of products and services, or the new version published in 2010, the *Publicly Available Specification* 2060, aimed at GHG emissions by organizations.

Different methodological frameworks require an international standardization process to encompass the existing proposals. In this direction, in 2007, the ISO, WRI and WBCSD announced their cooperation and signed a *Memorandum of Understanding* (ISO, 2008, pp. 2), to help normalization of accounting and verification of emission data.

Finally, the creation of a standard allowing simultaneous calculation of organizations' carbon footprint and that of its products is desirable (DOMÉNECH, 2004).

RESULTS AND DISCUSSION

Because of the foregoing, we propose hat companies in the lodging sector should include information about their energy consumption, greenhouse gas emissions and, finally, metric tons of carbon dioxide equivalent (CO_{2e}) emitted, which will allow it to accept a commitment to reduce these emissions, as their calculation will allow the sources of emissions of most impact to be detected and emission reduction and savings plans created for the critical points found.

For this purpose, we propose the following methods as an initial step towards calculation of the carbon footprint in the lodging industry, taking Carbon Dioxide (CO_2), Methane (NH_4), Nitrous Oxide (N_2O), Hydrofluorocarbons (HFC) and Perfluorocarbons (PFCs) into account, and including Scope 1 and 2 emissions, but initially excluding Scope 3 emissions, in order to establish, simple, clear, precise presentation rules, in accordance with the Uniform System of Accounts for the Lodging Industry (AHLEI, 2006). Direct emissions (Scope 1) will also be broken down into three types of source: Stationary combustion, Mobile combustion of fuels in transportation and *Fugitive*.

Emission data should be converted into a common measurement, carbon dioxide equivalent CO_2e, expressed in metric tons, which will make comparability of companies easier, but for this purpose we need the Emissions Factor and GWP (Global Warming Potential), published by the Intergovernmental Panel on Climate Change (IPCC, 2007).

Information should be provided about the current year, the previous year and the years corresponding to the base year. As DEFRA recommends (2009, pp. 26), the base year should be the first year for which emission data are available, either as a single year or as an average of several years.

In accordance with the above, there follow the methods we suggest should be adopted by companies in the lodging sector to calculate their greenhouse gas emissions (Scope 1 and Scope 2), as a step towards calculation of the full carbon footprint.

Direct emissions from stationary combustion: For calculation of direct emissions of CO_2, CH_4 and N_2O from stationary combustion, information about the type and amount of fuel used is needed, because emissions to air will depend on the type and amount of power used, being calculated as follows for each type of fuel:

Energy consumption * CO_2 Emissions factors	=	CO_2 emissions * GWP	=	**Stationary CO_2 emissions (MT CO_2e)**
Energy consumption * CH_4 Emissions factors	=	CH_4 emissions * GWP	=	**Stationary CH_4 emissions (MT CO2e)**
Energy consumption * N_2O Emissions factors	=	N_2O emissions * GWP	=	**Stationary N_2O emissions (MT CO2e)**
Total Emissions CO_2e from stationary combustion				

Direct emissions from mobile combustion: For calculation of direct emissions of CO_2, CH_4 and N_2O from mobile combustion, information about the types of vehicle the organization uses, their fuel consumption and the mileage or kilometres travelled for each type of vehicle.

The CO_2 emitted will be calculated from the fuel used and vehicle type and the CH_4 and N_2O will be calculated considering the type of vehicle and mileage or kilometres travelled, the calculation for each vehicle being as follows:

Gasoline usage * CO_2 Emissions factors	=	CO_2 emissions * GWP	=	**Mobile CO_2 emissions (MT CO_2e)**
mileage * CH_4 Emissions factors	=	CH_4 emissions * GWP	=	**Mobile CH_4 emissions (MT CO2e)**
mileage * N_2O Emissions factors	=	N_2O emissions * GWP	=	**Mobile N_2O emissions (MT CO2e)**
Total Emissions CO_2e from mobile combustion				

Direct fugitive emissions from the use of refrigeration and air conditioning equipment: For calculation of hydrofluorocarbon (HFC) and perfluorocarbon (PFC) emissions due to leaks from refrigeration and air conditioning systems, information is needed about the type and number of air conditioning units the organization has, the total refrigerant load, leak rates and types of refrigerant gas used. To do this, the company will have to make an inventory of units and the types of coolant gas used, and record any gas leaks.

The total emissions of each type of coolant due to leakage needs to be calculated, to do which one of these methods can be used: the *screening method, mass balance method* or *simplified mass balance method* (The Climate Registry, 2008, pp. 124-129). The calculation is as follows:

Total Leakage * Emissions factors	=	emissions * GWP	=	**Total refrigerant emissions CO_2e**

Indirect emissions from the electricity use: For calculation of indirect emissions from electricity usage, the annual electricity consumption of the lodging establishment needs to be known, and it is calculated as follows:

Electricity Purchases * CO_2 Emissions factors	=	CO_2 emissions * GWP	=	**Electricity Use CO_2 emissions (MT CO_2e)**
Electricity Purchases * CH_4 Emissions factors	=	CH_4 emissions * GWP	=	**Electricity Use CH_4 emissions (MT CO2e)**
Electricity Purchases * N_2O Emissions factors	=	N_2O emissions * GWP	=	**Electricity Use N_2O emissions (MT CO2e)**
Total Emissions CO_2e from electricity use				

Table 1. Proposed report of the Corporate Carbon Footprint: Scope 1 and Scope 2

Scope / Sources of Emissions	CURRENT YEAR Emissions (T CO2e / year)	%	PRIOR YEAR Emissions (T CO2e / year)	%	BASE YEAR Emissions (T CO2e / year)	%	Change, relative to base period
SCOPE 1 DIRECT GHG EMISSIONS							
Stationary fuel combustion:							
Fugitive Emissions: Stationary Air Conditioning and Refrigeration							
Mobile Fuel Combustion:							
Fugitive emissions: Mobile Air Conditioning.							
TOTAL SCOPE 1 EMISSIONS							
SCOPE 2 INDIRECT EMISSIONS FROM PURCHASED ELECTRICITY							
Purchased Electricity							
TOTAL SCOPE 2 EMISSIONS							
Total Emissions (Scope 1+Scope 2)	100%		100%		100%		

When all the greenhouse gas emissions have been calculated, the next step is to prepare a report distinguishing between direct (scope 1) emissions, indirect emissions caused by electricity used (scope 2) and other indirect emissions (scope 3) when these are included, these being the definitions of the *Greenhouse Gas Protocol Initiative* (GHG Protocol).

Information about emissions is useful, but for comparison of performance between hotels, it is easier to use intensity, calculated by dividing GHG emissions by a normalization factor.

For the normalization factor, THOMAS et al., (2000, pp. 27) points out that *"each industry sector has its own peculiarities and that normalization measures must be sector-sensitive"*, which is why we have included the rooms occupied (11) and total guests (23) defined in the USALI (AHLEI, 2006, p. 191-192), though other metrics such as the area in square feet (or m^2) of building could be included.

We have also included the net operating income (NOI), as this term is replacing *"Income before Interest, Depreciation, Amortization, and Income Taxes"*-(EBITDA), and *revenue*, both exported from the summary operating statement (AHLEI, 2006, pp. 35).

Intensity measurement CO_2e_1	=	Total CO2e (tonnes) produced by the hotel per annum rooms occupied (Total guests)

Intensity measurement CO_2e_2	=	Total CO2e (tonnes) produced by the hotel per annum NOI (EBITDA)

Intensity measurement CO_2e_3	=	Total CO2e (tonnes) produced by the hotel per annum revenue

CONCLUSION

For the *carbon footprint* to be included as an environmental indicator, it is essential that an international process of standardization is undertaken covering existing proposals, defining and delimiting the scope of calculation of the carbon footprint and resolving the ambiguity and discretionality in *scope 3*.

When a general consensus has been reached, the next step will be homogenization of calculation of the carbon footprint by companies in the lodging sector and development of its own measurement system, as well as the development of an internationally accepted carbon calculator specific to the lodging industry, because a host of calculators exists, but their results can vary considerably depending on the calculator used.

REFERENCES

Agence de l'Environnement et de la Maîtrise de l'Energie (ADEME) (2007). *Methodological Guide (Version 5.0): Objectives and Principals for the Counting of Greenhouse Gas Emissions (Bilan Carbone).* French Environment and Energy Management Agency.

Agence de l'Environnement et de la Maîtrise de l'Energie (ADEME) (2010). *Methodology guide (Version 6.1): objectives and accounting principles. (Bilan Carbone).* French Environment and Energy Management Agency.

American Hotel; Lodging Educational Institute (AHLEI) (2006). *Uniform System of Accounts for the Lodging Industry.* Hotel Association of New York City New York City. Lasing, Michigan.

British Petroleum (BP) (2007). ¿*What is a Carbon Footprint?.*

British Standards Institute (BSI); Department for Environment, Food and Rural Affairs (DEFRA); Carbon Trust (2008). *PAS 2050. Specification for the assessment of the life cycle greenhouse emissions of goods and services.* BSI. London, United Kingdom.

Carballo-Penela A. & Doménech, J. L. (2010). Managing the carbon footprint of products: the contribution of the method composed of financial statements (MC3). *International Journal of Life Cycle Assessment.*

Carbon Trust (2007a). *Carbon footprint measuring methodology. Version 1.3*

Carbon Trust (2007b). *Carbon footprinting. An introduction for organisations*

Chan W.; Wilco & Lam C. J. (2002). Prediction of pollutant emission though electricity consumption by the hotel industry in Hong Kong. *International Journal of Hospitality Management*, 21, 381-391.

Ciudad, A. (2009). *Uniform System of Accounts for the Lodging Industry: presente y future.* (Paper presented at the XV Congreso AECA Decisión en época de crisis: transparencia y responsabilidad. Valladolid - Spain).

Ciudad-Gómez, A. (2010). Principales cambios en la decima edición del sistema de reporting de la industria hotelera. *Partida Doble*, 221, 40-57.

Ciudad-Gomez, A. (2011). Cambios en el control y gestión del departamento de habitaciones. *Partida Doble*, 237, 26-45.

Ciudad-Gómez, A. (2012). The Uniform System of Accounts for the Lodging Industry and XBRL: Development and Exchange of Homogeneous Information. In Mondejar-Jimenez, J.; Ferrari, G. and Vargas-Vargas, M. (editors): *Research Studies on Tourism and Environment.* Nova Science Publishers, New York. Chapter 20.

Commission of the European Communities (2001). *Green Paper. Promoting a European framework for Corporate Social Responsibility.* COM (2001) 366 final, Brussels.

Commission on Sustainable Development -United Nations (2010). *Overview of progress towards sustainable development: a review of the implementation of Agenda 21, the Programme for the Further Implementation of Agenda 21 and the Johannesburg Plan of Implementation.*

Department for Environment, Food & Rural Affairs (DEFRA) (2006). *Environmental Key Performance Indicators. Reporting Guidelines for UK Business.* Department for Environment, Food & Rural Affairs (DEFRA) (2009). *Guidance on how to measure and report your greenhouse gas emissions.*

Department for Environment, Food & Rural Affairs (DEFRA) (2010). *Green Claims Guidance.*

Doménech, J. L. (2004). *La huella ecológica empresarial: el caso del puerto de Gijón.* (Paper presented at the 7º Congreso Nacional de Medio Ambiente. Madrid - Spain)

EMAS III (2009). *Regulation (EC) No 1221/2009 of the European Parliament and of the Council of 25 November 2009 on the voluntary participation by organisations in a Community eco-management and audit scheme (EMAS), repealing Regulation (EC) No 761/2001 and Commission Decisions 2001/681/EC and 2006/193/EC.*

European Commission (2007). *Carbon Footprint. What is it and how to measure it?* Global Footprint Network (GFN) (2007): *Footprint term glossary.*

Global Reporting Initiative (GRI) (2006). *Sustainability Reporting Guidelines (Version 3.0).* Amsterdam, the Netherlands.

Global Reporting Initiative (GRI) (2011). *Sustainability Reporting Guidelines (Version 3.1).* Amsterdam, the Netherlands.

Harris, P. & Brown, B. (1998). Research and development in hospitality accounting and financial management. *International Journal of Hospitality Management* 17, 161-181.

IPCC (1996). *Revised IPCC Guidelines for National Greenhouse Gas Inventories.* Greenhouse Gas Inventory Reference Manual; Volume 3. IPCC (2006): *IPCC Guidelines for National Greenhouse Gas Inventories.* Inter-Governmental Panel on Climate Change. IPCC (2007). *Climate Change 2007: The Physical Science Basis. Contribution of Working Group I to the Fourth Assessment Report of the IPCC.* Intergovernmental Panel on Climate Change. Geneva, Switzerland.

ISO (2008). *ISO International Standards practical tools for addressing climate change.* ISO Central Secretariat. Switzerland.

ISO 14031 (1999). *Environmental Management -Environmental Performance Evaluation Guidelines.* ISO Central Secretariat. Switzerland.

ISO 14064-1 (2006). *Greenhouse gases — Part 1: Specification with guidance at the organization level for quantification and reporting of greenhouse gas emissions and removals.* ISO Central Secretariat. Switzerland.

ISO 14064-2 (2006). *Greenhouse gases — Part 2: Specification with guidance at the project level for quantification, monitoring and reporting of greenhouse gas emission reductions or removal enhancements.* ISO Central Secretariat. Switzerland.

ISO 14066 (2011). *Greenhouse gases. Competence requirements for greenhouse gas validation teams and verification teams.* ISO Central Secretariat. Switzerland.

Parliamentary Office of Science and Technology (POST) (2006). *Carbon footprint of electricity generation.* Postnote 268. London, UK.

Perry, S.; Klemes, J. & Bulatova, I. (2008). Integrating waste and renewable energy to reduce the carbon footprint of locally integrated energy sectors. *Energy,* 33, 10, 1489-1497.

Rees, W. & Wackernagel, M. (1996). *Our ecological footprint. Reducing human impact on Earth.* New Society Publishers. Canada.

Ripoll, J. V. & Crespo, C. (1998). Costes derivados de la gestión medioambiental. *Técnica contable,* 591, 169-180.

Sasser, W.E.; Olsen, R. P. & Wyckoff, D. D. (1978). *Management of Service Operations.* Allyn and Bacon, Inc., Boston.

Schaltegger, S. & Sturm. A. (1989). *kologieinduzierte entscheidungsprobleme des managements. Ansatzpunkte zur ausgestaltung von instrumenten.* [Ecology induced management decision support. Starting points for instrument formation.] WWZ-Discussion Paper No. 8914. Basel, Switzerland: WWZ.

Schaltegger, S.; Sturm. A. (1998). *Eco-efficiency by Eco-controlling.* VDF, Zurich.

Schmidgall, R (1997). *Hospitality industry: Managerial accounting.* American Hotel & Motel Association. Michigan.

Schmidgall, R. S. & Damitio, J. W. (1999). *Hospitality Industry Financial Accounting.* American Hotel & Motel Association. Michigan.

The Climate Registry (2008). *General Reporting Protocol* Version 1.1. *Accurate, transparent, and consistent measurement of greenhouse gases across North America.*

The Climate Registry (2011). *2011 Climate Registry Default Emission Factors.*

The Environmental Technologies Action Plan (ETAP) (2007). *The Carbon Trust Helps UK Businesses Reduce their Environmental Impact*

Thomas, C.; Tennant, T. & Rolls, J. (2000). *The GHG indicator: UNEP guidelines for calculating greenhouse gas emissions for businesses and non-commercial organizations.* United Nations Environment Programme.

Weeks, I. A. (2000). Accounting for other Rooms Revenue and Average Rate Statics. *The Bottomline, the journal of the International Association of Hospitality Accountants*, 16, 3.

Wiedmann, T. & Minx, J. C. (2008). *A Definition of Carbon Footprint'.* In: Pertsova, C.C. (Coord.): *Ecological Economics Research Trends.* Nova Science Publishers, Hauppauge NY, USA. 1-11.

Wiedmann, T.; Lenzen, M. & Barret, J., (2009). Companies on the Scale: Comparing and Benchmarking the Footprints of Businesses. *Journal of Industrial Ecology*, 13, 3, 361–383.

World Business Council for Sustainable Development (WBCSD) (2000). *Measuring Eco-Efficiency: A guide to reporting company performance.*

World Business Council for Sustainable Development (WBCSD) (2009). *Corporate Ecosystem Valuation - Building the Business Case.*

World Resources Institute (WRI); World Business Council for Sustainable Development (WBCSD) (2004). *The Greenhouse Gas Protocol: A Corporate Accounting and Reporting Standard (Revised Edition).* GHG Protocol Initiative.

World Resources Institute (WRI); World Business Council for Sustainable Development (WBCSD) (2010). *Corporate Value Chain (Scope 3). Accounting and Reporting Standard.* Supplement to the GHG Protocol Corporate Accounting and Reporting Standard.

In: Methods and Analysis on Tourism and Environment   ISBN: 978-1-62417-824-5
Editors: J.M.Jiménez, M.V.Vargas, F.J.O.Rosell et al. © 2013 Nova Science Publishers, Inc.

Chapter 15

Environmental Management Systems, Financial Crisis and Competitive Advantage

Ricardo Martínez-Cañas, Pablo Ruiz-Palomino and Raúl del Pozo-Rubio

University of Castilla-La Mancha, Albacete, Castile–La Mancha, Spain

Abstract

After the eruption of the current global financial crisis, confidence in financial markets has been dramatically undermined. In this turbulent scenario, all progress made in implementing environmental management systems (EMS) could be jeopardized. Business managers can be seduced by the idea of implementation and follow-through of environmental activities is a cost that can lead to reduced profitability or increased losses. Nevertheless, from an ethical and operational point of view, this chapter analyzes why environmental management of business is needed more than ever to obtain a competitive advantage. Our analysis is based in the fact that EMS are not just the only right thing to do but are also an efficient option to reduce costs in the present crisis environment for holding competitiveness. Therefore, the assumptions of this chapter are that environmental commitment and international standard recognitions are likelier to be an important basis for competitive advantage that an economical burden. This paper also presents some conclusions derived from the conceptual model proposed and some future lines of research.

1. Introduction

Traditionally, maximization of value for shareholders has been the main purpose in business with a quasi-total obviation for the impact of their activities on the broader society (Melé, 2007). However, with the development and advancement of Corporate Social Responsibility (CSR), businesses have a set of multidimensional obligations to meet the expectations of society's global stakeholders by fulfilling economic, legal, ethical, ecological, and discretionary philanthropic responsibilities (Carroll and Buchholtz, 2008). Therefore, all those agents implied in the business decisions must be taken into account in the normal operations developed by the firm (Melé, 2007).

In order to create wealth and value in the long term, and in a sustainable way, there is a belief that modern corporations have a responsibility to society that extends beyond their economic responsibility to make money or profits for investors (Chandler, 2005). Therefore in this chapter, as a key important part of RSC in corporations, we focus on the role of environmental values that increasingly attract the attention of stakeholders.

The case for the environmental issue is an interesting one. During the last decades, the environmental issue and its perseverance have been highly impacting and interesting among an increasingly high economic and social force (Wenk, 2005). Therefore stakeholders expect corporations to assume responsibility for protection of the natural environment (Hoffman, 1999). This is not really surprising, mainly due to the high increase in population and consumption, which unfortunately has implied a higher generation of waste by every type of industry. Because such waste should be avoided to not negatively affect the natural and environmental ecosystems and also to preserve them, industries and the different agents and units involved in economical activities are especially implied in the new societal demands from business. These demands generally come from the Public Administration, clients and other socio-economic agents (Buysse and Verbeke, 2003; Rondinelly and Berry, 2000).

Indeed, meanwhile the Public Administration is increasingly being less considered as guarantor for the called "Welfare State", which includes the environmental issue,.Businesses are being perceived as units, which make up the social superstructure, with direct (and indirect) responsibility for respecting the welfare of society (Buysse and Verbeke, 2003). Different and increasing lobbies – associated with an increasing number of supporters – are now playing a significant role in defense for the environment. Also efforts are being increased by the Public Administration in western countries in terms of legislating and protecting the environment through a "pro-environment" social trend that involves the business world. Accordingly, businesses are making allowances in terms of the design of their business strategies and production processes to adapt their activity to the new competitive business scenario (Wenk, 2005).

Certainly, and although the importance of the environmental issue is being recognized in the business sector, it is still not being implemented in most of the productive processes. High costs and limits of all types of resources are some of the reasons underlying this negative situation (Del Brio et al., 2001), as well as the human belief that costs of implementation of environmental management systems are superior to benefits derived from it. However, social and environmental criteria are increasingly affecting the new decisions made for investment (De la Cuesta et al., 2002). Also, in addition to this fact there are a high and increasing number of environmental management system (EMS) programs that became involuntary certified international standards for reflecting the environmental engagement of the firm (Wenk, 2005). These EMS are management programs (physical or virtual) that offer (in a comprehensive, systematic, planned and documented manner) the organizational structure, planning and resources for developing, implementing and maintaining policy for environmental protection in firms.

In addition to these environmental programs and standards, some qualification agencies in Social Corporate Responsibility (SCR) issues (EIRIS, KLD, SAM, etc.) and new types of stock market indexes that are awarding those socially and environmentally responsible businesses (e.g. FTSE4Good IBEX, FTSE4Good, Dow Jones Sustainability Index, Domini

400 Social Index, etc.) exist. This increased investment rates for social and environmental issues probably has been governed by the important advantages that environmentally committed companies are thought to possess in contrast to others, and that previous research supports finding a direct positive association between their corporate social performance - including the environmental dimension (Stanwick and Stanwick, 1998) - and their corporate financial performance. However, vagueness and inconsistency in the causality and directionality of effects involved in the above relationship have been found in previous research (Waddock and Graves, 1997) which could bring about the thinking line that environmental responsiveness' advantages could really not exist. Indeed, previous research does not provide consistent results regarding the association between social performance (including the environmental dimension) and financial profitability, sometimes reporting a weak positive association (Preston, 1978), a neutral relation (Orliztky and Benjamin, 2001) or even a negative association (Patten, 2002).

Thus, in this chapter we try to theoretically justify why environmental management practices can be a basis for competitive advantage, even though in a global financial crisis context.

Therefore in the next epigraph we focus attention on the role of environmental issues in the corporate social responsibility dimension of the firm. Next, we study the links between environmental responsibility, EMS and competitive advantage. In the fourth epigraph, we propose a theoretical model explaining how firm competitive advantage is obtained based on environmental management practices and standards. Finally we remark on some conclusions and limitations together with possible lines of future research.

2. CORPORATE RESPONSIBILITY FOR ENVIRONMENTAL ISSUES

Although the classical Porter's (1980) five competitive forces model has served during the years as a principal reference framework for strategic decision making, in line with Waddock and Graves (1997), the impact of the different stakeholders' expectations is starting to be highly relevant in terms of influence on the business strategy to utilize. Prahalad and Hamel (1994) note that consumer's changing expectations, regulation changes, and environmental worries are starting to have an increasingly strong influence on the strategic decision making pattern utilized in the business sector, is also considered important to be advantageously competitive (Porter and van der Linde, 1995). More importantly, to be socially responsible is also being increasingly considered to be a potent source of innovation (Porter and Kramer, 2006).

Thus, the business sector is increasingly realizing this, and consequently tending not to limit the objectives to those strictly economic ones, but also to those of a social and environmental nature, mainly in an attempt to respond to demands of all stakeholders (Cuervo, 2005). Market (consumers), social (activist, non-governmental organizations) and governmental and investment agents are some of the principal drivers for the renewed and high interest given by businesses to the development of the corporate social responsibility issue (Melé, 2009).

Certainly, response to all types of social issues demanded in today's socio-economic context (e.g. defense of labor and human rights, product safety, consumer information, perseverance of certain goods and supply chain labor standards, labor relations, etc.) constitute a key pillar around which businesses are asked to operate to make ethically and socially responsible business.

Indeed, the key function of business is to satisfy human necessities through complying with quality criteria (García-Echevarría, 1994), and this fact indirectly implies to act, always thinking about the larger and wider societal context. However, the high relevance that responding to environmental concerns seems to have for fulfilling the key function of business should not be obviated, surely as it is key to developing the corresponding industrial and economical activity in a sustainable way, not only attentive to today's generation but more importantly, responsibly towards future generations.

According to Melé (2009) environmental problems seriously threatened the world society for more than 50 years.

Thus, although the high damage produced to the natural environment comes from so much earlier, seriously active social demands to business and government for a better environmental performance began to rise in the 1960s, mainly due to the appearance of some specific concerns related to the use of pesticides and/or the finding of highly toxic metals in rivers and oil-based waste in the oceans, among others (Melé, 2009). However, it was during the last decades of the past century, and at the turn of the 21st century, when social demands to business management for the reorienting of business activities towards an environmentally responsible behavior increased notably (Murillo-Luna et al., 2008).

When discussion arises about the root causes for current environmental problems, a wide variety are proposed: economic and cultural forms of late modernity, divine permission to subdue the earth, population explosion, consumption driven lifestyle, domination of a few over the majority in the today's society (Melé, 2009). However, consensus seems to come to light that logistic, market, transport, and industrial operations, that is, business activity in general, constitute the main direct and/or indirect responsible factors for present day problems of pollution and environmental damage (Del Brio and Junquera, 2002; Lorenzo, 2002). In addition, consensus seems to arise regarding how to move the business sector towards a more sustainable situation. Thus, the adoption of a reactive strategy, mainly associated with controlling pollution generated, and complying with current legislation (e.g. investments in sewage treatments) (Piñeiro et al., 2009) is a valid option, in reality the proactive strategy is optimally desired, in line with Piñeiro et al., (2009) rather than directing the focus of attention on control terms, it is associated with prevention of pollution and even anticipation of future legislation.

Indeed, the adoption of a proactive strategy implies a greater awareness of the importance of being environmentally responsible (Piñeiro et al., 2009), which is intimately related to the voluntary introduction of new productive techniques to reduce the damage produced to the natural environment (e.g. adoption of a cleaning technique to refine outflows) (Aragon, 1998). When an integral perspective is also considered, the proactive strategy permits the adoption of changing processes and designs intimately linked to favor the environment, leading to products more durable, reusable and recyclable and the avoidance of toxins in the productive process (Melé, 2009). Therefore, adopting an integral proactive strategy focuses basically on three key concepts: integrating science, knowledge intensity and productivity improvements; business organizations find an optimal way to create materials from renewable sources, develop less material intensive means and producing it more efficiently (Melé,

2009), which is crucial to develop the business activity in a sustainable, and also profitable way (Klassen and McLaughlin, 1996).

3. ENVIRONMENTAL RESPONSIBILITY, EMS AND VALUABLE BUSINESS ADVANTAGES

It is true that some controversy exists as to whether higher profitability is really associated to being environmentally responsible. Walley and Whitehead (1994) for example, discuss that economical efforts made to engage in environmental practices may cause rather negative impacts on profitability, and finally suppose an economical burden for the company, especially if competitors disregard investment in new technologies and processes to operate better environmentally. Some other studies, although limited, seem to reflect that implementing environmental policies and practices in isolation really does not pay, for the company (Barnett and Salomon, 2006). However, although certain strategic postures towards the environmental issue might produce a competitive disadvantage for businesses, there are other options to act relative to this issue.

Thus, although the adoption of a reactive strategy governed by the *end-of-pipe pollution control* likely only supposes a economical burden for the company (Melé, 2009), rather, the adoption of a proactive strategy governed by the *pollution prevention* philosophy drives financial gains (King and Lenox, 2002), leading to a better and more efficient use of economical resources utilized, and offering - through the implementation of new technologies and systems - opportunities to innovate and improve in terms of economical efficiency (Orlitzky, 2005).

Thus, to be proactively responsible, in environmental terms, does not suppose a competitive disadvantage at all, much less in the present and future socio-economic context (Barba-Sánchez and Sahuquillo-Martínez, 2010; Fernandez et al., 2003), in which the business sector is increasingly responding to social and environmental issues (Hsu and Cheng, 2011; Kuo et al., 2011).

Indeed, so high is the importance for being environmentally responsible in the present context that the new thinking and discourse which is emerging in society (e.g. the necessity for a sustainable development, safeguarding the natural environment and climate, etc.) is demanding a new paradigm of leadership to be practiced internally in organizations: the eco-leadership (Western, 2008), along with the corresponding instruments to make the organizations operate according to such discourse.

Thus, this new style of leadership, which *is about connectivity, interdependence and sustainability, underpinned by an ethical socially responsible stance* (Western, 2008: 183), recognizes a responsibility, connectivity and relationship to nature and the environment (Western, 2008) which partly is highly related to the adoption of an environmentally proactive strategy and also the implementation of an EMS in order to (Wenk, 2005):

- Be a tool to improve environmental performance.
- Provide a systematic way of managing an organization's environmental affairs.
- Address immediate and long-term impacts of its products, services and processes on the environment.

- Give order and consistency for organizations to address environmental concerns through the allocation of resources, assignment of responsibility and ongoing evaluation of practices, procedures and processes.
- Focus on continual improvement of the system.

And, it is along with the adoption of such a EMS how *saving costs in the production process* (e.g. productivity, efficiency, reduction of consumption of inputs and waste, saving in costs related to implementing control systems of pollution at the final stage of the production process, etc.) and *differential reputation towards stakeholders* – especially with regards to an emerging market share of ecological products – (Piñeiro et al., 2009) arise as specific business advantages.

Those advantages may be also be accompanied with likely environmental innovations in processes and also products, which surely would lead the company to ultimately improve in quality and market share terms (Shrivastava, 1995).

Therefore, as an extensive body of literature seems to indicate that "to be green ultimately seems to pay", and although improving the environmental performance may be costly, to environmentally perform poorly may likely impact more negatively on the companies' financial performance, bringing about negative media coverage, negative reputation towards stakeholders (Fombrum et al., 2000), numerous and large fines, and even shut-down of the business activity for a long period of time (Rees, 1994).

However, adopting a proactive strategy seems to be necessary to be successful (King and Lenox, 2002), which likely is highly and positively associated with the implementation of an EMS (Gonzalez-Benito and Gonzalez-Benito, 2008).

Indeed, since implementing an EMS supposes to establish the necessary procedures and controls to guarantee the successfully achievement of the company's environmental policy and objectives (Gonzalez-Benito and Gonzalez-Benito, 2008), an EMS is thought to be a facilitator of the right environmental performance of the company, or at least, of an improvement in its environmental performance.

The implementation of an EMS is thought to require high infrastructure investments and to involve the production plan, organizational structure and personnel training (Del Brio and Junquera, 2001). As a consequence, a high environmental engagement is expected on the part of the company (Del Brio and Junquera, 2001), and also an improvement in the management of such aspects like the use of natural (and also limited) resources, the water consumed, the spilling of residual water, the emission of contaminated particles to the natural environment, and so on.

Additionally, to have an EMS implemented under internationally well-recognized environmental standards such as the EMAS (Eco-Management and Audit Scheme) and the 14001 ISO facilitates the company to be included in social and environmental stock indexes – is very attractive for an increasing group of stock market investors (De la Cuesta et al., 2002), which brings about a better corporate reputation towards stakeholders and extra financial funding possibilities.

4. EMS AND COMPETITIVE ADVANTAGE: PROPOSAL OF A THEORETICAL MODEL

Following the arguments developed above, it can be remarked that an increasing number of firms are adopting EMS as a way of dealing with challenges from the natural environment. Many of these firms also voluntarily decide to have their systems certified according to one or both of the most accepted international standards (ISO 14001 and EMAS). These two voluntary activities can be the basis to obtain a competitive advantage (see Figure 1) because the implementation and recognition of those systems generally involves a significant investment of financial resources and a big management effort, which raises the question that: what benefits and competitive advantage might firms derive from these activities?

The first benefit, from an ethical-strategic point of view, is based on how the development of a pro-active strategy facilitates companies to improve their reputation in the market (sometimes being the first mover). The second benefit, from a more operational and internal point of view, is that environmentally responsible firms are favored to improve overall performance and efficiency together with better monitoring of the areas of the business that need an intervention.

Finally, as the third benefit, from a financial perspective, environmentally responsible firms are favored to improve their 1) cost savings through the reduction of waste and more efficient use of natural resources (e.g. electricity, water, gas and fuels), 2) avoiding fines and penalties derived from not meeting environmental legislation -thanks to better identification of environmental risks and better addressing operation weaknesses, and 3) reducing the level of insurance costs by demonstrating better risk management.

In sum, better competitive advantages, manifested in increased financial performance, are derived for socially and environmentally responsible companies that are involved in the implementation of an internationally recognized EMS.

Indeed, inclusion in Social Responsibility Investment Indexes, which are playing an increasingly important role in the stock markets (Adam and Shavit, 2008) and are increasing in number worldwide (FTSE4 Good, Ethibel Sustainability Index, Domini 400 Social Index, S&P ESG India Index, etc.) (cf. Marquez and Fombrun, 2005; Cheah et al., 2007; Sun et al., 2011), is easier when an EMS is implemented, which ultimately increases opportunities to attract financial capital (Giannarakis et al., 2009).

Also, these companies, as included in these investment indexes, usually make great efforts in terms of elaborating a policy of activities, implementing a system of management, publicly reporting activities and behavior conducted, and in the special case for climate change concerns, performing well relative to greenhouse gas emitted to the atmosphere.

Hence, companies included in such indexes, appear to be environmentally friendly and also contributors for a sustainable development of the business activity, which by their example of efficiency and reputation benefits, ultimately impacts positively on their financial performance, as some previous research seems to support (cf. Klassen and Whybark, 1999; Piñeiro et al., 2009; Porter and van der Linde, 1995).

The expected positive association between environmental engagement and financial performance is highly likely even in a context of financial crisis - characterized by a high volatile equity market - (Kimbro and Melendy, 2010), surely because those environmentally proactive companies which implement an EMS certified by an international standard are probably less sensitive to market oscillations.

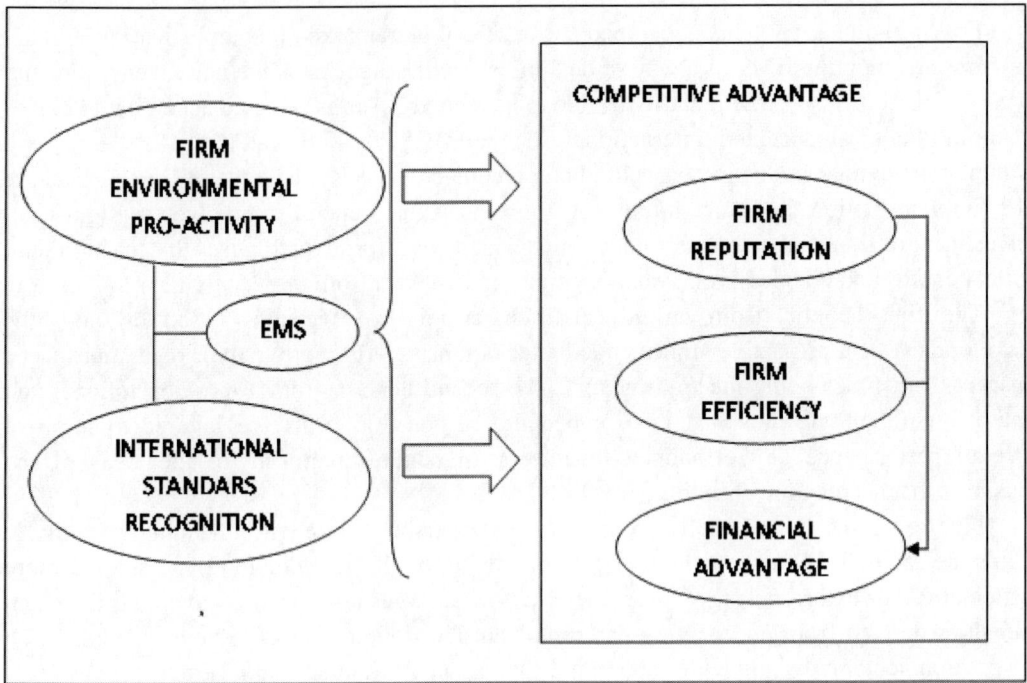

Figure 1. Theoretical model proposed.

CONCLUSION, LIMITATIONS AND FUTURE LINES OF RESEARCH

In line with previous research that theoretically proposes a positive association between environmental proactivity and competitive advantage in firms, it can be affirmed that complying with social and environmental responsibility criteria is associated with higher firm reputation, higher firm efficiency and better financial returns. In any case, it seems that the economic and management efforts made in terms of adapting and integrating a social and environmental philosophy and strategy into normal business activities do not pose a burden in terms of financial profitability, but permits the companies to adapt themselves to the new, growing and more demanding stakeholders' requirements in terms of social and environmental concerns, which ultimately is increasingly crucial to survive in today's competitive socioeconomic context.

In today's global financial crisis, problems of trust in the fragile economical-social-financial system need to be solved, and hence higher levels of a serious strong commitment to integrating social and environmental issues in business strategies are necessary, as it would reflect ethicality and ultimate seriousness in the involvement of the necessary sustainable development of global industrial activity. Therefore, the literature review effectuated along this chapter allows reflection of solid reasons for businesses to be involved in more serious social and environmental commitments in their normal business operations; such as a motivational sign for implementing an EMS and obtaining Environmental International

Standards certification is strengthened for the increasing market recognition, acceptance and importance of Social Responsibility Investment (cf. Florinda-Silva and Areal, 2011).

The main limitation of the present chapter is related to the conceptual and theoretical nature on which it is based. Thus we have argued exclusively on the theoretical importance of being proactive on environmental issues as a basis for competitive advantage. This first main limitation must therefore be the starting point for future empirical research to confirm our theoretical model by using data to compare significant differences between the market value of environmentally and non-environmentally responsible firms. Also the present chapter should promote and favor empirical research to analyze differences between performance measures such as financial performance, reputation and satisfaction of customers.

A second limitation is that the model proposed is not contingent on other influencing factors. The model proposed does not include such aspects as organizational structure, strategy and/or size of the company, all of which are potential determinants of the positive effect expected by implementing environmental policies and systems on the company's competitive advantage. However, the present chapter and our model could contribute to literature by reporting the important benefits that in a general way are supposedly derived to businesses that are environmentally proactive.

Finally, a third limitation is derived from the level of analysis used in designing our model since only the firm-level analysis was employed. In order to better understand, comprehend and elaborate the environmental phenomenon, a multilevel model that includes institutional-level and intra-firm level activities, is needed. As a result, a multilevel approach to the study of the competitive advantage to be obtained by environmentally responsible firms could be an interesting line for future research.

REFERENCES

Adam, A. M. & Shavit, T. (2008): How Can A Ratings-Based Method For Assessing Corporate Social Responsibility (CSR) Provide an Incentive To Firms Excluded from Socially Responsible Investment Index in CSR? *Journal of Business Ethics*, 82, 899-905.

Aragon, J.A. (1998): Strategic Proactivity and Firm Approach to the Natural Environment. *Academy of Management Journal*, 41, 556-567.

Barba-Sánchez, V. & Sahuquillo-Martínez, C. (2010): Integration of the Environment in Managerial Strategy: Application of the Resource-Based Theory of Competitive Advantage, Dynamic Capabilities and Corporate Social Responsibilities. *African Journal of Business Management*, 4, 1155-1165.

Barnett, M.L. & Salomon, R.M. (2006): Beyond Dichotomy: The Curvilinear Relationship Between Social Responsibility and Financial Performance. *Strategic Management Journal*, 27, 1101-1122.

Becchetti, L.; Di Giacommo, S. & Pinacchio, D. (2005): Corporate Social Responsibility and Corporate Performance: Evidence from a Panel of US Listed Companies. *Applied Economics*, 40, 541-567.

Brealey, R.A.; Myers, S.C. & Marcus, A.J. (2010): *Fundamentos de finanzas corporativas*. McGraw-Hill. Madrid. Spain.

Buysse, K. & Verbeke, A. (2003): Proactive Environmental Strategies: A Stakeholder Management Perspective. *Strategic Management Journal*, 24, 453-470.

Campbell, J.Y. & Hentschel, L. (1992): No News is Good News: An Asymmetric Model of Changing Volatility in Stocks Returns. *Journal of Financial Economics*, 31, 281-318.

Carroll, A.B. & Buchholtz, A.K. (2008): *Business and society: ethics and stakeholder management, 7th edition.* Cengage Learning, New York.

Chandler, D. (2005): *Strategic Corporate responsibility: stakeholders in a global environment,* Sage, London. United Kingdom.

Cheah, E.T.; Chan, W.L. & Chieng, C.L.L. (2007): The Corporate Social Responsibility of Pharmaceutical Product Recalls: An Empirical Examination of U.S. and U.K. Markets. *Journal of Business Ethics*, 76, 427-449.

Cuervo, A. (1991): *Rentabilidad y creación de valor en la empresa.* Real Academia de Ciencias Económicas y Financieras. Barcelona. España.

Cuervo, A. (2005): La Maximización del Valor para el Accionista versus la Responsabilidad Social Corporativa ¿Compatibilidad?. *Revista del Colegio de Economistas de Madrid*, 106, 13-21.

Del Brío, J.A. & Junquera, B. (2001): Posturas Directivas ante las Actuaciones Medioambientales en las Empresas Industriales Españolas. *Revista Galega de Economía*, 10, 1-21.

Del Brío, J.A.; Fernández, E. & Junquera, B. (2001): Impulso Medioambiental en las Industrias Españolas. El Papel de las Administraciones Públicas. *Economía industrial*, 339, 153-166.

Del Brío, J.A. & Junquera, B. (2002): Factores de Éxito en la Implantación de la ISO 14001: Un Análisis Empírico para las Empresas Industriales Españolas. *Revista Asturiana de Economía*, 24, 131-151.

De la Cuesta, M.; Valor, M. & Sanmartín, S. (2002): *Inversiones éticas en empresas socialmente responsables.* Universidad Nacional de Educación a Distancia. Madrid. España.

Fernández, E.; Junquera, B. & Ordiz, M. (2003): Organizational Culture and Human Resources in the Environmental Issue: A Review of the Literature. *International Journal of Human Resource Management*, 14, 634-656.

Florinda-Silva, M.C.C. & Areal, N. (2011): Socially Responsible Investing in the Global Market: The Performance of Us and European Funds. *International Journal of Finance & Economics*, (in press), DOI: 10.1002/ijfe.

Fombrun, C.J.; Gardberg, N.A. & Barnett, M.L. (2000): Opportunity Platforms and Safety Nets: Corporate Citizenship and Reputational Risk. *Business and Society Review*, 105, 85–106.

Freeman, R.E. (1984): *Strategic management: a stakeholder approach.* Pitman. Boston. Massachussets. Unites States.

French, K.R.; Schwert, G.W. & Stambaugh, R.F. (1987): Expected Stock Returns and Volatility. *Journal of Financial Economics*, 19, 3-29.

García-Echevarría, S. (1994): *Introducción a la economía de la empresa.* Díaz de Santos. Madrid. España.

Giannarakis, G.; Litinas, N. & Theotokas, I. (2009): Perceptions of Corporate Social Responsibility Concept in Greece. *International Journal of Social and Human Sciences*, 3, 663-669.

Gonzalez-Benito, J. & Gonzalez-Benito, O. (2008): Determinantes de la Proactividad Medioambiental en la Función Logística: Un Análisis Empírico. *Cuadernos de Estudios Empresariales*, 18, 51-71.

Haugen, R.A. (2001): *Modern investment theory*. 5th ed. Prentice Hall. London. United Kingdom.

Hoffman, A. (1999): Institutional Evolution and Change: Environmentalism and the U.S. Chemical Industry. *Academy of Management Journal,* 42, 351–371.

Hsu, J.L. & Cheng, M.Ch. (2011): What Prompts Small and Medium Enterprises to Engage in Corporate Social Responsibility?: A Study from Taiwan. *Corporate Social Responsibility and* Environmental Management (In press). DOI: 10.1002/csr.276.

King, A. & Lenox, M. (2002): Exploring the Locus of Profitable Pollution Reduction. *Management Science*, 48, 289–299.

Kimbro, M.B. & Melendi, S.R. (2010): Financial Performance and Voluntary Environmental Disclosures During the Asian Financial Crisis: The Case of Hong Kong, *International Journal of Business Perfomance Management*, 12, 72-85.

Klassen, R.D. & McLaughlin, C.P. (1996): The Impact of Environmental Management on Firm Performance, *Management Science,* 42, 1199-1214.

Klassen, R.D., Mc Laughlin, C.P. (1996): The Impact of Environmental Technologies on Manufacturing Performance. *Academy of Management Journal*, 42, 6, 599-615.

Kuo, L., Yeh, Ch.-Ch., Yu & H.-Ch. (2011): Disclosure of Corporate Social Responsibility and Environmental Management: Evidence from China. *Corporate Social Responsibility and Environmental Management.* (In press). DOI: 10.1002/csr.274)

Lorenzo, M.M. (2002): Marketing Ecológico y Sistemas de Gestión Ambiental: Conceptos y Estrategias Empresariales. *Revista Galega de Economía*, 11, 1-25.

Márquez, A. & Fombrun, C.J. (2005): Measuring Corporate Social Responsibility, *Corporate Reputation Review*, 7, 304-308.

Margolish, J.D. & Walsh, P. (2001): *People and profits?. The search for link between a company's social and financial performance.* Lawrence Erlbaum Associates Publishers. Mahwah. New Jersey.

Melé, D. (2007): Responsabilidad Social de la Empresa: Una Revisión Crítica a las Principales Teorías. *Ekonomiaz*, 65, 50-67.

Melé, D. (2009): *Business ethics in action. seeking excellence in organizations.* Palgrave Macmillan. London. United Kingdom.

Murillo-Luna, J.L.; Garcés-Ayerbe, C. & Rivera-Torres, P. (2008): Estrategia Medioambiental y Expectativas de Ventajas Competitivas. *Cuadernos de Estudios Empresariales*, 18, 9-31.

Orlitzky, M. (2005): Payoffs to Social and Environmental Performance. *Journal of Investing*, 14, 48-51.

Orlitzky, M. & Benjamin, J.D. (2001): Corporate Social Performance and Firm Risk: A Meta Analytic Review. *Business and Society*, 40, 369–396.

Patten, D. (2002): The Relation Between Environmental Performance and Environmental Disclosure: A Research Note. *Accounting, Organizations and Society*, 27, 763–773.

Peña, D. (2008): *Fundamentos de estadística.* Alianza Editorial. Madrid. España.

Piñeiro, P.; Quintas, M.A. & Caballero, G. (2009): Incidencia de la Proactividad Medioambiental en el Rendimiento de las Empresas Constructoras Españolas. *Revista Europea de Dirección y Economía de la Empresa*, 18, 79-106.

Porter, M.E. (1980): *Competitive strategy: techniques for analyzing industries and competitors.* Free Press. New York.

Porter, M.E. & Van der Linde, C. (1995): Green and Competitive: Ending the Stalemate. *Harvard Business Review*, 73, 120-133.

Porter, M.E. & Kramer, M.R. (2006): Strategy and Society: The Link between Competitive Advantage and Corporate Social Responsibility. *Harvard Business Review*, 84, 78-92.

Prahalad, C. K. & Hamel, G. (1994): Strategy as a Field of Study: Why Search for a New Paradigm?. *Strategic Management Journal*, Summer Special Issue, 15, 5-16.

Preston, L.E. (1978): Analyzing Corporate Social Performance: Methods and Results. *Journal of Contemporary Business*, 7, 135–150.

Rees, J. (1994): *Hostages of each other: the transformation of nuclear safety since three mile island.* University of Chicago Press. Chicago. Illinois. United States.

Rondinelly, D.A. & Berry, M.A. (2000): Environmental Citizenship in Multinational Corporations: Social Responsibility and Sustainable Development. *European Management Journal*, 18, 70-84.

Shrivastava, P. (1995): The Role of Corporations in Achieving Ecological Sustainability. *Academy of Management Review*, 20, 936-960.

Stanwick, P.A. & Stanwick, S.D. (1998): The Relationship between Corporate Social Performance and Organizational Size, Financial Performance and Environmental Performance: An Empirical Examination. *Journal of Business Ethics*, 17, 195-204.

Sun, M.; Nagata, K. & Onoda, H. (2011): The Investigation of the Current Status of Socially Responsible Investment Indices. *Journal of Economics and International Finance*, 3, 676-684.

Waddock, S.A. & Graves, S.B. (1997): The Corporate Social Performance-Financial Performance Link. *Strategic Management Journal*, 18, 303-319.

Walley, N. & Whitehead, B. (1994): It's Not Easy Being Green. *Harvard Business Review*, 72, 46-52.

Wenk, M. (2005): The European Union's Eco-Management and Audit Scheme (EMAS), Springer. The Netherlands.

Western, S. (2008). *Leadership: A critical text.* Sage Publications. London. United Kingdom.

In: Methods and Analysis on Tourism and Environment   ISBN: 978-1-62417-824-5
Editors: J.M.Jiménez, M.V.Vargas, F.J.O.Rosell et al. © 2013 Nova Science Publishers, Inc.

Chapter 16

CONFRONTING SPANISH TEXTILE'S INDUSTRY FUTURE THROUGH SUSTAINABLE MANAGEMENT

Lluís Miret-Pastor[1], Ángel Peiró-Signes[1],
María-del-Val Segarra-Oña[1,3]
and José Mondéjar Jiménez[2,3]

[1]Universitat Politècnica de València, Spain
[2]Universidad de Castilla La Mancha, Spain
[3]INERTE, International Network of Economic Research on Tourism
and Environment, Oviedo, Spain

ABSTRACT

The Spanish textile industry is going through a hard structural crisis. Previous studies have pointed out the sector´s need of innovation and productivity improvement but no research has been done analyzing how environmental sustainable orientation may help companies to survive and achieve competitiveness advantages. In this research 7296 Spanish textile firms are analyzed and economic data of companies that have implemented the ISO14001 and those that have not have been studied using statistical analysis. Results show significant differences between both groups.

1. INTRODUCTION

The European textile industry, with a 205'3 billion euros of total income and employing more than 2.6 million workers in more than 186,000 businesses in the European Union is facing important challenges in the near future. Spain ranks fifth as a textile producer, behind Germany, Italy, UK and France (Euratex, 2007).The Spanish textile sector is in a deep structural crisis. This crisis is similar to that of other developed countries, where the textile industry is facing a major transformation, caused in part by changes in the distribution and consumption, but above all, by strong international competition (Puig et al., 2009).

Due to this situation, the textile industry can choose between two options; to relocate (Dunford, 2006) or to adapt production and strategy to the new competitive environment (Lane and Probert, 2004; Abedecassis-Moeda, 2007). In this sense, the only way left for the textile industry of developed countries to maintain their competitiveness without relocation is to lay down on innovation and differentiation, ultimately, the search for a new type of textile industry (Jones and Hayes, 2004, Pla-Barber and Puig, 2009).

Some studies have focused on the ability of differentiation through innovation in the textile sector by the development of technical materials, new uses, new markets and new organizational forms (Enkell and Gassman, 2010, Kirner et al., 2009). But little has been studied so far about the possibilities that sustainable innovation can deliver to the industry. Society evolves and demands innovative products that meet the social and cultural changes from the companies. In this sense, environmental concern is a fact. We live in a society increasingly concerned about the environment, with consumers more aware and demanding about environmental matters (Steg and Vlek, 2009). This may pose a threat to certain companies, but also an opportunity for those who opt for environmentally friendly products, those who are committed to eco-innovation and to adopt eco-friendly production technologies (Porter and VanderLinde, 1995, Esty 2006).

Many studies can be found in the literature on business proactivity applied to specific sectors. For example, in Spain Aragón-Correa et al., (2008) found that in the automotive repair industry, firms with the most proactive practices exhibited a significantly positive financial performance. Martín-Tapia et al., (2009) studied the food industry and found a correlation between advanced environmental strategies and export intensity of SMEs.

Some authors have shown relationship between environmental responsibility and the financial performance of hotels (García and Armas, 2007). A correlation has also been found between environmental orientation and performance in the tourist sector (Claver-Cortés et al., 2007, Tarí et al., 2009, Molina-Azorín et al., 2009). Among the studies dealing with the implementation of environmental management tools, McKeiver and Gadenne (2005) analyzed both the external and internal factors that influenced the implementation of an environmental management system and Bonilla (2008) studied the situation of environmental certification in the Spanish hotel industry.

The implementation of environmental management systems and how this affects the economic performance of enterprises has been studied in recent years, especially the application of ISO14001 systems (Segarra-Oña et al., 2011).

This research line follows our previous work, with the main objective of analyzing the implementation of Environmental Management Systems in the Spanish textile industry, and to determine if this has any impact on business results. Our research question will study if there is any the relationship between the environmental management certification systems and economic performance of companies.

To validate this hypothesis we designed a multi-stage work. At the introduction the situation, the purpose and the hypotheses to be tested are explained. The second section presents the relationship between competitiveness, innovation and environment.

The situation of textile industry in developed countries in general and in Spain in particular is highlighted at the third section. Then, the methodology used is explained, results´ analysis is presented and, finally, conclusions of the study as well as limitations and future research are discussed.

2. COMPETITIVENESS, INNOVATION AND ENVIRONMENT

The search for competitiveness through innovation is a recurring theme for the academia (Bercovitz and Mitchell, 2008, Boutellier et al., 2008). Innovation generates benefits associated to cost, productivity or access to new markets (Crespi and Pianta, 2008, Van Leeuwen and Klomp, 2006) and represents a key aspect in competitiveness (Hidalgo and Albors, 2008, Calia et al., 2007). Over the Spanish textile sector several studies have been done studying the introduction of innovations such as distribution networks (Pla Barber et al., 2007), competitive strategy (Puig et al., 2007) and technical textiles (Grael, 2003; Tecnitex, 2003). So far, few studies on the attempts of the Spanish textile industry in carrying out environmental innovations, however, other studies have shown the benefits of this strategy in developed countries (Søndergård et al., 2004; Getzner, 2002; Babool and Reid, 2010).

Andersen (2008) establishes links between environmental innovation and competitiveness. In fact, The European Union establishes eco-innovation as a key to achieve the objectives set in the Lisbon strategy: "The most competitive and dynamic knowledge-based economy in the world capable of sustainable economic growth with more and better jobs and greater social cohesion"(European Commission, 2004).

The term eco-innovation was defined in 1996 by Fussler and James, as "new products and processes which provide customer and business value but significantly decrease environmental impacts"

Innovation and sustainability are two separate concepts that impact the competitive position of companies (Hitchens et al., 2005) and that together, act synergistically (Esty, 2006). The intersection between business and the environment is transforming existing markets, creating new ones (Beise and Rennins, 2005), and more and more, including the principles of sustainability in business strategies (Montalvo, 2007).

One problem for the analysis of eco-innovation is its measurement, since it involves the same problems that hinder innovation measurement. Measuring eco-innovation means finding indicators that cover both, economic and environmental aspects. The work on this topic (Kemp and Pearson, 2008; Arundel and Kemp, 2009, Huppes et al., 2008) provide different methods and indicators, but recognize that they are all inadequate. In addition to the problems mentioned there are other difficulties like the fact that eco-innovation is not an official industry.

One of the options proposed by the literature to measure eco-innovation is the use of environmental certifications (Foxton, Pearson and Speirs, 2008, Kemp and Pearson, 2008) adapting what is already stated in the report of the OECD (Governance of Innovation Systems) Remøe et al., (2005) for the use of certification in innovation studies in general.

Certification can be defined as a voluntary process that checks, audits and provides written assurance that a process, product or service meets a series of specific standards (Bien, 2003). These standards, in regard to environmental management, provide guidance to implement an Environmental Management System (EMS). An environmental management system (EMS) is a continuous cycle of planning, action, reviewing and improving the environmental performance of the company in relation to the nature, magnitude, and environmental impacts of its activities, products and services. An EMS is based on the realization of an environmental assessment to identify, assess, reduce and prevent environmental impacts on the environment, making a commitment to continuously improve the impact of the company in the environment. The two environmental certification systems most widely used are ISO 14001 and EcoManagement and Audit Scheme (EMAS). These two systems are the most used and are cited in the work of Pearson et al., (2008) and Kemp and Pearson (2008) as indicators of eco-innovation.

The ISO 14001 is a standard developed by the International Standardization Organization aimed at providing companies with an effective Environmental Management System (EMS), contrasted and integrated in other productive activities. (ISO, 1996).

In this paper, we selected the ISO 14001 standard as it is the most widely used environmental management system. From 1996 to 2006 certifications increased from 1491 to 129,199 licenses worldwide and growth in recent years has been exponential. 40% of these certificates are produced in the European Union.

In recent years, different studies have appeared analyzing the economic impact of the implementation of ISO 14001 (Melnyk et al., (2003), Kelly et al., (2007) and Montabon et al., (2002), Segarra et al., (2011)), but none has been applied to Spanish textile industry.

3. ANALYSIS OF THE SPANISH TEXTILE INDUSTRY SITUATION

The choice of this industry to develop research is justified because it is a traditional industry undergoing a deep competitiveness crisis, which is leading to a rethink on their competitive strategies (Shafaei, 2009).

The textile industry in developed countries is undergoing a crisis stage, where it faces changes and challenges for the future (Puig et al., 2009). There are different explanations for the crisis causes in textiles, but the two main causes of the crisis would be the changes in consumption patterns that lead us to define the industry as mature (Belussi, 1996) and the exponential growth of Asian competition, consequence of the globalization of world economy and trade liberalization (Pla and Puig, 2009).

With respect to consumption patterns, if we analyze the evolution of spending on clothing and footwear (see Table 10), we can observe a decrease in the spending percentage that purchases of clothing and footwear are accounting.

Table 1. Distribution of total expenditure on clothing and footwear in %

1958	1964	1973	1980	1985	1990	1996	2006
13'6	14'9	7'7	8'5	10'4	10'1	7'6	6'86

Source: INE.

Data confirm clothing and footwear market as a mature product market, tracing a line of changes in consumption patterns, that in junction with increased foreign competition hinder the survival of European industry (De Brito et al., 2008). The increased competition comes from international agreements on textile trade. In 1994, the "Agreement on Textile and Clothing" (ATC) was signed in Marrakesh. This agreement established quotas on the amount developing countries could export to developed countries for a ten year period. Effective January 1 2005 there are no such quotas. Since that date, the global textile trade is being transformed (Bailey et al., 2010). Before the abolition of trade barriers textile trade was a fragmented (OECD, 2004). Low-wage countries were specialized in the early stages of textile production chain (eg. production raw materials pre-cut) while developed countries were limited to end the production and distribution.

We are currently experiencing a change in the global textile model, with the emergence of a number of developing countries with significant comparative advantages (China, India, Turkey and Morocco) who are creating strong textile sectors that comprise the entire value chain (Tewari, 2006). The textile industry is both an example of an internationalized industry and of a highly localized and concentrated industry (Buxey, 2005). This is an industry that tends to relocate in low-wage countries because it is labor intensive and its products are easy to transport (Grandys and Grandys, 2008). The labor costs' comparative exhibit (see exhibit 1) helps to explain many of the problems being experienced by the textile industry in developed countries and how EU´s trade balance has been declining (see table 2).

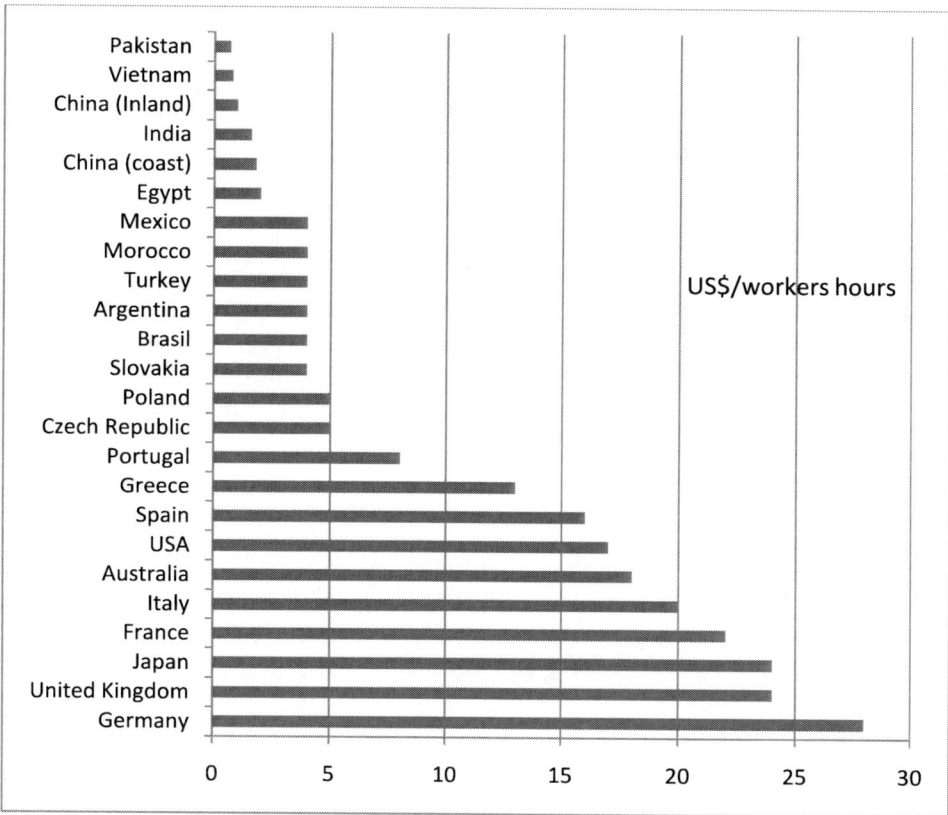

Source. Compiled by authors from Werner International data (2007).

Exhibit 1. Table comparing labor costs at the textile industry.

Table 2. EU trade balance for textile materials

2004	2005	2006	2007	2008
927 m€	408 m€	-649 m€	-1537 m€	-1441 m€

Source: Eurostat.

Therefore, the crisis´ consequences in the Spanish textile industry can be seen through several indicators in table 3.

Table 3. Evolution of main economic indicators of the Spanish textile industry

	2005	2006	2007	2008	2009
Production (m€)	11650	11415	11390	10390	8800
Export(m€)	6659	7356	7814	8005	7821
Import(m€)	11011	12336	13383	13281	13971
Employment(num)	223200	206000	196500	182300	150000
Ner. of companies	9412	9116	8716	7668	7037

Source: Compiled by authors from *CITYC and DIRCE data.*

Data show the consequences of a deep crisis sector since 2001. Both Maluquer (2003) and Moral and Pazo (2004) considered that the adjustment of Spanish textile is being even more drastic than other developed countries, as other economies began prior to restructure its textile industry. Lane and Probert (2004) indicated that the two possible strategies for the European textile industry come, either by relocation or by adapting the production and the strategy to a new competitive environment. Abedecassis-Moedas (2007) raises the same dichotomy but considering that the two strategies are not mutually exclusive but complementary. Similar conclusions seem to be getting different studies on the textile industry in developed countries as Buxey (2005) concerning Australia, Gullstrant (2005) concerning Sweden or Bilalis (2006) concerning France and Germany.

The keys to' competitiveness come through adaptability, uses cutting-edge and differentiation (Llach et al., 2009). As noted by Jones and Hayes (2004) in a study of the British textile industry "a new type of textile industry is emerging from the ashes of the old textile industry". The importance of innovation and the environment must play a key role in the new European textile industry.

4. OBJECTIVES AND METHODOLOGY

In order to analyze whether there is any relationship between the companies that survived the first stage of the structural crisis experienced by the industry in Spain and the fact of being innovation-oriented enterprises, especially eco-innovation oriented, we have analyzed economic data from 7296 textile companies, of which 27 were certified to ISO 14001. The data used are from 2008, since it was the latest year for which data were available for the entire population. Over this population we have applied quantitative methods of statistical analysis.

Firstly, to validate our hypotheses, we applied the ANOVA test that can detect mean differences across business functions comparing ISO 14001 certified with non certified firms, using specific performance indicators such as Return on Capital Employed; Net Assets Turnover; Net sales; profit margin; EBIT y EBITDA. While textile companies with ISO 14001 are on average 110 employees, textile companies without ISO 14001 have an average of 16 employees. To mitigate the effect of company size (no. of employees) may have on the results, these parameters are calculated per the same indicators had previously been used to analyze economic performance in Spain (Albors et al., 2008, Hervás, 2004, Albors et al., 2009). To construct the indicators, information was taken from the SABI database and was subsequently processed.

The ANOVA analysis seeks to break down the variability in a study into independent components that can be assigned to different causes. It is a statistical technique designed to analyse the significance of the mean differences of the different populations, and as such, it is considered as an extension of the means difference test, and is used to study the relationship between nominal, ordinal and interval variables (Hair et al., 1998). The ANOVA technique indicates whether or not we reject the null hypothesis that reflects the equal means value for each α level of significance. In this way we confirm whether the mean of the variable performance is significantly different for the firms according to their ISO 14001 environmental certification. The database was analysed using SPSS.17.0.

5. RESULTS

The analysis of variance of each of these variables were performed and the results are shown in the table 4, below.

Table 4. Variance analysis results

		Mean	Std dev.	F	Sig.
Number of employees	0	16,236	84,115	33,179	,000
	1	110,667	219,129		
	Total	16,602	85,216		
Profit per Employee (t€)	0	-0,680	78,185	3,769	,052
	1	30,470	138,605		
	Total	-0,571	78,482		
Oper. Rev. per Employee (t€)	0	127,590	293,262	11,724	,001
	1	334,277	652,063		
	Total	128,315	295,432		
Return on Capital Employed (%)per employee	0	3,143	48,235	,010	,921
	1	2,188	5,844		
	Total	3,140	48,149		
Net Assets Turnover per employee	0	1,627	78,603	,009	,925
	1	0,141	0,408		
	Total	1,622	78,462		
Net salesper Employee (t€)	0	142,954	313,210	11,457	,001
	1	356,496	630,287		
	Total	143,728	315,105		
EBIT per Employee (t€)	0	-0,565	98,702	4,121	,042
	1	39,662	145,740		
	Total	-0,420	98,925		
EBITDA per Employee (t€)	0	3,609	91,872	6,188	,013
	1	49,530	150,336		
	Total	3,774	92,172		

Analysis of variance of the different variables studied show significant differences between those companies certified to ISO 14001 and which are not, in fact the average of all variables is much higher among those certified. The results confirm that companies with ISO environmental certification, considered companies with active environmental management policies, get significantly better financial results, which is in line with previous work (Aragon and Correa, 2008; Martin-Tapia, 2010). Other work on similar technology sectors such as ceramics and food industries (Segarra et al., 2011a and Segarra et al., 2011b) show similar findings.

CONCLUSION

Through the statistical technique, analysis of variance between group(ANOVA), that compares the mean values between to different groups hypothesis set in this chapter: "the implementation of an environmental management system positively affects business performance" was contrasted. It has been shown that the use of ISO 14001 environmental management tool has a major impact on several indicators of business profitability. It seems clear that there is a relationship between having a proactive environmental attitude and business results achieved.

In the analysis of results has emphasized the important differences in size between certified companies and those which were not. Logically, there is a relationship between size, organizational innovation and performance. In any case, the indicators are calculated "per employee" to mitigate this effect.

One of the main conclusions of this analysis is that the number of environmentally certified companies in the textile industry is still very low compared with other industries. This is probably because it is an industry formed mainly by family businesses and small enterprises, which add difficulties to adopt proactive environmental strategies. In any case, in an industry with so much competition and where the old wage cost advantage has become the biggest drag on, the industry should rethink in differentiate from Asian competitors in areas such as environmental care and responsibility. However, the implementation of environmental management systems in the Spanish textile industry is still very limited and confined to medium or large businesses. The administration or the industry should expand the environmental management system to the textile SMEs, which should stop to consider the environment as a cost to consider it a competitive opportunity that positively affects various financial ratios.

The findings of this analysis may have important consequences for the implementation of sectorial policies or business practices that can help an industry undergoing a deep crisis. However, this line of work can be extended with future work which should consider other forms of environmental innovation in the textile industry based on patents, eco-labeling, etc. It would also be interesting to deepen into the factors that drive or hinder the eco-innovation as size, exterior orientation or formal innovation.

ACKNOWLEDGMENTS

The authors would like to thank the Spanish Ministry of Economy and Competitiveness for its financial support through the research project (EC02011-27369). Also the Universitat Politècnica de València for its research funding to the environmental performance Project (PAID-06-2011- 1879) and for its support to the "Globalización, terciarización, turismo y patrimonio: hacia una gestión sostenible del pasado como futuro" research microcluster.

REFERENCES

Abecassis-Moedas, C. (2007). Globalization and Regionalization in the Clothing Industry: Survival Strategies for UK Firms. *International Journal Entrepreneurship and Small Business*, 4, 3, 291–304.

Albors-Garrigós, J.; Hervas-Oliver, J.L. & Marquez, P.B. (2008). When technology innovation is not enough, new competitive paradigms, revisiting the Spanish ceramic title sector. *Int. J. Technology Management*, 44, 3/4, 406–426.

Albors-Garrigós, J.; Márquez-Rodríguez, P. & Segarra-Oña, M.V. (2009). Internet como herramienta de creación de valor en sectores maduros. El caso de los productores y distribuidores cerámicos en España. *Boletín de la Sociedad Española de Cerámica y Vidrio*, 48, 279-288.

Andersen, M. M. (2008). Eco-innovation.Towards a taxonomy and theory. DRUID Conference. Copenhagen.

Aragón-Correa, J.A.; Hurtado-Torres, N.; Sharma, S. & García-Morales, V.J. (2008). Environmental strategy and performance in small firms: A resource-based perspective. *J Environ Manager,* 86 ,88-103.

Arundel, A. & Kemp, R. (2009). Measuring Eco-innovation. *Working paper series*. United Nations University.

Babool, A. & Reid, M. (2010). The Impact of Environmental Policy on International Competitiveness in Manufacturing. *Applied Economics,* 42, 16-18, 2317-26.

Bailey, D.; Bellandi, M.; Caloffi, A. & De Propris, L. (2010). Place-renewing leadership: trajectories of change for mature manufacturing regions in Europe. *Policy Studies,* 31, 4, 457-474.

Beise, M. & Rennings, K. (2005). Lead markets and regulation: a framework for analyzing the international diffusion of environmental innovations. *Ecological Economics,* 52, 5-17.

Belussi, F. (1996). Local systems, industrial districts and institutional networks: Towards a new evolutionary paradigm of industrial economics? *European Planning Studies ,* 4, 1, 5-26.

Bercovitz, J. & Mitchell, W. (2008). When is more better? The impact of business scale and scope on long-term business survival, while controlling for profitability. *Strategic Management Journal,* 28, 1, 61-79.

Bilalis, N.; Van Wassenhove, L.; Maravelakis, E.; Enders, A.; Moustakis, V. & Antoniadis, A. (2006). Insights from Research. An Analisis of European Textile Sector Competitiveness. *Measuring Business Excellence,* 10, 1, 27-35.

Bonilla, M.J. & Avilés, C. (2008). Analysis of Environmental Statements Issued by EMAS-Certified Spanish Hotels. *Cornell Hospitality Quartely,* 49, 4, 381-394.

Boutellier, R.; Gassmann, O. & Zedtwitz, M. (2008). *Managing Global Innovation. Uncovering the Secrets of Future Competitiveness.* 3rd ed, Springer.

Buxey, G. (2005). Globalisation and Manufacturing Strategy in the TCF Industry, *International Journal of Operations and Production Management,* 25, 2, 100–114.

Calia, R. C.; Guerrini, F. M. & Moura, G. L. (2007). Innovation networks: From technological development to business model reconfiguration. *Technovation,* 27,426–432

Claver-Cortes, E.; Molina-Azorín, J. F. & Pereira-Moliner, J. (2007). Competitiveness in mass tourism. *Annals of Tourism Research,* 34, 3, 727–745

Crespi, F. & Pianta, M. (2008). Demand and innovation in productivity growth. International. *Review of Applied Economics.* 22, 6, 655–672.

De Brito, M.; Carbone, V. & Blanquart, C. M. (2008). Towards a sustainable fashion retail supply chain in Europe: Organisation and performance. *International Journal of Production Economics,* 114, 2, 534-553.

Dunford, M. (2006). Industrial Districts, Magic Circles, and the Restructuring of the Italian Textiles and Clothing Chain. *Economic Geography,* 82, 1, 27–59.

Enkel, E. & Gassmann, O. (2010). Creative imitation: exploring the case of cross-industry innovation. *R&D Management, Special Issue: The Future of Open Innovation,* 40, 3, 256–270.

Esty, D.C. & Winston, A.S. (2006). *Green to Gold, How smart companies use environmental strategy to innovate, create value, and build competitive advantage.* John Wiley and Sons, Hokoben, New Jersey.

Euratex (2007). *EU25 Data Digest of EU-25 Textile and Clothing Industry,* http://www.euratex.org/download/publications/others/eu25_textile_and_clothing__industry_2006_digest.pdf.

European Commission (2004). *Stimulating Technologies for Sustainable Development: An Environmental Technologies. Action Plan for the European Union.*

Fussler, C. & James, P. (1996). *Driving Eco-Innovation: A Breakthrough Discipline for Innovation and Sustainability,* Pitman Publishing: London,

García Rodríguez F. J. & Armas Cruz, Y. M. (2007). Relation between social-environmental responsibility and performance in hotel firms. *International Journal of Hospitality Management,* 26, 824-39.

Getzner, M. (2002). The Quantitative and Qualitative Impacts of Clean Technologies on Employment. *Journal of CleanerProduction,* 10, 4, 305-319.

Graell, J. (2003). Nuevas Oportunidades: los textiles técnicos. *Boletín Económico del ICE,* 2768, 85-90.

Grandys, E. & Grandys, A. (2008). Outsourcing-An innovation tool in clothing companies. *Fibres&Textiles in Eastern Europe,* 16, 5, 13-16.

Gullstrand, J. (2005). Industry Dynamics in the Swedish Textile and Wearing Apparel Sector, *Review of Industrial Organization,* 26, 349-370.

Hair, J.F.; Anderson, R. E.; Tatham, R. L. & Black, W. C. (1998). *Multivariate data analysis: with readings,* 5th ed.. Englewood Cliffs, NJ: Prentice-Hall.

Heim, E. H. (1997). Dimensions of Decline: Industrial Regions in the United States and Europe, 1970-1990. *International Regional Science Review,* 20, 3, 211-221.

Hervas-Oliver, J.L. & Albors-Garrigos, J. (2009). The role of the firm's internal and relational capabilities in clusters: when distance and embeddedness are not enough to explain innovation. *J Econ Geogr.*, 9, 2, 263-283.

Hidalgo, A. & Albors-Garrigos, J. (2008). Innovation management techniques and tools: a review from theory and practice. *R&D Management*, 38, 2, 113-127.

Hitchens, D.; Thankappan, S.; Trainor, M.; Clausen, J. & De Marchi, B. (2005). Environmental performance, competitiveness and management of small businesses in Europe. *Royal Dutch Geographical society, KNAG.* 96, 5, 541–557.

Huppes G.; Kleijn R.; Huele R.; Ekins P.; Shaw B.; Schaltegger S. & Esders M. (2008). *Measuring eco-Innovation: Framework and typology of indicators based on Casual Chains.* Ecodrive Project.

Jones, R. M. & Hayes, S. G. (2004). The UK Cloting Industry: Extinction or Evolution? *Journal of Fashion Marketing and Management*, 8, 3, 262-278.

Kelly, J; Haider, W; Williams, P. & Englund, K. (2007). Stated Preferences for EcoEefficient Destination Planning Options. *Tourism Management*, 28, 2, 377-390.

Kemp, R. & Pearson, P. (2000). *Final report of the project 'Measuring Eco-Innovation' (MEI)* . Available in: http://www.merit.unu.edu/MEI/ index.php.

Kirner, E.; Kinkel, S. & Jaeger, A. (2009). Innovation paths and the innovation performance of low-technology firms—An empirical analysis of German industry. *Research Policy, Special Issue: Innovation in Low-and Meduim-Technology Industries*, 38, 3, 447-458.

Lane, C. & Probert, J. (2004). Between the Global and the Local: a Comparison of the British and German Clothing Industry, ESRC *Centre for Business Research, Working Paper*, Cambridge University, 283.

Llach, J.; Bikfalvi, A. & Marques, P. (2009). What are the success factors for textile Spanish firms? An exploratory multiple-case study. *Fibres&Textiles in Eastern Europe*, 17, 2, 7-11.

Maluquer, S. (2003). La industria textil-confección europea en el umbral del siglo XXI. *Boletín económico del ICE*, 2768, 35-40.

Martín-Tapia, I.; Aragon-Correa, J.A. & Rueda-Manzanares, A. (2010). Environmental strategy and exports in medium, small and micro-enterprises. *Journal of World Business*, 45, 266-275.

Melynk, S.; Sproufe, R. & Calantone, R. (2003). Model of Site-Specific Antecedents of ISO 14001 Certification. *Production and Operations Management*, 12, 3, 369-387

Molina-Azorín, J.F.; Claver-Cortés, E.; Pereira-Moliner, J. & Tarín, J.J. (2009). Environmental practices and .firm performance: an empirical analysis in the Spanish hotel industry. *Journal of Cleaner Production*, 17, 516–524.

Montalvo, C. (2008). General wisdom concerning the factors affecting the adoption of cleaner technologies: a survey. *Journal of Cleaner Production*. 16, 1, s7-s13.

Moral, M. J. & Pazó, C. (2004). El sector textil y confección en España ante un futuro incierto. *Economía industrial*, 355/356, 273-282.

OECD (2004). *A New World Map in Textiles and Clothing*, OCDE, París.

Pla Barber, J.; Puig, F. & Linares, E. (2007). Crisis, actitudes directivas y estrategia en los sectores manufactureros tradicionales: el sector textil español. *Universia Business Review-Actualidad económica*, 68-82.

Pla-Barber, P. & Puig, F. (2009). Is the influence of the industrial district on international activities being eroded by globalization? Evidence from a traditional manufacturing industry. *International Business Review,* 18, 5.435-445.

Pla, J. & Linares, E. (2007). Crisis, Actitudes, Directivas y Estrategias en los Sectores Manufactureros Españoles: el Sector Textil Español. *Universia Business Review,* 68-83.

Porter, M.E. & Van der Linde, C. (1995). Toward a new conception of the environment competitiveness relationship, *Journal of Economic Perspective,* 9, 4, 97–118.

Puig, F.; Marques, H. & Ghauri, P. N.(2009). Globalization and its impact on operational decisions: The role of industrial districts in the textile industry. *International Journal of Operations & Production Management,* 29, 7, 692 – 719.

Puig, F. & Marques, H. (2011). The Dynamic Evolution of the Proximity Effect in the Textile Industry, *European Planning Studies,* 19, 8, 1423-1439.

Remøe, S. (2005). *Governance of innovation systems.* Organisation for Economic Co-operation and Development. OECD.

Segarra-Oña, M.; Peiró-Signes, A.; Albors-Garrigós, J. & Miret-Pastor, L. (2011,a). Impact of Innovative Practices in Environmentally Focused Firms: Moderating Factors. *International Journal of Environmental Research,* 5, 425-434.

Segarra-Oña, M.; Peiró-Signes, A.; Miret-Pastor, L. & Albors-Garrigós, J. (2011,b). Eco-innovación, una evolución de la innovación? Análisis empírico en la industria cerámica española. *Boletín de la Sociedad Española de Cerámica y Vidrio,* 50, 5, 253-26.

Segarra-Oña, M.; Peiró-Signes, A.; Miret-Pastor, L. & Albors-Garrigós, J. (2011,c). Uncovering Non-obvious Relationship Between Environmental Certification and Economic Performance at the Food Industry. *Information Technologies in Environmental Engineering,* 3, 3, 325-338.

Shafaei, R. (2009). An analytical approach to assessing the competitiveness in the textile industry, *Journal of Fashion Marketing and Management,* 13, 1, 20 – 36.

Smith, A.; Pickles, J.; Begg, R. & Roukova, P.(2005). Outward Processing, EU Enlargement and Regional Relocation in the European Textiles and Clothing Industry: Reflections on the European Commission's Communication on 'the Future of the Textiles and Clothing Sector in the Enlarged European Union, *European Urban and Regional Studies,* 12, 1, 83-91.

Sondegard, B.; Hansen, O. & Holm, J. (2004). Ecological Modernisation and Institutional Transformation in the Danish Textile Industry. *Journal of Cleaner Production.* 12, 4, 337-352.

Steg, L. & Vlek, C. (2009). Encouraging pro-environmental behaviour: An integrative review and research agenda, *Journal of Environmental Psychology,* 29, 3, 309-317.

Tewari, M. (2006). Adjustment in India´s textile and apparel industy technological legacies in a post-MFA world, *Environment and planning,* 38, 2325-2344.

Van Leeuwen, G. & Klomp, L. (2006). On the Contribution of Innovation to Multi-Factor Productivity Growth, *Economics of Innovation and New Technology,* 15, 4/5, 367–390.

Werner Internationally (2007). International Comparison of the Hourly Labour Cost in the Primary Textile Industry 2007, *New Twist Werner Intl. Newletter,* 3.

In: Methods and Analysis on Tourism and Environment   ISBN: 978-1-62417-824-5
Editors: J.M.Jiménez, M.V.Vargas, F.J.O.Rosell et al. © 2013 Nova Science Publishers, Inc.

Chapter 17

ASSESSMENT OF THE IMPACT OF BUSINESS ACTIVITY IN SUSTAINABILITY TERMS: EMPIRICAL CONFIRMATION OF ITS DETERMINATION IN SPANISH COMPANIES

María Luisa Pajuelo Moreno
Universidad de Extremadura, Extremadura, Spain

ABSTRACT

Because the issue of sustainability presents urgent problems crucial to the future of mankind, there has been serious discussion of the role accounting should play. In this context, a new line of research, still at a relatively unexplored, embryonic stage, has arisen, which tries to establish measurement of business sustainability and so compensate for the lack of information currently existing about the net impact of the company's activity. After establishing a simple theoretical model which supports integration of social and environmental information and accounting in the company, we choose the more mature Full Cost Accounting as the most suitable method for this aim. This tool allows sustainability to be translated into the language of business, together with analysis and comparison of its progress, making it the most appropriate vehicle for more participatory, democratic accounting, with greater dialogue, giving the accountant a much more active role.

1. INTRODUCTION

Although most studies have focused on *analysis of the environmental information published in companies (*as evidenced in the work of Gamble et. al., 1995; Deegan & Rankin, 1996; Cormier & Magnan, 1999; Moneva & Llena, 1996, 2000, 2006; Cormier & Gordon, 2001; Toms, 2001; Larrinaga et al., 2002; Carvalho & Monteiro, 2002; O'Dwyer, 2003; Walden & Stagliano, 2004; Cowan & Gadenne, 2005; Rodrigues et al., 2005; Monteiro & Aibar, 2005; Llena et al., 2007; Blanco et al., 2008; Crespo et al., 2009), *annual reports*, in recent decades, study of the *role of accounting as a support for environmental management* has also been empirically analysed (Monteiro & Aibar, 2009), mainly covering the following subjects:

- *The links existing between accounting and environmental management* (Bartolomeo & James, 1999; Bouma & Wolters, 1999a; Bartolomeo et al., 2000; Carvalho & Monteiro, 2002; ICAA, 2003; Masanet-Llodrá, 2006; Albelda et al., 2007; Monteiro & Aibar, 2009).

- *Management accounting system elements used in environmental management* (For example, the use of sustainability indicators (GRI, 2000; Lange, 2007; DETR, 1999,2000; Fowler & Hope, 2007; Dierkes & Preston, 1977; Walter & Stützel, 2009; Lamberton, 2000; Chambers & Lewis, 2001; Jones & Matthews, 2000; Jones, 2003) and environmental management systems (Ditz et al., 1995; EPA, 1995; Blanco, 1996; Tibor & Feldman, 1997; Shields et al., 1997; Bennett & James, 1998a,b; Ritchie & Hayes, 1998; Bouma, 1998; Kitzman, 2001; Bartolomeo et al., 2000; ICAA, 2003; Rogers & Kristof, 2003; Llena, 2008).

- *The active role of accounting in the organizational change related with interaction with society and the introduction of environmental management practices* (Hopwood, 1985; Gray, 1990a,b; Carrasco & Larrinaga, 1995; Power, 1994; Carmona et al., 1993; Gray et al., 1995; EPA, 1995; Burns & Scapens, 2000; Hibbit & Kamp-Roclands, 2001; Larrinaga et al., 2001; Larrinaga et al., 2006; Larrinaga & Bebbington, 2001; Crespo, 2002; Burrit, 2004; O´Dwyer, 2005; Kaplan & Norton, 2005; Moneva & Llena, 2006; Scavone, 2006; Curkovic & Sroufe, 2007; Brown, 2009; Da Silva & Amaral, 2009; Berbeeten & Blessings, 2009; Hopwood, 2009; Utne, 2009; Länsiluoto & Järvenpää, 2008, 2010; Ahlroth et al., 2011).

- *Definition of the Environmental Management Accounting and information about its current practice* (Mathews & Perera, 1991; Anderson, 1992; Christiphe, 1992; Belkaoui, 1992; Carrasco & Larrinaga, 1995; Birkin, 1996; Ansari et al., 1997; IFAC, 1998; Bartolomeo et al., 1999; Bennett & James, 1998, 2000; EPA, 2000; Schaltegger & Burritt, 2000; UNDSD, 2001; Jasch, 2002, 2003, 2006; O´Donovan, 2002; Burritt & Schaltegger, 2202; Burritt, 2004; IFAC, 2005; Burritt & Saka, 2006; Gray & Bebbington, 2006; Jasch & Lavicka, 2006; Staniskis & Stasiskiene, 2005; Henri & Journeault, 2010).

From these studies, it is concluded that the traditional accounting model, with its narrow focus on accounting figures, does not adequately capture the consequences of the company's activities on the environment. For this reason, there has been a recent increase in the number of studies proposing different *models to try to assess the contribution of business activity to Sustainable Development* (hereafter SD) (for example: Linowes, 1968; Ramanathan, 1976; Estes, 1976; Parker, 1986; Gray, 1992; Milne, 1992; Rubenstein, 1994; EPA, 1996; Bebbington & Thomson, 1996; CICA, 1997; Boone & Rubenstein, 1997; Atkinson, 2000; Bebbington & Gray, 2001; Bebbington et al., 2001; Grittiths, 2001; Howes, 2002, 2003; Baxter et al., 2002, 2003; Antheaume, 2004, 2007; Figge & Hahn, 2004; Gauthier, 2005; Herborn, 2005; Bebbington & MacGregor, 2005; Taplin et al., 2006; Fernández & Larrinaga, 2006; Bebbington, 2007; Bebbington et al., 2007; Xing et al., 2009, Davies, 2009a, 2009b;

Frame & Cavanagh, 2009; Jones, 2010), which highlight the need for more critical reflection about the consideration and internalization of external factors.

With the aim of contributing towards this recent line of research, we have expanded the theoretical model established by Jones (2010) to treat the need for social and environmental information and accounting theoretical. We end with a series of conclusions.

2. THEORETICAL MODEL

Based on Jones's model (see Jones, 2010), we shall now set out a multilayer model which adds three premises to the former and which will turn on the role of accounting (external and internal) in the determination of company (un)sustainability, for consideration in administration functions and rendering of accounts (Figure 1).

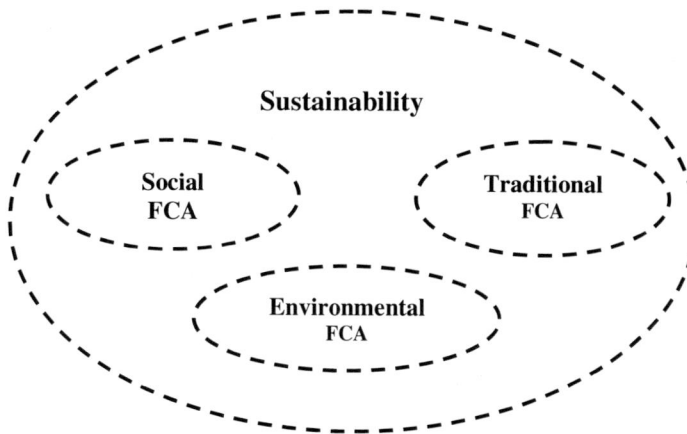

Figure 1.

1. *Environmental risks place the planet at risk:* This premise argues that, while the nature and seriousness of the threat are not confirmed, there is a general awareness of deterioration in the planet's health (PNUMA, 2007), because, essentially, reputable scientific sources are in agreement that we are faced with a cocktail of serious environmental problems, which do not respect the borders between countries (for example: ozone erosion (Farman, 1990; Stern, 2006); climate change (Bradley, 2003; Carter, 2007; IPCC, 2007; Lewis, 2007; Morris, 1997; Schneider, 1990; Stern, 2006); acid rain (Wilkinson & Woodin, 1990); decline of biodiversity (Bhattacharya, 1990; Harmon, 1990; Kovel, 2007; Prance, 1990; Myers, 1985; Prettty, 1990; Teer & Berwick, 1987).

2. *Corporate social responsibility:* Within this broad concept, three premises developed for the model are discussed:

    2.1. *Industry has a big impact on the environment:* As Malthus (1798) conjectured, the Earth's ecosystems cannot sustain present levels of economic activity and consumption, and new management frameworks are necessary to alleviate this pressure and ensure social integrity (Wackernagel & Rees, 1996). Industry is directly responsible for major environmental incidents such as the Exxon Valdez oil spill in Alaska (1989) or habitat loss such as the deforestation of the Amazon and other tropical rainforests by logging companies. Moreover, industry is very wasteful of materials, recycling little (Ayres, 2004). Indirectly, the increasing usage of agricultural pesticides and herbicides causes biodiversity loss, while industrial activity causes air, land and water pollution (see, Jones, 2010). In this context, because companies cause many environmental impacts and even catastrophes, society has begun to demand that they accept their responsibility (Moneva & Llena, 2006), so driving the expansion of corporate responsibilities in social and environmental matters (Nieto & Fernández, 2004; Escobar & González, 2005; Garrigues & Trullenque, 2008).

2.2. *Search for social legitimation:* The legitimation described by Shocker & Sheti (1973), is proposed as an alternative to the profit model (Gray et al., 1996; Friedman, 1962, 1970; Hetherignton, 1973; Benston, 1982), and offers companies the opportunity to legitimate their behaviour and procedures in the eyes of society. By virtue of a "social contract" (Schuman, 1995; O'Donovan, 2002), companies begin to assume that, unless they want to see their survival threatened, they need to operate with a value system in accordance with that of the society in whose eyes they are being legitimated (Gray et al., 1987; Wicks, 1992; Gray et al., 1996; Husillos, 2007; Moneva, 2008). This will shape their strategies (Gray et al., 1995), and one of the basic functions of the Social and Environmental Accounting (Richardson, 1987; Mellemvick et al., 1988; Carmona, 1989; Escobar & González, 2005), such as the publication of social and environmental information (Lindblom, 1994). However, in practice, it is used by companies to influence public opinion, being heavily biased towards whatever puts companies in a good light, making it impossible to analyse it and draw a reliable conclusion about business behaviour (Brown & Deegan, 1998; Deegan & Rankin, 1996; Deegan et al., 2000; Deegan et al., 2002; Husillos, 2007; O'Donovan, 2002; Patten, 1992, 1995, 2005).

2.3. *Individuals, the administration and industry have the duty to act and cooperate:* The fourth premise means that no-one, i.e., neither corporations, individuals (including managers and accountants), or governments (Bebbington & Thomson, 1996; Fernández & Larrinaga, 2006), can stand aside given the legal and moral responsibility we have to our environment, because the environment provides resources and satisfactions to everyone, accumulates waste and supports life (Pearce, 1976; Turner et al., 1994:17). This awareness has been reflected in profound political, economic and social changes and in a call to action (Goldsmith et al., 1972) in a global framework (even a binding one like the Kyoto Protocol).

3. *A new relationship between industry and its environment:* If we accept these four premises, the limited traditional model (Aragón, 1996; Gladwin et al., 1995; Daly & Cobb, 1994; Pauchant & Fostier, 1990; Shrisvastava & Hart,1994) becomes the *"new model of sustainability",* producing a necessary, radical reorientation of human relationships, and therefore, relationships of companies, with their environment, where SD becomes the immediate goal, because, as Pearce et al., (1989) point out, from a realistic point of view this is a pragmatic, practical response, allowing more radical reorientations to be sought later and undertaken as long-term goals. SD is thus

a pragmatic and practical initial response, upon which more radical future reorientations such as long-term zero growth (Daly, 1985), population control and deep ecology (Naess, 1985) could be built, but, in the short term, although ecologically desirable, would be socially, economically' and politically impossible to achieve. SD covers a practical theoretical umbrella, with environmental indicators such as sustainable performance indicators, FCA and natural inventories, allowing a variety of options for putting into practice, motivating and integrating social, environmental and ethical concerns about the social accounting and responsibility of companies (Unerman et al., 2007), changing them into "sustainable companies".

4. *Measure the impact of the company's activity:* From both the anthropocentric and non-anthropecentric points of view, consensus recommends that the Earth's resources must be protected (Jones, 2010) to guarantee at minimum, a "sustaining level of activity." Essentially, sustainability is the maintenance of at least a certain stock of resources such as natural habitats, fauna, water or air, and worldwide global sustainability should be attained (Simon, 1989, Turner, 1987). In the business context, this means at minimum that companies should not leave the environment worse than it was at the beginning of the accounting period ("maintaining the capital stock") (s.e. Gray, 1992; Barton, 1999; Ekins et al., 2003; Fernandez & Larrinaga, 2006). It is, therefore, imperative that the impact of their activity be measured, because companies may have positive indicators of success in the shape of growth and profits, while at the same time they pollute the air and water, fire employees, destroy habitats and devastate communities (Bebbington & Gray, 2001). To carry out this measurement and provide the decisive answers to the environmental threat, it will be necessary to influence economic decision making and involve accounting (Larrinaga & Bebbington, 2001). So if this need is accepted, there are two interrelated premises:

    4.1. Conventional *accounting is inadequate:* Traditional accounting practices are deficient (Larrinaga, 1997) because they do not include sustainability quantitatively, a situation which has endured because of its capitalist orientation, business focus, confidence in neoclassical economics, the predominance of numerical quantification, monetary dependence and various technical aspects to these practices (Jones, 2010). This has caused unsustainable decisions (UNCSD, 2001) due to the existence of incorrect prices (Bebbington et al., 2001), or cost-saving opportunities to be missed because of the lack of information (Jasch, 2001; Gale, 2006a,b) or aggregation in general expense accounts (Savage et al., 2001).

    4.2. *Need for active, participatory, democratic, dialogic accounting:* The increase in research and development into Social and Environmental Accounting has developed internationally in parallel with the international debate about the phenomena of greenhouse gases, global warming, human rights, deforestation, land degradation and pollution (Parker, 2011). So we advocate a form of accounting which can give a suitable, up-to-date view of the world (Turner & Anderson, 1989), models reality (Blanco, 1993) and be a participant in company strategy and in the creation of its information systems (Simons, 1990), which cannot be separated from the company's internal and external social processes (Choudhury, 1986). As Gray et al., (1996:64) point out, accounting might not be the best field from which to begin the necessary social changes, but once they have begun, it is an important element to achieve them. Although other authors go further and, based on the "Theory of Accounting Change", consider that accounting can be deliberately designed to trigger or contribute towards social change and, specifically, to change perception of the ecological problem (Larrinaga, 1999; Carmona & Gutiérrez, 2003). For all these reasons, a proactive and participatory (Gray, 1993), multidimensional (integrating economic, social and environmental aspects) and dialogic (taking not only shareholders but also a wide variety of stakeholders into account) (Brown, 2009) and, therefore much more democratic and pluralist form of accounting needs to be developed. The goal will be the search for transparency and the discharge of accountability, which will be achieved by combining the functions of financial accounting, to guarantee that this form of accounting is minimally obligatory, and general accounting, to guarantee the necessary willingness to achieve "self-regulation," with flexibility.

4.2.1. *External or obligatory accounting: financial accounting:* Because of this deficiency, and the disparity of criteria (Silva & Aibar, 2007), heterogeneousness and lack of comparability of traditional accounting systems (Archel et al., 2000), numerous authors (e.g. Gray, 2002; Larrinaga et al., 2002) and international organizations of various kinds (e.g. European Commission, 1992, 1998, 2001; CICA, 1993; AAF, 1995; ISAR, 1998; UNCTAD, 1998; FEE, 1996, 2000) have declared the need for this information to be included in annual accounts, as well progressive international harmonization (European, IASSB and FASB).

4.2.2. *Internal or voluntary accounting: management accounting:* Because the traditional accounting system does not take in what is required (Atkinson, 2000; Gray, 2002; Stewart, 1994:68), environmental management systems and environmental management accounting can provide the opportunity to adapt knowledge to new realities and increase the social utility of relationships between business and nature. This subdiscipline of management accounting will therefore cover both monetary and physical aspects, making it suitable for performing a huge variety of relevant functions in company management (Staniskis & Stasiskiene, 2006), one of which is measurement of the net impact of its activity, which has aroused great interest among managers (Ansari et al., 1997; Burritt & Schaltegger, 2001; Burritt & Saka, 2006; Bebbington & Gray, 2001; O'Donovan, 2002). In addition, it can provided different perspectives and indicators, the FCA being a perfect tool for monetary measurement of the sustainability of an activity and the net social result.

5. *Administrative and management functions:* The ninth element is related with the fact that, given the broad recognition, both within and outside of the field of accounting, of the need for new forms of participation in accounting, which are provided by administrative and management functions (Brown, 2009; O'Dwyer, 2005; Gray, 2002; Boyce, 2000; Gray et al., 1997; Morgan, 1988; Mouck, 1995; O'Ceary, 1985). To achieve this, it is essential that managers help to develop and implement the

environmental management accounting and its different tools (Starik & Rank, 1995), which will integrate and seek sustainability through performance of these functions:

5.1. Planning and decision making: Information is not an end in itself, but rather its purpose is to be useful for planning and decision making (operative, tactical and strategic decisions) (FASB, 1991) in the field of environmental management (EPA, 1995; Gray et al., 1993).

5.2. Rendering of accounts: As Meadows et al., (1992) say, "Information is key to transformation". For this reason, in recent years the rendering of sustainability accounts and transparency in the Corporate Social Responsability (Ballou et al., 2006; Hedberg & von Malmborg, 2003) have been developed and have spread rapidly in recent years, as companies have been required to act more coherently with SD and social and management accounting (Milne et al., 2009).

It should not be forgotten that accounting and all its disciplines are essentially a field of applied research, so it is difficult to imagine such research without detailed examination of current practices (Ittner & Larcker, 2002). For this reason, after the theoretical model had been developed, empirical analysis was carried out using the survey method.

CONCLUSION

Sustainable Development has become the most pragmatic, popular way to seek global sustainability mainly because more extreme positions are not socially, economically or politically acceptable, and to the fact that it includes a broad umbrella of options allowing its interpretation in very different ways being the possible result of very different actions.

As we have found, although there is a great deal of talk about the need to measure the "Sustainable Develpment result" or determine the "sustenance level of the activity," to render accounts based on transparency and the discharge of accountability, immediate measures should be taken in all fields, because: i) there has not been much practical application, mainly because of companies' reluctance to declare the non-sustainability of their activities, with the consequent effect on their image and reputation, and ii) empirical accounting research has been insufficient, sporadic and unconnected, because, based on such a "politically plastic" concept, it should play a far more active, participatory and dialogic role, even turning researchers into (co) creators of a kind of accounting which deals with understanding, which means that it needs to be developed by experts with experience of this subject, in a limited number of companies which are receptive to the idea.

With this aim, to determine the company's contribution to Sustainable Development, FCA presents itself as a perfect tool to establish this sustenance level, at which the production process can have more value than the financial figure obtained. In this regard, because there is a wide variety of terms used to refer to FCA, or FCA is used to refer to very different matters, it needs to be delimited. In this context, the following classification and/or nominations takes the three dimensions of Sustainable Development – economic, social and environmental – into account:

I.   When only the economic dimension is analysed (FCA from a traditional point of view, i.e., only taking internal production factors into account): *"Full Cost Accounting"*.
II. When only the social dimension is analysed: *"Social Full Cost Accounting"*.
III. When only the environmental dimension is analysed: *"Environmental Full Cost Accounting"*.
IV. When the three dimensions, i.e., the economic, social and environmental dimensions are analysed together, with the additional inclusion of the ethical dimension: *"Sustainability Full Cost Accounting"*.

Furthermore, although all our theoretical base has been developed around the sustenance level of an industrial company's activity, it is perfectly applicable to any other type of company (e.g., public sector) or unit of analysis (e.g., country, product, activity or process).

REFERENCES

Ansari, S.; Bell, J.; Klammer, T.V & Lawrence, C. (1997). *Management Accounting. A Strategic Focus: Measuring and Managing Environmental Cost*. McGraw-Hill.

Antheaume, N. (2004). Valuing external costs-From theory to practice: Implications for full cost environmental accounting. *European Accounting Review*, 13, 443-464.

Antheaume, N. (2007). Full Cost Accounting: Adam Smith metes Rachel Carson?. En Unermann, J., O'Dwyer, B. & Bebbington, J. (Eds.): *Sustainability Accounting and Accountability*. London.

Aragón-Correa, J.A. (1998). Strategic proactivity and firm approcach to the natural environment. *Academy of Management Journal*, 41, 5, 556-567.

Ballou, B.; Heitger, D.L.; Landes, C.E. & Adams, M. (2006). The Future of Corporate Sustainability Reporting. *Journal of Accountancy*, 202, 6, 65-74.

Barton, A. D. (1999). A trusteeship theory of accounting for natural capital assets. *Abacus*, 35, 2, 207–222.

Baxter, T. Bebbington, J. & Cutteridge, D. (2003). Sustainability assessment model: modeling economic, resource, environmental and social flows of a project. En A. Henriques & J. Richardson (Eds.): *The triple bottom line, does it all add up?: Assessing the sustainability of business and CSR*. London: Earthscan.

Bebbington, J. (2007). *Accounting for sustainable development performance*. London: CIMA.

Bebbington, J., Gray, R., Hibbitt, C. & Kirk, E. (2001). *Full cost accounting: an agenda for action*. Certified Accountants Educational Trust: London, ACCA Research Report, 73.

Bebbington, J.; Brown, J. & Frame, B. (2007). Accounting technologies and sustainability assessment models. *Ecological Economics*, 61, 224-236.

Bebbington, J.; Brown, J.; Frame, B. & Thomson, I. (2007). Theorizing engagement: The potential of a critical dialogic approach. *Accounting, Auditing and Accountability Journal*, 20, 356-381.

Bebbington, J. & Gray, R. (2001). An Account of Sustainability: Failure, Success and a Reconceptualisation. *Critical Perspectives on Accounting*, 12, 5, 557-605.

Bebbington, J. & Thomson, I. (1996). RR48: Business conceptions of sustainability and the implications for accountancy. *ACCA Research Report* No. 48, London.

Bebbington, J. & Macgregor, B. (2005). *Modelling and Accounting for Sustainable Development*. RICS Foundation, London.

Boone, J. & Rubentein, D.B. (1997). Natural solution: Full Cost Accounting can help companies to integrate environmental considerations into decision making. *CA Magazine*, 130, 4, 18-22.

Boyce, G. (2000). Public discourse and decision making: exploring possibilities for financial, social and environmental accounting. *Accounting, Auditing and Accountability Journal, 13*, 1, 27-64.

Brown, J. (2009). Democracy, sustainability and dialogic accounting technologies: Taking pluralism seriously. *Critical Perspectives on Accounting*, 20, 313-342.

Brown, N. & Deegan, C. (1998). The public disclosure of environmental performance information –a dual test of media agenda setting theory and legitimacy theory. *Accounting and Business Research*, 29, 1, 21-41.

Burritt, R. & Saka, C. (2006). Environmental Management Accounting applications and eco-efficiency: case studies from Japan. *Journal of Cleaner Production*, 14, 1262-1275.

Burritt, R. & Schaltegger, S. (2001). Eco-efficiency in corporate budgeting. *Environmental Management and Health*, 12, 2, 158-174.

CICA (1993). *Environmental Cost and Liabilities: Accounting and Financial Reporting Issues*. Toronto.

CICA (1997). *La comptabilisation du coût complet du point de vue de l'environment*. Toronto.

Choudhury, N. (1986). The Seeking of Accounting Where it is Not: Towards a Theory or Non-Accounting in Organizational Settings. *Accounting, Organizations and Society*, 13, 6, 549-557.

Daly, H. E. (1985). Economics and sustainability: In defence of a steady-state economy. En Tobias, M. (Ed.): *Deep ecology*. California: Avant Books, 90-100.

Daly, H. & Cobb, J. (1989). *For the common good: Redirecting the economy toward community. The environment and a sustainable future*. Massachusetts: Beacon Press.

Deegan, C. & Rankin, M. (1996). Do Austalian companies report environmental news objectively? An analysis of environmental disclosures by firms prosecutes successfully by Environmental Protection Authority. *Accounting, Auditing & Accountability Journal*, 9, 2, 50-67.

Deegan, C., Rankin, M. & Voght, P. (2000). Firms' disclosure reactions to major social incidents: Australian evidence. *Accounting Forum*, 24, 1, 101–130.

Deegan, C., Rankin, M. & Tobin, J. (2002). An examination of the corporate social and environmental disclosures of BHP from 1983-1997: A test of legitimacy theory. *Accounting, Auditing & Accountability Journal*, 15, 312-343.

Ekins, P.; Simon, S.; Deutsch, L.; Folke, C. & De Groot, R. (2003). A framework for the practical application of the concepts of critical natural capital and strong sustainability. *Ecological Economics*, 44, 165-185.

Environmental Protection Agency (EPA) (1995). *Full Cost Accounting for Municipal Solid Waste: A Handbook*. EPA530-r-95-041. Washington, DC: US.

Environmental Protection Agency (EPA) (2000). *Full Cost Accounting. Practical Guidance on converting to FCA*. Washington, DC: US.

Escobar, B. & González, J. (2005). Responsabilidad Social Corporativa: ¿Compromiso u oportunismo? *Revista de Contabilidad*, 8, 16, 67-98.

Estes, R.W. (1976). Socio-economic accounting and external diseconomies. *The Accounting Review*, 47, 284-290.

Fernández, M. & Larrinaga, C. (2006). Percepciones sobre Contabilidad de Costes Ecológicos Completos: Análisis empírico en el sector energético español. *Revista Española de Financiación y Contabilidad*, 131, 225-254.

Figge, F. & Hahn, T. (2004). Sustainable Value Added-Measuring Corporate contributions to sustainability beyond eco-efficiency. *Ecological Economics*, 48, 173-187.

Frame, B. & Cavanagh, J. (2009). Experiences of sustainability assessment: An awkward adolescence. *Accounting Forum*, 33, 195-208.

Friedman, M. (1970). The social responsibility of business is to increase its profit. *The New York Times Magazine*, 122–126.

Gale, R. (2006a). Environmental Management Accounting as a reflexive modernization strategy in cleaner production. *Journal of Cleaner Production*, 14, 1228-1236.

Gale, R. (2006b). Environmental costs al a Canadian paper mill: a case study of Environmental Management Accounting (EMA). *Journal of Cleaner Production*, 14, 1237-1251.

Garrigues, A. & Trullenque, F.E. (2008). Responsabilidad Social Corporativa: ¿papel mojado o necesidad estratégica? *Harvard Deusto Business Review*, 164, 19-36.

Gauthier, C. (2005). Measuring corporate social and environmental performance: The extended life-cycle assessment. *Journal of Business Ethics*, 59, 199–206.

Gladwin T.N., Krause T.S. & Kennelly J.J. (1995b). Beyond Eco-efficiency: Toward Socially Sustainable Business. *Sustainable Dev*elopment. 3, 35-43.

Gladwin, T.N., Kennelly, J. & Krause, T.S.(1995). Shifting Paradigms for Sustainable development Implications for Management Theory and Research. *Academy of Management Review*, 20, 4, 874-907.

Goldsmith, E., Allen, R., Allaby, M., Davoll, J. & Lawrence, S. (1972). *A blueprint for survival*. Penguin: Harmondsworth.

Gray, R. (1992). Accounting and environmentalism: an exploration of the challenge of gently accounting for accountability, transparency and sustainability. *Accounting, Organizations and Society*, 17, 399-425.

Gray, R. (1993). *Accounting for the Environment*. Paul Chapman Publishing, Londres.

Gray, R. (2002). The social accounting Project and Accounting Organizations and Society: privileging engagement, imaginings, new accounting and pragmatismo ver critique? *Accounting, Organizations and Society*, 27, 687-708.

Gray, R. (2009). Is accounting for sustainability actually accounting for sustainability. . .and how would we know? An exploration of narratives, of organisations and the planet. *Accounting, Organizations and Society*, 34.

Gray, R.; Bebbington, J. & Walters, D. (1993). *Accounting for the Environment*. ACCA, London.

Gray, R.; Dey, C.; Owen, D.; Evans, R. & Zadek, S. (1997). Struggling with the praxis of social accounting: stakeholders, accountability, audits and procedures. *Accounting, Auditing and Accountability Journal*, 10, 45-60.

Gray, R.; Kouhy, R. & Lavers, S. (1995). Corporate social and environmental reporting: a review of the literature and a longitudinal study of UK disclosure. *Accounting, Auditing & Accountability Journal*, 8, 2, 44-77.

Gray, R.; Owen, D. L. & Maunders, K. T. (1987). *Corporate social reporting: Accounting and accountability*. Hemel Hempstead: Prentice Hall.

Gray, R.; Owen, D. & Adams, C. (1996). *Accounting and accountability: Changes and challenges in corporate. In Social and environmental reporting*. London: Prentice Hall.

Griffiths, E. (2001). *Environmental accounting in the construction industry*. In Advances in Environmental Accounting, Proceedings of the ACCA/Environment Agency Seminar , 47–55.

Hedberg, C.J. & Von Malmborg, F. (2003). The Global Reporting Initiative And Corporate Sustainability Reporting In Swedish Companies. *Corporate Social Responsibility And Environmental Management* 10, 153-164.

Herborn, K. (2005). A full cost environmental accounting experiment. *Accounting, Organizations and Society*, 30, 519-536.

Howes, R. (2002). *Environmental Cost Accounting: An Introduction and Practical Guide*. London. CIMA Publishing/Elsevier.

Husillos, F.J. (2007). Una aproximación desde la teoría de la legitimidad a la información medioambiental revelada por las empresas españolas cotizadas. *Revista Española de Financiación y Contabilidad*, 36, 133, 97-121.

Ittner, C.D. & Larcker, D.F. (2002). Empirical managerial accounting research: are we just describing management consulting practice? *The European Accounting Review*, 11, 4, 787-794.

Jasch, C. (2001). Environmental Management Accounting Procedures and Principles. United Notions Division for Sustainable Development. *United Nations Department of Economic & Socials Affairs,* New York, 4-10.

Jones, M.J. (2010). Social and environmental report assurance: some interview evidence. *Accounting Forum*, 34, 1, 20-31.

Larrinaga, C. (1997). Consideraciones en torno a la relación entre la contabilidad y el medio ambiente. *Revista Española de Financiación y Contabilidad*, 26, 957-991.

Larrinaga, C. (1999). ¿Es la contabilidad medioambiental un paso hacia la sostenibilidad o un escudo contra el cambio? El caso del sector eléctrico español. *Revista Española de Financiación y Contabilidad*, 28, 645-674.

Larrinaga, C. & Bebbington, J. (2001). Accounting change or institutional appropriation?- A case study of the implementation of Environmental Accounting. *Critical Perspectives on Accounting*, 12, 269-292.

Larrinaga, C.; Carrasco, F.; Correa, C.; Llena, F. & Moneva, J.M. (2002). Accountability and accounting regulation: the case of Spanish environmental disclosure standard. *The European Accounting Review*, 11, 4, 723-740.

Linowes, D.F. (1968). Socio-economic accounting. *Journal of accountancy*; 126, 37-42.

Meadows, D.H.; Meadows, D.L. & Randers, J. (1992). *Beyonf the Limits: Global Collapse or a Sustainable Future*. London: Earthscan Publications Ltd.

Milne, C. (1992). *Handbook of Environmental Law*. Royal Forest and Bird Protection Society, Wellington.

Milne, M. J., Tregida, H. & Walton, S. (2009). Words not actions! The ideological role of sustainable development reporting. *Accounting, Auditing and Accountability Journal*, 22, 8, 1211–1257.

Moneva, J.M. & Llena, F. (2006). Contabilidad e Información Medioambiental de la Empresa. Antecedentes y situación actual. En Gallizo, J.L. (Coord.): *"Responsabilidad Social e Información Medioambiental de la Empresa"*. AECA, Madrid, 57-82.

Monteiro, S. & Aibar, B. (2009). Las prácticas de contabilidad medioambiental en las grandes empresas que operan en Portugal. *Revista Iberoamericana de Contabilidad de Gestión*, 13, 1-16.

Morgan, D.L. (1988). *Focus groups as qualitative research*. London: Sage.

Mouck, T. (1995). Financial reporting, democracy and environmentalism: a critique of the commodification of information. *Critical Perspectives on Accounting, 6,* 535-553.

Naess, A. (1985). Identification as a source of deep ecological attitudes. En Tobias, M. (Ed.): *Deep Ecology* . California: Avant Books, 256-270.

Nieto, M. & Fernández, R. (2004). Responsabilidad Social Corporativa: la última innovación en management. *Universia Business Review-Actualidad Económica*, 28-39.

O'Donovan, G. (2002). Environmental disclosures in the annual report:extending the applicability and predictive power of legitimacy theory..*Accounting, Auditing & Accountability Journal*, 15, 344-371.

O'Dwyer, B. (2005). The construction of a social account: A case study of overseas aid agency. *Accounting, Organization and Society*, 30, 3, 279-296.

Parker, L.D. (1986). Polemical themes in Social Accounting: scenario for standards setting. *Advances in Public Interest Accounting*. 1, 67-93.

Parker, L.D. (2011): Twenty One Years of Social and Environmental Accountability Research: A Coming of Age. *Accounting Forum*, 35, 1, 1-10.

Patten, D.M. (1992). Intra-Industry Environmental Disclosures in Response to the Alaskan Oil Spill: a Note on Legitimacy Theory. *Accounting, Organizations and Society*. 17, 5, 471-475.

Patten, D. M. (1995). Variability in social disclosure: a legitimacy-based analysis. *Advances in Public Interest Accounting*, 273–285.

Patten, D. M. (2005). The accuracy of financial reports projections of future environmental capital expenditures: a research note. *Accounting, Organization and Society*. 30, 457-468.

Pauchant, T.C. & Fortier, I. (1990). Anthropocentric ethics in organizations. Strategic management and the environment: a Eypology. En: Shrisvastava, P. & Lamb, R., (Eds.) *Advances in Strategic Management*, vol.6, JAI Press, Greenwich, CT: 99-114.

Pearce, D.W. (1976). "The Limits of Cost Benefit Analysis as a Guide to Environmental Policy", *Kyklos*, 29, Fasc.1, 97-112.

Pearce, D., Markandya, A. & Barbier, E. B. (1989). *Blueprint for a Green Economy*. Earthscan Publications Ltd, London.

Ramanathan, K.V. (1976). Toward a theory of corporate social accounting. *The Accounting Review*, 51, 3, 516-528.

Rubenstein, D.B. (1994). *Environmental Accounting for the Sustainable Corporations: Strategies and Techniques*. Quorum Books, Westport, Connecticut and London.

Savage, G.T., Nix, T.W., Whitehead, C.J. & Blair, J.D. (1991), Strategies for assessing and managing organisational stakeholders. *Academy of Management Executive*, 5, 2, 61-75.

Shocker, A.D. & Sethi, S.P. (1973). An approach to developing societal preferences in developing corporate action strategies. *California Management Review*, 97-105.

Shrivastava, P. & Hart, S. (1994). Greening Organizations-2000. *International Journal of Public Administration*, 17, 607-635.

Simon, D. (1989). Sustainable development: theoretical construct or attainable goal? *Environmental Conservation*, 41–48.

Staniskis, J.K & Stasiskiene, Z. (2006). Environmental Management Accounting in Lithuania: exploratory study of current practices, opportunities and strategic intents. *Journal of Cleaner Production*, 14, 1252-1261.

Starik, M. & Rands, G.P. (1995). Weaving an Integrated Web: Multilevel and Multisystem Perspectives of Ecollogically Sustainable Organizations. *Academy of Management Review*, 20, 4, 908-935.

Stewart, G.B. (1994). EVA: Fact and Fantasy. *Journal of Applied Corporate Finance*, 7, 2, 71-84.

Taplin, J.R.D.; Bent, D. & Aeron-Thomas, D. (2006). Accounting for the social dimensión of sustainability: Experiences from the biotechnology industry. *Business Strategy and the Environment*, 15, 347-360.

Turner, R.K. (1987). Sustainable global features. Common interest, interdependency, complexity and global possibilities. *Futures*, October, 574-82.

Turner, R.K, Pearce. D. & Bateman, I. (1994). *Environmental Economics*, Harvester Wheatsheaf, England.

Unermann, J.; Bebbington, J. & O´Dwyer, B. (2007). *Sustainability Accounting and Accountability*. Taylor & Francis, Colchester, Essex.

Wackernagel, M. & Rees, W.E. (1996). *Our Ecological Footprint:Reducing Human Impact on the Earth*. Gabriola Press New Society Publishing, B.C.

Wicks, C. (1992). Business and the environmental movement. En D. Owen (Eds.): *Green reporting: Accountancy and the challenge of the nineties*. London: Chapman and Hall, 102-106.

Xing, Y.; Horner, R.; El-Haram, M. & Bebbington, J. (2009). A framework model for assessing sustainability impacts of urban development. *Accounting Forum*, 33, 209-224.

INDEX

I

J

Q

R

S

T

U

V

W

Y

Z